Routledge Revivals

Palestine To-day and Tomorrow

First published in 1930, *Palestine To-day and Tomorrow* provides a comprehensive overview of John Haynes Holmes's experiences in Palestine. Chapter one is a running account, written on the spot, of his experiences in Palestine. Chapter two presents a brief statement of the facts and forces in Jewish history culminating in Zionism, is intended primarily for readers who may not be familiar with them. Chapter three is intended to be a careful and rather elaborate presentation of the difficulties and dangers which beset the path of Zionism in Palestine. Chapter four is an account of what has been done by the Jews in Palestine during a period of fifty years. Chapter five, in many ways the most important in the book is a discussion of the ideas and ideals of Zionism as these have appeared again and again in author's presentation of the more practical aspects of the movement. This book is an important historical reference work to understand the history of the Arab Jewish situation and the question of the English mandate.

Palestine To-day and Tomorrow
A Gentile's Survey of Zionism

John Haynes Holmes

First published in 1930
by George Allen & Unwin Ltd in Great Britain

This edition first published in 2024 by Routledge
4 Park Square, Milton Park, Abingdon, Oxon, OX14 4RN

and by Routledge
605 Third Avenue, New York, NY 10017

Routledge is an imprint of the Taylor & Francis Group, an informa business

© copyright in U.S.A.,1929

All rights reserved. No part of this book may be reprinted or reproduced or utilised in any form or by any electronic, mechanical, or other means, now known or hereafter invented, including photocopying and recording, or in any information storage or retrieval system, without permission in writing from the publishers.

Publisher's Note
The publisher has gone to great lengths to ensure the quality of this reprint but points out that some imperfections in the original copies may be apparent.

Disclaimer
The publisher has made every effort to trace copyright holders and welcomes correspondence from those they have been unable to contact.

A Library of Congress record exists under LCCN:

ISBN: 978-1-032-76262-3 (hbk)
ISBN: 978-1-003-47777-8 (ebk)
ISBN: 978-1-032-76264-7 (pbk)

Book DOI 10.4324/9781003477778

PALESTINE
TO-DAY AND TO-MORROW

A GENTILE'S SURVEY OF ZIONISM

BY
JOHN HAYNES HOLMES

LONDON
GEORGE ALLEN & UNWIN LTD.
MUSEUM STREET

Copyright in U.S.A. 1929
First published in Great Britain 1930

ROWORTH & COMPANY
LONDON

TO
NATHAN STRAUS
IN GRATITUDE AND REVERENCE

FOREWORD

I

THE writing of this book has been a remarkable experience. I began it in the elaborate notes I made during my visit to Palestine in February of this present year (1929). I continued it in a series of articles which I sent from Palestine to my paper, *Unity* (Chicago), large portions of which I have included in these pages. I set myself to the task of preparing the book itself in the leisure hours of my summer vacation, and had just completed the third chapter when suddenly, at the end of August, there broke in Palestine the terrific storm of rioting and bloodshed.

I stopped my work. For days I could think of nothing but the horror of what was transpiring in the land through which I had so recently traveled. Towns and villages which I had visited were being sacked and burned; homes in which I had been graciously entertained were being looted and destroyed; men and women who had been my hosts and had become my friends were being killed, wounded, maimed, driven in terror to strange places. Surely, I could not now continue my book. In the face of such a cataclysm as this, what was my story worth? When these riotings were done, what would there be left of what I had seen and known? Zion suddenly was gone, and there was nothing for me to tell.

Then, as days passed and violence subsided, I took thought again. This uprising of the Arabs against the Jews had been terrible, but it was nothing new. It was a repetition, more extensive and more disastrous, of the wild outbreaks of 1920 and 1921. Zion was wounded grievously, but by no means fatally. This tragic experience, as Nathan Straus so accurately and nobly said, was but an "interruption" to the inevitable progress of the movement to its appointed goal. A storm had swept the landscape and scattered the people; but the landscape was the same, and the people would return to replant their fields and rebuild their homes.

I reread the text of my completed chapters, and was surprised to discover that they needed no revision. The facts which I had presented, and the problems I had discussed, were all unaltered. My tale was as valid as before—and a thousand times more vivid and pertinent! For here were described the very forces which had led to this vast upheaval. What had happened, to be sure, had darkened the colors of my picture and deepened its outlines; but, by the same token, had illuminated its meaning with terrifying brilliance. So far from stopping my book, I should continue it with all speed as a fitting introduction to, and interpretation of, events which hold such enormous significance for the Jews, and also for the world.

I therefore set to work again, and have finished my task along exactly the lines projected in the beginning. So precisely have I kept to my notes, and to my original plan of writing, that I doubt if any reader would have guessed, apart from this Foreword and occasional footnotes in the text, that the book was in actual course of composition when the riots came, and that chapters four and five were written after, as chapters one, two and three were written before, this tragic episode in Zion's history. If there be those disappointed that I have not commented more directly upon recent events, I can only plead that my purpose in undertaking this book was to describe not events,

FOREWORD

but the facts and forces which lead to events. I went to Palestine to see and report a situation. The fact that out of this situation, like lightning from a storm cloud, there leaped a sudden, dramatic, and very terrible event, only makes it the more important that I should not be diverted from my appointed task. One is not neglecting an explosion, when one turns from the event itself to a study of the conditions which have produced it, and the remedies which must be applied to prevent its recurrence. I shall be surprised if, from this standpoint, the readers of this book do not find the August (1929) riots on nearly every page.

II

Meanwhile, in view of the special character of my book, it may be well to set down in this place a few words of direct and summary comment upon what has happened in Palestine. I would emphasize four facts as yet but dimly seen, and for this reason, perhaps, seldom mentioned, which I regard as fundamental to the present situation and its remedy. These facts, which may be taken as a kind of summary of the Palestinian problem to-day, are as follows:

First, the riots which shocked the world were not really riots at all, but *war*. The Arabs who engaged in the upheaval were prevailingly savage tribesmen, not the laborers of town and village in friendly relationship with the Jewish pioneers, and these practiced looting and burning on a wide scale. But their motive was not plunder, but revolt.

Secondly, the war was not a "holy war," prompted by religious fanaticism, but a political and social uprising, prompted by nationalistic pride. The dispute at the Wailing Wall was merely a spark which kindled the long-accumulated fuel of a people's grievances. And these grievances, carefully nursed by native politicians who see in the advancement of Jewish culture under the sanction of English law, a menace of Western against Eastern civilization, were quite as much against the English as against the Jews. If the Arabs struck at the Jews, it was because they regarded them as the occasion, and thus gladly made them the victims, of their resentment against the English, at whom they dare not strike.

Thirdly, this war, now temporarily repressed, cannot be ended, since its issues cannot be settled, by the Mandatory. That the English administration can, and under the terms of the Mandate must, maintain the peace and protect the Jews from violence and death, is elementary. Britain has accepted the obligation of the police power, and cannot be relieved of its responsibilities. But the authority of administration and the power of arms are no solution of the problems involved. On the contrary, under the conditions now prevailing in Palestine, they can serve only at bottom to aggravate and thus perpetuate the existing situation. As the government has disappointed the Jews, so it has outraged the Arabs, and thus has alienated both the races which it would reconcile.

Lastly, the war *should* not be ended by the Mandatory. The permanent solution of the difficulties between the Jews and the Arabs belongs of necessity not to the English at all, but to the Jews and Arabs themselves. Zion would be destroying its future by betraying its ideals if it were content to fall back upon British bayonets for the advancement, or even the ultimate protection, of its cause. The one permanent security of the Jews in their new homeland, as the Zionists have proclaimed and in their own constructive work made manifest, is the confidence and good will of their Arab neighbors. The hearts of these natives must be won to friendship. For which victory the Jews must trust not to the English but to themselves—to their prophetic ideals of peace and brotherhood, their spirit of justice, and that innate capacity for strength through suffering which has enabled them to survive the hatred of the centuries.

The pages of this book, in so far as they bear upon the question of Jews, Arabs, and English, are an amplification, and I trust a· justification, of these ideas. If they contain any message, it lies in the presentation of this point of view.

III

The plan of the book is evident. Chapter one is a running account, written on the spot, of my journeyings and experiences in Palestine. It can claim to be little more than a series of quick, vivid impressions of the land and its people as I saw them, and is included here as a background against which to set my study of the Zionist Movement.

Chapter two, a brief statement of the facts and forces in Jewish history culminating in Zionism, is intended primarily for Gentile readers who may not be familiar with them. Jewish readers can be interested in this chapter only as a summary, from a Gentile point of view, of what they already know in great and glorious detail.

Chapter three is intended to be a careful and rather elaborate presentation of the difficulties and dangers which beset the path of Zionism in Palestine. It is useless, it seems to me, to deny the existence of these problems, or to underestimate their seriousness. To do so is to prepare trouble in the end, and also to depreciate the value and diminish the splendor of the achievements which have been wrought in the new homeland by heroic men and women. It is in this chapter that I state the Arab-Jewish situation, and the question of the English Mandate, as I see them at the present moment.

Chapter four is an account of what has been done by the Jews in Palestine during a period of fifty years. It is also a description of Zion as "the national homeland" exists to-day. What we see is a deep-founded, full-rounded civilization, reared in an inhospitable country, amid a primitive people, by the labor of men's hands and the sacrifice of their heroic hearts. I know of nothing in history to compare with it, unless it be the early settlement of New England.

Chapter five, in many ways the most important in the book, is a discussion of the ideas and ideals of Zionism as these have appeared again and again in my presentation of the more practical aspects of the Movement. In this chapter I have aligned myself with those who look to Zion as fundamentally an ethical and spiritual phenomenon, and find its destiny in a deliberate surrender of the "things of this world" to those high ideals of the Law which are Israel's unique and precious contribution to mankind. I have found comfort in the discovery, amply revealed in this chapter, that the limitations which compass Zion, the very difficulties which inescapably beset her, are the conditions which dictate success in terms not of wealth and power and national greatness, but of those cultural concepts which are the light and leading of any happy people. In the new Zion as not in the old, the prophets and not the kings must prevail.

IV

I am indebted to Nathan Straus, who made possible my journey to Palestine; to Dr. Hans Kohn, of Jerusalem, who led me to the heart of Zionism, and revealed to me its inner life; to Henrietta Szold, Judah L. Magnes, Zvi Shwarz, and other friends in Palestine too numerous to mention, who guided my steps through the land, and opened all doors to my inquiry; and to Dr. Kohn, Rabbi D. de Sola Pool, and Rabbi Stephen S. Wise, who have read my manuscript, and, without assuming responsibility for ideas and opinions which are my own, have generously given me the priceless benefit of their superior knowledge and wise counsel. To all of these honored friends, named and unnamed, I offer here my humble gratitude and reverence.

J. H. H.

October 1, 1929.

CONTENTS

	PAGE
FOREWORD	vii

CHAPTER I—JOURNEYINGS

THE MEDITERRANEAN	3
ALEXANDRIA	5
CAIRO	8
ON TO JERUSALEM	9
THE HOLY CITY	11
JORDAN AND THE DEAD SEA	16
SAMARIA AND THE SAMARITANS	18
INTO THE MOUNTAINS	20
DAMASCUS AND SYRIA	25
AN ANCIENT SHRINE—SAFED	27
A MODERN SHRINE—HAIFA	32
NAZARETH	36
TEL-AVIV	40
AN ADVENTURE	44
JERUSALEM AGAIN	53
BETHLEHEM AND HEBRON	56
ON THE MOUNT OF OLIVES	59
THE FLIGHT INTO EGYPT	60

CHAPTER II—ZIONISM

THE DIASPORA	65
MESSIANISM	68
ZIONISM	71
SUMMARY OF A MOVEMENT	77

CONTENTS

CHAPTER III—PROBLEMS

	PAGE
First Impressions	87
Land—Palestine	90
People—the Arabs	105
Government—the English	144
Zion—the Jews	162

CHAPTER IV—ACHIEVEMENTS

Background	171
Agriculture	172
The Colonies—Three Types	175
The Kvutzoth, or Communal Colonies	188
Industry	207
Schools	210
Health Work	219
Cultural Work	223
The Hebrew Renaissance	227

CHAPTER V—THE PROMISE

Success	239
What Kind of Success	242
What Such Success Means	263
Conclusion	270

"Gentiles shall come to thy light" . . .
Isaiah 60:3

CHAPTER I [1]

JOURNEYINGS

The Mediterranean

It was a voyage on new seas when our ship passed the Pillars of Hercules and breasted the clear blue waves of the Mediterranean. I had never before sailed beyond the bounds of the Atlantic, and as I gazed at Gibraltar on my left and the dark hills of Africa on my right, I suddenly remembered that these two elevations marked the end of the world to the peoples of ancient times. Through all the centuries preceding the discovery of America, this vast inland sea was the center of civilization.

Every mile of our progress from west to east unfolded to our gaze the undying tale of ships and men and empires. The Riviera was beautiful with the charming villas and thriving towns of our own day. But crumbling watchtowers here and there bore mute testimony to the centuries when pirate craft swept through these waters to deeds of rapine and horror. The scattered Roman ruins on these same shores told how the Roman triremes journeyed westward and nosed their way into inlets and harbors. The Phoenician fleets, frail galleys and larger sailing ships, came this

---

[1] This Chapter consists exclusively of travel notes, largely written on the scene. I have placed them here in evidence of where I went, what I saw, and how I felt during my stay in Palestine. Readers not interested in these details of personal experience are advised to begin with Chapter II.

far. Across these blue waves the Carthaginians moved on to Spain, and made this land a Carthaginian possession. In Genoa we met the crowded shipping of to-day, with memories of the medieval times when Genoa ruled the western as Venice the eastern stretches of this great sea. In Naples, lost in clouds of fog and rain, we saw nothing. I thought of my visit to Milan where I did *not* see the Cathedral, and to Lucerne where I missed the Lion, as we crept into this far-famed bay and saw neither the city on the left nor Vesuvius on the right. In the chill of the evening, as we sailed away after a six hours' stay in port, the air had cleared a bit. We saw the lights of the city, the slopes of Vesuvius (not the smoking crater), and the rocky shores of Capri. But it was wet and dismal, and discouraging. Not until the next morning, in Syracuse, where we lay at anchor beneath a typical Italian sky, did we find heart to dream again. We thought of the Athenian fleet, and Alcibiades, and of the great battle where the Grecian ships were sunk beneath these waters by the Syracusans and their allies, while the Greek soldiers on the hills yonder looked down in terror and dismay. Then we sailed east, into waters over which Grecian mariners and Roman conquerors had coursed for centuries. I thought of Sulla and Cæsar, of Pompey, Antony and Augustus. I remembered Paul journeying along these pathways on his long voyage to Italy. Later times brought the fleets of Venice and the Turks. What a pageant of the ages!

As I stood on deck and listened to the throbbing of the ship, it seemed suddenly as though I heard the beat of oars, and saw coming out of the darkness a lurching trireme. There were the galley slaves, chained naked, sweaty and bleeding to their benches. There were the legionaries, with helm and shield and gleaming spear. High up aloft, dimly disclosed by the trembling lantern, was the captain, driving his craft through the night to some dread deed of pillage. What scenes these waters have beheld, what cries they have echoed, what mysteries they have swallowed up forever! And here I was sailing along in comfort, happiness and safety. The ships we met were friendly ships, the shores we passed were peaceful shores. We had our slaves—the stokers far below. Only a few years ago this sea was filled with terror, and every drifting wisp of smoke an occasion of fear. But still, there is progress. Like Milton's lion, we are clawing our way out of the past that still confines us into the future when we shall be free. Who can despair of what lies ahead when he sees in this portion of the world what lies behind?

ALEXANDRIA

But I was eager to get on, as Palestine to-day, and not the Greece, or Rome, or Venice of yesterday, was the goal I sought. So I welcomed the cool and cloudless dawn of that January morning which unveiled the shores of Egypt, the Nile, and Alexandria. But I would gladly have had night again and quiet seas could we have escaped that landing upon Egyptian soil. Had an ancient pirate ship suddenly boarded us, and plundered us from stem to stern, the experience could scarcely have been more terrible.

From the moment when our docking steamship was surrounded by rowboats filled with clamoring hotel and tourist agents, to the moment when the last persistent peddler was thrust from the departing train, it was one hideous bedlam of noise and confusion. The shouts and screams, the pulling and hauling, the angry struggling and fighting, the porters toiling under their burdens of baggage, the officers striking madly with their canes, the money changers clanking their silver and calling out for business, the news venders, fruit sellers, souvenir peddlers, jugglers, fakers, and innumerable loafers—was there ever such a turmoil? It was in the beginning so sudden and in its continuance so appalling, that one lost all reason and self-control. I found myself stricken by a kind of subconscious panic of emotion, and without realizing it was passing out silver to outstretched palms like a drunken millionaire. Hell hath no terror for me after this experience. I shall be able to face undismayed its deepest rounds of horror, for I have endured a boat landing in Egypt.

I had expected to be thinking in Alexandria of the library destroyed in ancient days, of the quay where Cæsar bade good-by to Cleopatra on his last departure for Rome, of the harbor where rode the fleets of Greece and Tyre and the Roman Empire. But instead I found myself meditating in my railroad carriage, after the landing was over, on the phenomenon of porters. Who are these fellows who are fighting like flame-beset demons for the privilege of lugging from a steamship the back-breaking baggage of foreign tourists? What a sight! Here is a man sweating and panting with five dress-suit cases lashed together by an enormous strap about his neck and back. Here is another bent almost double to the ground with two trunks piled up, one atop the other, on his shoulders. And here is still a third carrying two enormous bags on his back, two more in his hands, and a fifth dangling from his teeth in a knotted handkerchief. How can muscles bear such burdens, and bones not crack beneath such strains? Talk about overloading animals! I had no sympathy for struggling donkeys and camels inland after seeing the human beasts of burden upon the docks. If men can thus be treated, why be surprised if animals are abused? And these men were abusing themselves. They were not slaves, driven to this killing toil for others. No master lashed them to obedience as in the grim days of the Pharaohs. No, these porters were free men, freely choosing thus to labor and earn.

Or so it seemed! But deep down in these lives were forces more terrible than any foreman's whip or conqueror's sword. This fierce lifting and carrying on the docks were all that stands between these men and starvation. They *must* have those few coins tossed to them by contemptuous passengers if they and their families are to eat. It is thus that we organize society—place at the bottom vast hosts of ignorant, helpless, hopeless men who shall be driven by the sheer struggle for physical survival to do the dirty and burdensome work of the world. These porters, like all other toilers in our Western nations, are free politically. We have abolished the laws and institutions which make one man the property of another. But these same porters are still subject to another law—the law of economic necessity; they are bound by another institution—the institution of wage labor. Free politically, they are slaves economically. They tug and toil at our bags not because they love us, not because they enjoy such work, not because they are filled with the spirit of service, but simply and solely because they *have* to do it if they are not to starve like dogs in a famine-stricken town. Outwardly I saw this fearful sight of men racing madly across the pier to bow themselves down beneath the burden of our baggage. Inwardly I saw another and truly lovely sight of men carrying their own baggage off the boat, the stronger among them sharing the burden of the weaker, and all rejoicing in the dignity of labor and the joy of mutual help. Some time that day will come when there will be no more outcasts and slaves and human beasts, but all of us will be brothers together in the common labor of the common life.

Cairo

We were not happy on the trip to Cairo—the memory of that landing was too much with us! Yet were we wooed from the panic and pain of the experience, in spite of ourselves, by the strange sights that greeted us through the windows of the train as we flashed along. First, a woman with a veiled face, then flocks of dirty but picturesque Arabs trudging along the roads or toiling in the fields, then mud villages overtopped by tall, waving palm trees, donkeys galore, and then a camel, another camel, lots of camels. Later, after some days in Jerusalem, I became *blasé* on the camel question. But those first camels discovered from the car windows were worth going miles to see. The real thing, however, only came after some three hours, when the scene had begun to pall upon us a bit. This stretch of country, through the flat Delta region of the Nile, was all much the same—unchanging areas of cultivated land cut crosswise with irrigation ditches, occasional Arab villages, groups of workers or travelers along the highways, donkeys, camels, bullocks, and dogs. The ploughing interested us—the primitive wooden ploughs, pulled by donkeys or bullocks and turning the soil only a few inches deep. But it was much the same everywhere, and we were getting impatient for Cairo. Suddenly, I heard a cry of surprise. "The pyramids!" We leaped to the windows—and there over the distant city, clearly outlined against the sunlight, loomed the unmistakable bulks of two pyramids. The spell of Egypt was upon us. The huge piles were too far away to be impressive, but we stared and stared, until intervening buildings shut out the awesome sight. Immediately upon our arrival at Cairo, we wanted to rush to the desert, and behold these mightiest of monuments. But we had no time. In the few hours between trains, we could only walk the streets of this curious and noisy city, and wait until our return to "see the sights."

ON TO JERUSALEM

At six o'clock, we were on the train for Kantara; and at nine-thirty we were at the Suez Canal for the crossing from Africa to Asia. We were doing three continents in four days.

I shall not soon forget that little but momentous waterway. Was there ever such a motley gathering of humans as crowded on the dimly lit ferryboat that night? There were perhaps a hundred of us. The omnipresent American was there, of course, in full force. An equally large group was composed of silent Arabs, wrapped securely in their mantles and squatting on their enormous packs. There were several English military officers. Two Japanese were talking to an American about Tokyo. Egyptians and a Nubian or two were scattered here and there. I heard the German language at my right. On the other side of the boat was a Greek Orthodox priest—an important dignitary who at Cairo had had a large group of devotees to bid him farewell with much kneeling and kissing of hands. Among the passengers were also numerous Jews. The tribes of earth and the religions of all the gods were represented on that ferry craft.

We pushed off into the placid stream, bathed in the cold splendor of a full moon. It was a narrow canal. Could two ships pass? Yet this little stream outweighed the seven seas. For here was the central link of England's empire—the greatest empire since the passing of the vast sovereignties of classic days. Suez it was which held Egypt in occupation, Palestine under the Mandate, India in subjection, and East and West under single political control. Snap this link of the English chain of military and political dominance, and the globe would fall apart. But it will never be snapped—not while England lives! In the Great War, the best planned, most ably led and most triumphant campaign of the Allies was that conducted by the English, Arabs and Jews [2] under General Allenby in this region for the conquest of Palestine, the destruction of the Turkish army, and incidentally and primarily the protection of Suez. In the next war, if it ever comes, English lives will be poured out like water to protect this artificial lane of communication between the Mediterranean and the Red seas. Chamberlain had this canal in mind when he wrote his so-called reservations to the Briand-Kellogg Treaty. And here it lay in the moonlight, crossed by a little band of ill-assorted travelers, who at that peaceful moment were sheltered, protected, guided, controlled and mastered by Britain. Rome herself never ruled this world with half so great a power.

On the journey to Jerusalem, we traveled on the railroad built along the coast line and over the desert by English engineers for the passage of Allenby's great host. Prior to this campaign of arms, there was no entrance to the Holy Land through this region except by the ancient caravan trail, and by occasional by-paths fit only for donkeys' feet. But Allenby's base of supplies was Egypt, and communications must be kept open through all this desert country. So the road was constructed with matchless skill and devoted labor, and now, rebuilt along permanent lines, does the work of peace. My pacifist conviction that war can do no good thing was shaken just a bit as I lay in my comfortable de luxe "waggon lit," and reflected that, had the

---

[2] Three battalions of General Allenby's army were Jewish. These battalions were especially recruited in the United States and in England from men who volunteered. None were drafted. Jewish graves can be seen to-day in the military cemetery on the Mount of Olives.

English not conquered this country, I should be sleeping in some caravan camping ground, or daring the perilous landings at Jaffa or Haifa.

I saw little of the country till morning, when I was awakened by the zealous porter at Ludd, the railroad junction town, for a cup of tea and a bit of bread. Then I watched the slow winding of the train up and up, around and around, as it slowly scaled the twenty-seven hundred and more feet to the hilltop of Jerusalem. It seemed incredible that an army had ever crossed these hills, yet it had been done with a skill which makes Allenby one of the great strategists of all time. The hills were mostly barren, but they were terraced here and there, and in sheltered spots appeared traces of cultivation. I could see that the railway with its few trains was still a novelty, for camels bolted and ran as the engine puffed laboriously by, and workers stopped to stare as in a fascinated trance. This was an Arab country, and the people were primitive and miserably poor. There was little of beauty or cheer till the end of the journey drew near, and I saw the outskirts of Jerusalem. I was disappointed at the first glance, for I saw nothing of the old city. These were suburbs, comparatively modern—one of the older Jewish settlements, then an Arab village, and at last the farthest houses of the city proper. It was not Jerusalem as I had expected it. But a few moments' drive from the station brought me to the Jaffa Gate, and I was supremely happy. Here was the city of my dreams. My long journey across two oceans, through six countries, and touching four continents, was ended.

The Holy City

A half, or even a tenth, of what I did in this holy city of Jews, Christians and Moslems, cannot be set down in this book, which is intended to be something other and more than a book of travels. I was in Jerusalem a week before I started off on my automobile tour of the country, and saw all that to me was so strange and beautiful.

Such streets! As narrow as the alleyways of Naples, as deep and dark as the subterranean passages of a coal mine. In and out, a turn here, steps going up there, a tortuous wall to get 'round yonder—as easy to get lost as in a maze. What houses and shops! Built of stone like fortifications, the homes like cells in a prison or the chambers of the cliff dwellers, the shops like booths of a bazaar, mere holes in these huge walls, open in front, lost in darkness and cold in back. What peoples—all the tribes of earth! Bedouins wrapped warm in their abundant and picturesque robes of varied colors; Arabs distinguished in bearing, some of them cultured scholars, others wild barbarians from the desert; Jews with their long beards, hanging curls, and queer hats and gabardines; veiled ladies, from the Moslem homes; superb women, young and old, bearing with noble carriage their baskets or jars or bundles upon their heads; English soldiers and officers; the local police, a uniformed and trained body of men; a water carrier with his goatskin water bag across his back; a letter writer squatting on the pavement with ink, pen and paper; a Nubian peddler blacker than any Negro; a blind beggar whining for alms; an alert native boy eager to serve as interpreter with either Arab or Jew; little children playing about the stalls and gutters; a donkey boy leading his patient beast; a camel driver guiding one, two, three lordly camels with packs so bulky that they threaten to crush the passer-by against the unyielding wall; a rabbi, an Abyssinian priest, a Moslem effendi. There is no end to the variety and picturesqueness of this spectacle. "Stand at the Jaffa Gate," said a Palestinian friend to me, "and in fifteen minutes you will see as many different kinds of Jews—Jews from Arabia, from

Syria, from Afghanistan, from Persia, from Russia, from Morocco, from South Africa, from America." They are all distinctive in dress, in language, in type, in character. For the dispersion was wide, and it lasted long. But here is the homeland, and the tribes are gathering.

All this is endlessly fascinating. I walk down David Street, and step into a coffee-shop. In the center of the large room is a group of Arabs puffing silently and contentedly at their shining brass houkahs. On the right are two picturesque old Jews, playing the same game of backgammon that was taught me years ago in New England, surrounded by five or six onlookers arrayed in every style of Eastern garb. On the left are two black men, in vivid turbans, absorbed in some kind of card game. A picture from the Arabian Nights, if there ever was one!

I turn a corner, and find myself in a pottery, with the bearded potter at his wheel. I see him slap on a shapeless mass of moist clay, then dip his hands in a bowl of water, and proceed to smooth and mold the yielding lump. Suddenly the wheel begins to turn, and, fascinated, I watch him slowly, surely, expertly stretch out the clay into an urn-like shape, then quickly insert first his thumb and then gradually his whole hand into the mass, hollowing it out from top to bottom. Turns, turns the wheel; rhythmically the deft hands dip into the water, then touch the clay; beautifully the jar swells into its perfectly proportioned lines; at last, the wheel is still, and the jar is done. For how many thousand years, here in the patient East, has this potter been at his task, working to-day precisely as in the day of Abraham?

I dive into a low archway in the heavy stone, make my way through a damp, dark passage, climb a winding stair of worn stone steps, and find myself looking into the homes of the very poor. Here is a single room, with stone floor, plastered stone walls, a single window tight shut against the cold. Under the window, sitting cross-legged on a piece of dirty matting, is the father of the family, a typical Jew with scraggly beard and curled earlocks, a tinsmith working busily at his trade. In a corner is a tumbled bed, in another corner a box of drawers, some petrol tins filled with filthy water, a few rags of clothing tossed about on the floor, some shivering children, a tired mother, a mangy cat. I stoop along other dark stone passages, climb other stairs, and always I see other rooms, each one with its shivering and crowded family. "Shalom" (Peace) is the friendly greeting at every door; the mother not infrequently snatches up a child and exhibits him with smiling pride; lean and hungry cats dodge in and out. These houses, or some of them, date back to the time of the Crusades. They resemble forts more than homes. They seem to have been built with the idea of protection from some enemy. It would be easy to hide in these endless passages, and not difficult to wall up these low arches. For centuries they must have been inhabited by people who lived in terror of the sword. Now poverty haunts these nooks and corners, and hunger is the lurking terror of their denizens.

These sights interest me far more than doubtful historical buildings and alleged historical monuments. I have seen the Church of the Holy Sepulchre, and found it a grimly impressive memorial to the ignorance, superstition and intolerance of men—a sepulchre not of the Christ, but of his hopes and dreams. I have stood in the Mosque of Omar, and seen its perfect beauty marred by the evidence that Moslems are as credulous as Christians. I have trod the "Via Dolorosa" from the house where Pilate condemned Jesus to the slopes of Calvary, and found only so many "stations" established to entice offerings from the pocketbooks of Christians. I have found that David's Citadel is not David's, and that Solomon's Stables are neither Solomon's nor stables; I have looked on two sepulchres of Christ, three gardens of Gethsemane, and one of I know not how many graves of Moses. All this rubbish is disappointing, disillusioning, disgusting. It is a relief to turn from shams of this scandalous order to the picturesque realities of the daily life of this ancient town. The money changer clanking his coins at his little booth is a truer evidence of Jesus's day than all the tombs and churches in Jerusalem. The shepherd with his sheep on the road to Bethany brings back the olden time more vividly than any shrine or altar. These innumerable churches are encumbrances upon sacred soil, but this "city set on a hill" to-day as yesterday "cannot be hid."

This last gives illustration of what are the genuine satisfactions of the Holy City, apart from its swarming peoples from all the East. We have only to remember that Jerusalem has been destroyed some seven or eight times since the opening of the Christian era, and that the present level of the city is some sixty feet above the level of the old city, to understand that no edifice or even stone within these walls is genuinely ancient. No monument, with certain exceptions like Herod's wall, dates back more than a thousand years, and no tradition is earlier than the reign of Constantine. Why get excited about holy places? But one can get excited about other things. There is the Mount of Olives, for example, the same hill upon which Jesus stood; here was the city upon which he looked; and along some road between these two spots the Master must have walked on that first Palm Sunday. It was just about at this point that he passed the gates of the city, and precisely at this point that he found the Temple. Take the road to Jericho, and two miles out is Bethany. Not Jesus's Bethany—but a later town on the site of Jesus's Bethany!

Here within the range of a few hundred square feet was the home of Mary and Martha; and along this road, or some similar road, to Jerusalem, Jesus must have passed and repassed during that last week. Stand on Mt. Scopus! There are the Jordan and the Dead Sea, just as Moses, Joshua and Jesus must have known them; over there, to the north, is the birthplace of Jeremiah; on that hilltop yonder Samuel denounced the cry of Israel for a king. This is the country that the kings and the prophets, the priests and the apostles knew. This is the river over which Joshua led his host, and in which John baptized. These are the hills that Jesus saw, and the roads over which he walked. Sites can be identified, the landscape remains the same. For all the sham and roguery that deface this land, no one can look upon it without profound emotion, nor, having seen it, ever again read his Bible or ponder the origins of his religion without a consciousness of revelation as if from the very mind of God. Palestine, as well as its people, has in its essence a divine reality.

JORDAN AND THE DEAD SEA

This was our first trip, on the one good day of our first week. Speeding by the contemporary Jewish cemeteries, and skirting the Mount of Olives, we came to Bethany. Then we moved for miles of swiftly descending, frequently precipitous road, through the wilderness of Benjamin—that vast stretch of barren, unwatered mountain country between Jerusalem and the Jordan. The endlessly rolling hills were beautifully colored in the alternating sunshine and shadow of the changing day, but they were so dry and bleak as to chill the heart. No villages, no gardens, no people! It was easy to believe that we were approaching the very wilderness in which Jesus lost himself for forty days. I think that as I looked upon this waste and empty land, I understood for the first time the nature of Satan's temptation of Jesus, that he take these stones and make them bread.

At last, fourteen hundred feet below sea level, we emerged from the arid mountains, and came to the desert. Slowly we plowed our way through this dead soil and came at last to the shores of the Sea. Here, in a few miserable Arab huts, we found a chance to go in bathing; we stripped, and plunged into the saltiest water in the world. All the stories were true. To sink in this flood was impossible; to swim was almost impossible, the body floated so high above the surface. Curling ourselves up, we bobbed upon the tide like rubber balls. A queer experience!

From the Dead Sea we went to the shores of the Jordan. What a surprise! *This* the most famous, the most holy river in the world! A little, muddy stream, more like a swollen brook than the great watercourse which I had imagined. Here was a genuine disappointment. Yet I am told that hosts of pilgrims seek this place, plunge ecstatically into the water, bathe in it, drink it in eager gulps, and think themselves saved. Great is the capacity of man to deceive himself.

It was a relief to turn away from this depressing sight, and go to Jericho. This is in an oasis as green and beautiful as in the days of the city which Joshua destroyed. No Old Testament site in Palestine is better authenticated than this. Here are the ruins of the old city, and here the lovely little modern town which serves as a winter resort for the chilled citizens of Jerusalem. Sober Arabs sat sunning themselves beneath vine-clad walls, handsome girls carried gracefully their water jars, donkeys trotted patiently along the streets, camels peered contemptuously from the courtyard of an inn. By the Pool of Elijah, the rushing spring that feeds the oasis, I found an Egyptian girl as lovely as a story book, accompanied by two musicians with viol and drum. She smiled at me, held out her arms, and jangled her beads. The toss of a coin, and the musicians were playing and singing some weird refrain, and the girl was dancing like a wondrous houri! Was there ever such a moment of pure fantasy? Joshua was dead these many centuries. The fortress walls of this old town had risen and been battered down again and yet again. In this plain moldered the bones of the thousands slain in the last overthrow of the Israelites by the hosts of Nebuchadnezzar. The glory was departed, and Jericho at this moment but a lovely Oriental beggar girl dancing for a tourist clergyman from New York. The music ceased, and the tripping feet were still. I looked on the waving palms about me, and beyond to the barren hills, and pondered the destiny of man and of his works upon the earth. Why do we strive and cry, and fight and kill? A little hour, and all is over, save a song in desert places.

Samaria and the Samaritans

After a week in Jerusalem, we started north on a ten days' automobile tour through Galilee and Syria.[*] Two days on the road plunged us into storms almost unprecedented for this country. Continual rains swept the mountains and drenched the plains. Farther north and west, heavy snows were falling. Everywhere roads were washed away or blocked, railway service was suspended, telegraph and telephone lines were down. The winds were high, the cold severe, and the population generally miserable. We saw the Near East under conditions which resemble our Far West.

Starting from Jerusalem on a lowering Monday morning,

[*] On this trip I visited many of the colonies, schools, industries of Zion, but have postponed description of them to Chapter IV.

we drove north on the highroad to Nazareth and Tiberias. The country was lonely, but speedily gave signs of being much more fertile than the wilderness country to the east. This was land which could be cultivated, and could sustain a population. We were interested, as we sped along, in passing camel trains, herds of sheep and cattle, wayfarers with or without donkeys on their way to the city for a day's trading, Arab villages in the distance, and occasional ruins of crusading or earlier times. Now and again our host, Dr. Judah L. Magnes, Chancellor of the Hebrew University in Jerusalem, pointed out mounds, or "tels," as he called them, which marked the sites of ancient fortresses or cities, and contained successive layers, like geological strata, of the remains of the passing civilizations and cultures of ancient days. Certain of these "tels" are being excavated, with results not gorgeous like those of Egypt, but immensely satisfying to historian and archæologist. Dr. Magnes, learned in the lore of the land, showed us famous Biblical scenes and brought to mind many a chapter of Old and New Testament.

After some two hours of riding, we came to the town of Nablus, better known as the ancient Shechem. Readers of John's Gospel will remember that "Jacob's well was there." Here on the outskirts of the present town live a group of Samaritans, one hundred and fifty in number, who are the sole survivors of that Samaritan community which played so large a part in Jewish life in the New Testament and earlier days. For some twenty-five hundred years these Samaritans have endured as a separate people, and these survivors, as independent and proud as ever, still maintain the traditions of their tribe and the sanctity of their altar.

Into narrow streets we went, passed through dark and foul-smelling alleys, stooped under low arcades, climbed stairways between cold, damp walls, and came at last, as through a maze, to the miserable homes of the Samaritans. We were met by a tall, gaunt man, arrayed in bright-colored robes, who introduced himself as the son of the high priest who was at the moment absent in Egypt on a mission. He offered to show us the synagogue, which was solemnly opened by three men, each holding a separate key for the release of a separate lock. For centuries, we were told, the synagogue has been in the custody of three priestly families, each one of which has clung tenaciously to its high privilege and responsibility. The synagogue proved to be a single, low-vaulted chamber, with the familiar paraphernalia of worship. The scroll of the Law was brought out for our inspection, and the text written on ancient parchment was said to date from the seventh year after the death of Moses. We were polite enough to look properly impressed, and generous enough to give the tips for which eager palms were eagerly extended. It was a rather pitiful experience. Back through the arches and alleys we made our way, and rejoiced again to feel the fresh air on our faces. I looked up at Mt. Gerizim, towering into the mist on our right, and remembered gratefully that it was "neither in this mountain, nor yet in Jerusalem, that (men) worshipped the Father." The great Nazarene had little use for these things.

Into the Mountains

Another hour, and we were out of the mountains and descending easily into the rich plain of Esdraelon. Here was the great highway and battle-ground between East and West. Like a gash from some giant hand, it cut the mountains, and gave access from the Mediterranean to the Euphrates and beyond. Through this valley had passed and repassed every army from the days of the most ancient Egyptians to the days of the English and the Turks in 1917.

Tiglath-pileser and Sennacherib, Nebuchadnezzar and Cyrus, Alexander and Pompey, Godfrey de Bouillon and Richard Cœur de Lion, Ali and Saladin, Napoleon and Allenby, had all crossed this valley and looked upon these hills. Deep in the rich soil of the plain mingled the bones and arms of Philistines, Chaldeans, Babylonians, Persians, Greeks, Romans, Saracens, Turks, and all European peoples. Here was the spring where Gideon chose his three hundred men for the defense of Israel; there was Gilboa where Saul was defeated and slain with Jonathan, his son; yonder was Beison where Saul's head was nailed up for all to see after his overthrow. If nature were not kind, these stones and dust would bear the stains of all the wars of all the last five thousand years. But nature *is* kind, and Esdraelon lies green, beautiful and peaceful beneath the gaze of the passing traveler.

On the edge of this plain it had been agreed that the Chancellor of the University and I should leave the car and take horses into the mountains, to visit two remote and highly interesting Zionist colonies of the communist order. In one of these colonies the mosaic floor of an ancient Jewish synagogue had recently been uncovered in the course of some ditch digging, and the Chancellor was going in to examine and photograph the "find." I was to accompany him, and survey the colony as an important specimen of Zionist colonization of the homeland.

It had rained for days, and the roads were wet and muddy. The sky was now dark and threatening. Nevertheless, here were the horses, brought to the roadside by one of the colonists, and everything was ready. So we mounted our steeds, said good-by to the folks, and rode away. Within a hundred yards, we passed through an Arab village of five hundred souls. All the houses were of mud, built low to the ground, with a hole here and there as a vent, and a door through which crawled man and beast to the foul straw within. They reminded me more of Eskimo igloos than of anything else of which I could think. Behind the houses were huge piles of dried camel dung, for fuel. Mud and filth were everywhere. A dog was eating some kind of dead animal by the road; a forlorn figure was passing between the houses; two barefooted women were trudging over the fields bearing huge bundles of brush upon their heads. Of all the five hundred persons, these were the only ones we saw.

As we moved through the village, four horses in single file, it began to rain again. We buttoned up our coats securely, wrapped the saddle robes about our legs, and pushed ahead. Within an hour, we had reached a Jewish colony upon our way—Ain Harod, by name—with the rain pouring down upon us in torrents. We dismounted for a few moments' rest and refreshment, were cheered by some food and cups of hot tea, spent an hour or so splashing 'round the settlement, and then, in a heavier rain than ever, mounted our dripping horses, and started down the lonely road.

The way was now a bog, deep with mud and pouring with water. The horses plunged into the mud well up to their knees. My horse was tired, and again and again stopped in sheer despair at the prospect. Frequently we would leave the road and try the pastures, only to find ourselves more deeply in the mud than ever. Mile after mile we went on, encouraging the struggling horses, and shifting our wraps to keep ourselves in some way warm and dry. Now and again something would happen to enliven our melancholy journey. We met a caravan of five camels, which our horses refused to pass. Nothing to do but lash the animals across a ditch, and make a wide detour through the mucky fields! We passed a shepherd on the hillside, with his shivering sheep gathered about him as though for shelter. We encountered a lone horseman—the veterinary, so we were told, traveling from village to village to tend the stock. A moment of genuine excitement came when three wild boars went dashing across the road. But most of the time there was nothing but rain and the mud and the chilling cold. The valley stretched out green and beautiful on our left, the mountains loomed rocky and steep on our right; but we saw little but the road, and felt little but the wet.

As we struggled along, I thought of wet days on the Maine coast. Then I thought of the blazing hearth fires before which we dried our clothing, warmed our chilled limbs, and toasted our apples and marshmallows. Then I recollected that there was no fuel in this country—no coal, and no wood—and that when we arrived at our destination, we should find no warmth of any kind. The anticipation was fulfilled. About four o'clock in the afternoon, with the rain heavier than ever, we reached the colony of Beth Alpha. We dismounted in a sea of mud, stalked into the dining hall which was as cold as all outdoors, and there, without removing a garment or even our hats, we sat till nine o'clock, sipping hot coffee, munching dry bread, eating a dinner of soup, boiled cauliflower and more coffee, and talking Zionism, communism and pacifism. On our way to bed, we visited various buildings of the settlement, inspected the work, questioned the members; then, cold, forlorn, and apprehensive of the morning, we went to our room, and snuggled into bed.

All night long the storm raged. In the morning, the land looked like Noah's flood. Our plan was to take horses again, ride three miles into the valley to a railroad station, and there catch a train for Tiberias, where we were to rejoin our automobile. In the early hours of what for a time promised to be a better day, we started off, only to be overtaken by a renewal of the storm. The road was now quite turned to water. As we descended into the valley, we went splashing through plunging torrents which seemed like brooks or even rivers. At last, when our haven by the railway was just looming into view, we found that a veritable cataract had swept across the road during the night and carried it entirely away. Up the raging stream and down we sought a place where it would be safe to drive or swim the horses across, but all in vain. No horse could live in such a flood as that. Nothing to do but turn back, and retrace all that frightful road over which we had struggled the day before! Not until hours beyond the appointed time did we reach Tiberias, and get started upon our scheduled journey into Syria.

By three o'clock we were off by automobile over that "road to Damascus" over which Paul was journeying when he was smitten by the vision of the risen Christ. For four thousand years it has been the highway from south to north—we were traveling the trail of countless caravans and myriads of pilgrims. In all that time I doubt if the road was ever darker or more forbidding. Suddenly, after some two hours' riding, we were stopped by the loud horn-blasts of a passing automobile. The water was pouring over the highway some miles ahead, the road was in bad condition and might go out at any time, we would be wise if we turned back. What should we do? The gathering night decided the question. Better the bad but still passable conditions behind us, than the uncertainties and dangers ahead! So back we went, back along the shores of the Sea of Galilee, back to Tiberias, now as squalid as it was once glorious. A warm hotel and a good dinner awaited us. By ten o'clock we were in bed, anxious as to the adventures which awaited us upon the morrow.

JOURNEYINGS

Damascus and Syria

Not in the space of a single generation had Palestine and Syria been swept by such devastating storms as had prevailed during the past week. Beirut was cut off from all communication with the rest of Syria, and our projected trip to this seacoast town must be abandoned. Heavy snow blocked all the roads, a railroad train from Damascus was lost in the mountains, telephone and telegraph wires were all down. Damascus had had no mail from the west for five days, and none from the south for four days. The train from Tiberias to Damascus was blocked by washouts, and its shivering passengers had spent the night and most of the next day in the cars. Automobiles had been ditched in every direction, and miserable stories were coming in of nights spent on the wet ground in the chill darkness of Arab huts. Jerusalem was in the midst of a deluge, and tourists were huddling in the hotels shivering with cold and desperate with disappointment.

These were the reports that came to us at Tiberias the morning after we had turned back. This next morning was gloomy enough, and prospects of a change in the weather were like the snakes in Ireland—there were none! After some hesitation, we decided to try for Damascus again. We at least had all the day before us; there was no danger of darkness, and our worst fate would be to turn back again. So we started out!

A fitful gleam of morning sunshine showed us the beauty of the Sea of Galilee, with its shining waters and its sheltering hills. This was where Jesus walked and talked, and stilled the storm (we knew something about these storms!), and crossed to the opposite shore of the Gadarenes. It was not difficult to imagine Jesus here, especially when we saw some fishers in their heavy fishing boats. In all these years the fishing has been the same—the boats have not been changed by so much as a single nail. As we climbed the hills, away from the lake, the country became desolate again. There were no villages, only the wretched goatskin tents of nomads here and there. There were no people, save an occasional shepherd wrapped close in his enfolding mantle, a lonely Arab road mender, or a wandering trader with his plodding camels. In a little over an hour we reached the banks of the upper Jordan, the border line between Palestine and Syria. The incessant rains now began falling again in floods. We bumped and skidded over roads which were more like bogs than highways. But these roads were not impassable. Even where lakes of muddy water in the fields and ditches on both sides had flowed together over the way, we were able to push through, though the flood mounted to our axles. Once at least, where a miniature waterfall was overflowing the road, it looked like ticklish business. But courage, a skillful driver, and abundant good luck carried us through. Before noon, we had reached Damascus, and the skies were blue.

How old this Moslem city is, I doubt if anybody really knows. Located in the middle of one of the great oases of this Eastern world, it has for ages been an important caravan station, and the center of the trading for near and distant regions. Through the center of Damascus runs the river which changes the arid sands to pleasant verdure. Climb the hills, and you see the crowded town ringed around by the beautiful gardens of the oasis, and beyond, on every side, the desert. The Arab poet was right when he called it a pearl set in emeralds. Mohammed was stirred by real emotion when he said that it was the dream of Paradise come true.

But Damascus is more beautiful afar than it is close at hand. Its streets are narrow, crowded, and dirty. Its famous bazaars are extensive enough, but rather shabby. Its important buildings and beautiful houses are set in poor quarters or hidden behind high walls, and are wonderful within rather than without. Even its women, undoubtedly lovely, are veiled, and invariably clad in gloomy black. If anything is perfect, as a fulfillment of expectations, it is the minarets, which rise with infinite grace above the many mosques. Especially are these beautiful when they ring with the voices of the muezzins in their calls to prayer. On every tower is that lordly figure, chanting in his clear, musical, far-sounding voice. Echoes come from all directions, till the sky seems vocal with solemn melody. We heard these muezzins elsewhere, but never as in Damascus.

But our visit to Syria was only a short detour from the main road of travel through Palestine, and does not concern us here. On the second day we were headed back toward the Jordan frontier, to resume our journey through Galilee to the west.

An Ancient Shrine—Safed

Our first destination was Safed—an ancient Jewish town, lost in the mountains above the Sea of Galilee, the same to-day as in the Middle Ages, or earlier in the creative days of Talmud lore. It is mentioned by Flavius Josephus, and must have existed as early at least as 200 A.D. How much farther back the old town goes, nobody has any idea. For centuries Safed was a center of Jewish learning and piety in Palestine. Its saints and religious mystics made it for a time an even greater and more significant center than Jerusalem. Renowned teachers gathered in this town as in a university; students came from far and near to sit at the feet of these learned men; by the light thus kindled

* Looted and burned, with loss of property and life, in the August (1929) riotings.

all the realms of the Diaspora were illumined. The climax of Safed's glory came in the sixteenth century when flourished the famous Isaac Lurya, known popularly as Ha-Ari, "the Lion." He was the founder and leader of the great mystical movement in Judaism, associated with the famous cabalistic practices of the Chasidic Jews. This movement had a twofold significance. On the one hand, it was a reaction against and an attack upon the extreme intellectualism of the Jews in their exclusive study of the Law. On the other hand, it was a democratic uprising of the people against the pretensions of the rabbis and scholars generally to a monopoly of piety and virtue. Not in learning, said these mystics, but in the inner spiritual experiences of each humble but devoted soul, lies the way of salvation. In Isaac Lurya this movement found its inspired teacher and exemplar, and in Safed, the home of "the Lion," its seat of authority and center of influence. From this new Sinai went forth this new Law of inner sanctity. Around this new Moses of the spirit gathered disciples of every clime, and Safed became a very "holy of holies." Long after "the Lion's" death, Safed held its position of peculiar primacy in Israel—and might have held it to this day, had it not been for the great earthquakes of 1800 and 1837. The terrible devastation wrought by these visitations frightened the emotional inhabitants into the conviction that God had punished them for preferring Safed to his own holy city, Jerusalem. Immediately there began an exodus to this latter city, which has continued to this day. Safed is a dying community. Its forty-six synagogues, of which no less than twenty-eight lie idle and empty, are a monument at once to its ancient glory and its present fall. Only three thousand persons remain, Arabs and Jews together. Both groups are miserably poor, the Jews kept alive only by the pious offerings of the faithful the world around. Orthodox of the orthodox, wearing the garb and practicing the habits of former times, living in low stone houses which have not changed in a thousand years, these Jews are like a ghetto community of the Middle Ages suddenly come to light. The men with their round caps and long beards, the women clustered at evening with their water jars about the running springs, the children bowing and swaying in their schools as they chant the Torah, the Sabbath unbroken by the turning of a wheel or the lifting of a stone, the synagogues with their absorbed, silent and venerable students of the Book, all testify to a world forgotten and to an age gone by. Where in Palestine, or in the world, is there a place like this?

Up from the Sea of Galilee we climbed, to reach this ancient town, three thousand feet above sea level. Behind us shone the Sea, with the dark mountains beyond, just as Jesus must have seen them many a time when he fled into the hills for rest and prayer. Before us ran the narrow road, a mere shelf between the looming cliffs upon the one side and the precipitous ravines upon the other. It was as though our automobile were an aeroplane, so swiftly did it sweep through the defiles and mount aloft to the towering crests. At last, and suddenly, as we flew around the side of the mountain, we saw Safed lying in a cup-like hollow beneath us, spilling over the farther side into the distant valley. We sped by a shepherd waving his staff protectingly over his huddled flocks; dipped into the hollow, like a swooping bird; moved rapidly up the main street between the old, one-storied, dirt-roofed houses, and stopped before the inn amid an excited crowd of bearded, hawk-faced, swarthy Jews who darkened every window of the car with peering faces. It was winter, and no tourists had been in Safed for a long time.

Our first business was with our host, a handsome, dignified, hospitable man of early middle age, with beard, skullcap, and long frock coat. Would we have a meat dinner, or a milk dinner? We could have either, for we were the only guests and all the resources of the house were at our disposal. But we could not have both, or any mixture of the two, for the laws of the Jews forbade. Not even the same plates and eating utensils could be used for these two kinds of meals, for such confusion was impiety. So we chose a meat dinner and a milk breakfast. And I duly observed that all the equipment of the table was different for the two repasts.

Our dinner ordered, and the hour being late, we took a guide and went into the town. What a plunge it was into the past! We moved along main streets too narrow for a loaded camel to pass. We went down side streets which were mere flights of rude stone steps from level to level. We peered into homes which were single rooms crowded with parents and children. We entered a school, and were met by two venerable men, clad in noble flowing robes, who were just dismissing a clamorous crowd of boys whom a moment before we had heard chanting the verses of the ancient lore. We looked into synagogue after synagogue, all of them small, most of them empty, the relics of the mighty days gone by. Torrential rains had made the streets muddy and unclean. The drains running through the middle of the streets were open and "smelly." From the dark, damp, unventilated houses came noisome odors. But as we reached the far edges of the town, we saw distant hills and lofty skies—a panorama of earth and heaven so beautiful as to grip the throat with tears. Did the people ever come out of their ancient hovels to gaze upon these mountains? Did these bearded men ever look up from their Talmud long enough to watch the sunset dying on these western summits?

I pondered such questions as we were asked to turn away from these glories of the land to the hoarded glories of the builded town. In the heart of Safed was a "holy of holies" —the synagogue and house of Isaac Lurya, Ha-Ari, "the Lion." The synagogue was much like the others we had seen, but we were ushered in as to a shrine. From a guarded cupboard the silver decorations of the sacred scroll, used by "the Lion" himself, were lifted down by reverent hands and exhibited to each one of us. Then we were taken into the house where the great teacher had lived. In the central room, on the eastern wall, was a small aperture. This aperture admitted to a cell-like chamber, scarcely four feet square, which had neither door nor window. Here in silence and alone, in darkness lit only by a lighted candle, day and night together for years, "the Lion" read his scripture and meditated upon its wisdom. Here he tortured his flesh with ascetic exercises, and moved himself to ecstatic visions of the inner spirit. Buried in the depths of cold stone walls, cut off from air and light and human intercourse, it was a living tomb in which a great soul had immured itself for years. "Was 'the Lion' buried here," I asked. No, not here. But quickly we were led back into the outer air, and shown far down in the valley a cemetery, and there beneath the tallest monument reposed the body of the great man.

It was dark, now. The day in Palestine is followed immediately by the night, without dusk or twilight. We threaded hurriedly the narrow streets, for it was cold as well as dark. We passed the windows of a dimly lighted synagogue, and I went in. The place was dark, save at the farther end, where hung an oil lamp. In this pool of light, there sat a group of aged men. Their long beards swept their breasts; their keen eyes fixed themselves upon the huge tomes which they were reading; their faces, gaunt with hunger and quick intelligence, were lit in silhouette by the hanging flame. One man with burning eyes was expounding the sacred text—the others were nodding in assent, or listening with an intentness that was painful. It was like a Rembrandt canvas. I stood silently among these men. Save for a whispered "Shalom," they noticed me not at all. After a little time I turned away, and as I passed the door saw a strange figure—a young man with hanging earlocks, bent shoulders, and eager, questing eyes, leaning forward upon a desk, and reading, as by the light of his inner spirit of devotion, the darkened text before him. He was too young to be received among the elders. But with him as with them, the Law was the life of men, and he was preparing himself for the august succession. I bowed to him and went out into the cold, wet night. The spirit of "the Lion" was living on.

A Modern Shrine—Haifa

The night in Safed was one of the coldest I have ever known. It was a cold from which there was no escape. It sat with us after dinner, as we huddled about a small brazier and held our hands over the glowing ashes. It crawled in under the bed clothes, and slept with us through the dark hours. In the morning we ate breakfast wrapped in every coat and sweater we had with us, our frosted breaths steaming the air about us. I wondered how the people in the town endured such nights as these in their cavernous houses and on their meager diet. Fortunately the winter season is as short in Palestine as in California.

By eight o'clock we were speeding down the mountain highway to our next stop, Haifa. This city is the port of Palestine, now a dangerously open roadstead where ships can land only in small boats and in good weather, but soon to be made by extensive building operations the finest harbor on this Mediterranean coast. I was coming here to examine this project, and visualize the fleets of ships which would be floating in years to come upon these waters. I wanted also to see certain schools and other public institutions. But most I wanted to see in this place the head of the world-wide Bahai movement, Shoghi Effendi, and make my pilgrimage to the graves of the immortal prophets of this noble faith. This was my desire on behalf of American friends, and in expression of my own devout reverence for this great inclusive religion of our time.

Our first view of Haifa was from Mt. Carmel, where Elijah in the ancient day confounded the prophets of Baal. What a place from which to summon the witness of Jehovah! On the left, the dazzling blue of the Mediterranean; on the right, the wide curve of the beach sweeping to the walls of Acre; in front the bay, with two large ships and numerous smaller craft peacefully at anchor; below, like a tumbling waterfall, the white stone houses of the town; and just in the center, like a lovely gem, the garden in which repose the bodies of the honored Bahai dead.

We visited this garden the next morning, after a special audience with the head of the Bahai church. In the center towered the cluster of noble cypresses, beneath whose grateful shade the venerable Abdul Baha sought quiet and refreshment. Around these trees, winding from terrace to terrace, and lined with giant hedges of geraniums, were paths, paved with broken fragments of red tile, which tempted the feet to meditative wandering. Rose bushes, gorgeous with blossoms a few weeks hence, broke frequently the stretches of fresh, deep-rooted grass. On the lowest terrace, facing a straight avenue which shot down, and then on like an arrow, to the sea, was the granite mausoleum. We removed our shoes, in accordance with Arab custom, and stepped into the large room, dimly lighted through stained windows, in which lay the body of Abdul Baha. I remembered him as the wise and gentle sage with whom I had talked on his last visit to America. Now his noble face was still in death beneath this richly inscribed drapery upon the floor. We stood shoeless upon rugs so soft and heavy as to be warm to the feet. We saw silver vases laden with flowers standing like candles about the grave. A great peace lay upon the place. I had never seen a tomb so beautiful. After long moments of reverent salutation, we moved away, and entered a second room where lay the body of the Bab. This great forerunner of the faith, martyred in the awful persecutions of the early days, for years had had no rest. His body had been snatched secretly from place to place by loyal disciples, hidden wherever a moment's security could be won. But here at last it had found peace, and therewith itself had become a shrine. In this room, as in the other, were the rugs, the vases and the flowers. This dauntless hero of the spirit was not without his great reward.

Baha O'Llah, the third of the great trinity of Bahai leaders, was buried across the bay in Acre. In the afternoon, under the escort of a cousin of Shoghi Effendi, also a grandson of Abdul Baha, we started for this ancient city. Our way led us first along the hard, clean beach of sand which stretched across the roadstead. It had been storming, and the waves were running high and breaking in wild cascades of foam. Fishermen were busy, as high winds and dark skies drove in the fish. Some were launching their huge boats through the breakers; others, far out upon the waves, were dragging their heavy nets along the deep; still others had landed and were laboriously hauling their catch to the shore. At intervals among the fishers walked long caravans of camels, each patient beast contrasting strangely with the background of sea and sky. Far ahead loomed the ancient city, its ridge of close-packed houses surmounted by the huge bulk of the mighty citadel and a minaret so graceful as to suggest a dream of Paradise. Here, in this bay, had floated long ago the fleets of the Phœnicians. Later ages saw the ships of Genoese, Venetians and Pisans, for Acre was a great port. Paul came to this city, and stayed a day. Richard Cœur de Lion landed here with his mailed warriors of the Third Crusade, and defeated Saladin in one of the fiercest sieges of the time. Napoleon six hundred years later was not so happy, for against this citadel his artillery beat in vain, and his dream of an Eastern empire faded away forever.

We went to the citadel, incidentally to see this relic of the Crusaders, primarily to visit the prison cell where Baha O'Llah had been held captive through so many awful years by his persecutors. As we mounted the huge walls, twenty feet thick, we heard the muezzin chant his call to prayer from the nearby mosque. The Moslem rules this battleground to-day. Our escort was influential and tried hard, but we did not see Baha O'Llah's cell. For the citadel is still a prison—we saw the striped convicts in the yard—and visitors could not be admitted. We sought consolation in walking the corridors where centuries before the mailed feet of knights and squires had noisily trod, and in visiting the astounding subterranean church built by the Crusaders *beneath* the citadel. It had been filled up with dirt and rubbish long ago by the Saracens. We stood on the *top* of this mass of dirt and touched the capitals of the huge pillars which supported the groined roof just above our heads. Very soon now the church would be excavated and its grandeurs brought to light. Meanwhile, we had had this curious experience of entering the edifice from above instead of from below.

Another fifteen minutes, and we were in the Bahai garden where lay the remains of Baha O'Llah. Huge cypresses and palms were close about; the same red-tiled walks threaded their way through luxurious grass and flowers. A strange peace again dropped down upon us from the encompassing atmosphere of beauty. With eager reverence we once more removed our shoes, and stepped into the sacred presence of the prophet's tomb. Was it because this great man reposed alone that I was so deeply touched? Or was it because a sense of the man's greatness came sweeping suddenly upon me? Baha O'Llah was not only the supreme genius of the Bahai movement; he was without question one of the supreme spiritual geniuses of history. There have been few in any age to compare with him in point of insight, vision, lofty thought and noble speech. I felt this as I stood within this quiet place. Were it possible to stand by the grave of Jesus, I felt I should be moved in this same way. Here, appropriately, was not darkness, but light; not gloom, but glory. These prophets' shrines are truly among the sacred spots of earth.

NAZARETH

No place in Palestine, not even Jerusalem itself, held more interest for me than Nazareth. I knew perfectly well that the sacred places were spurious. No house in all the town existed in the days of Jesus; no site has even a remote possibility of being real, save only the well where Mary is reputed to have come in the eventide for water. This spring must have been running in her day as in ours, and have given water to her as to the other women of the place. But the location of the town itself is beyond all question. Here between these hills, in this gentle hollow of the land, stood the house where Jesus was born, the home wherein he lived, the streets upon which he played. Though I saw no other place, I must see this.

My first glimpse of Nazareth was on the way to Haifa.

The rains had ceased for a few moments. All day that extraordinary succession of sunshine and storm, which is characteristic of Palestine in the winter season, had tantalizingly beset us. Sometimes it was shining from one portion of the sky and raining from another. Not infrequently, amid the heaviest downpours, we saw rainbows so glorious and so near at hand as to baffle all description. But these rainbows meant nothing—Noah was arguing from inadequate premises when he interpreted the rainbow as a promise of the Lord that the flood was over! The floods came to us even while the rainbows were flaming from the skies. But at this moment, as we rode through Nazareth, it was pleasant for a little time.

We caught sight of the town as we crested the hills, and dipped into the valley. There it was, far below us—the famous Nazareth! It looked right—as I wanted and expected it to look. It was larger and more prosperous than the village in which Joseph and Mary lived. Those huge churches and monasteries did not occupy the landscape in that early day. But these low, stone houses were not unlike those which Jesus knew; this shepherd and his sheep the young lad must have seen a thousand times; and the shelter of the hills, threaded by its deep paths and winding camel tracks, must have looked to him precisely as it did to me. The bright sunshine on the wet vineyards and pastures helped to make the picture infinitely charming. As our machine sped past high walls and leaning house fronts, dodging sheep and donkeys and playing boys, it seemed as though the years had rolled away, and we were back in the days of the Nazarene.

Our second glimpse of the town came two days later, in the dark hours of a drenching afternoon. The approach from the low plains of the seacoast was not impressive. It was too wet and cold for any of us to enthuse over anything. At the inn we found that we were the only guests, and that the house was ours. A good dinner, a parlor warmly heated by an oil stove, quiet hours of reading and writing, put us in excellent spirits for the morrow. But, alas, the next day—Sunday—was wetter than all preceding days, and sight-seeing was rendered almost impossible. Yet our visit was not disappointing, for Nazareth is a place not to be seen but to be felt.

What is there to see? Churches covering so-called holy places—monasteries crowded with idle monks, the so-called guardians of these holy places—the synagogue in which Jesus preached, and which (curiously enough) dates from many years after Jesus's death—sites identified so perfectly with Bible scenes as to defy criticism and credence! Next only to Jerusalem and Bethlehem, Nazareth is cluttered up with empty churches and idle churchmen. For years it has become the custom in Palestine to cover every alleged holy place with a church. A Parisian roué is not more eager to cover his bald spot than Christianity is eager to cover Bible scenes with churches and cathedrals. Then, when the shrine is duly built, to stand empty and useless save for the credulous pilgrims and gullible tourists who will pay good money to take a look, it must of course have guardians and gate-keepers. So the sacred orders erect their monasteries and scatter monks all over the place. It is a beautiful system—build a church, give it a reputation through the world as the place where Jesus did something or other, and then sit at the seat of customs and rake in the money of those who have to see everything that is properly advertised!

The Franciscan church which covers the site of Joseph's carpenter shop is a perfect example of what I mean. This shop, of course, is in a different part of the town from Joseph's home, in spite of the invariable fact that, in a village like Nazareth, an artisan worked where he lived.

But to admit this fact would be to forfeit the chance to have two churches, and two sources of income, instead of one. So this church covers only the shop. It was Sunday morning when we visited it, but the place was closed. To have it opened for divine worship would give a person a chance to see it, I suppose, without paying. So we stood moodily in the rain while the custodian turned a rusty key in a rusty lock, and let us in. "Any services in this church?" —"Oh, yes! on Fridays! But this service is open only to the members of the Franciscan order." We were shown the dirty chancel, the shabby altar; then, with much mumbo-jumbo, taken down a flight of stone steps, into a dark, cold chamber lit by hanging lamps, to see the place where Joseph, the carpenter, had done his work. "The very place?" "Oh, yes, the very place." "Right here where we are standing?" "Oh, yes—no doubt about it." A touching sight—especially to the pocketbook. But it left my heart as untouched as my mind was unconvinced.

No! Nazareth is not a place to be seen, unless one would have every illusion shattered, every dream dispelled. Spurious scenes, itching palms, whining beggars, inescapable brigands in the form of guides and postcard merchants, these spoil everything to the sensitive and reverent soul. I am glad that bad weather kept us off the streets and thus saved us from disillusion. What we did was not to see Nazareth, in the ordinary tourist style, but to *feel* it. We let our imagination play upon it. The spring there, where we had seen the women with their water jars! This is the only place within the town which has reality. Mary must have come here in her day, for the valley has no other source of water. Her boy must have been with her on occasion— this is a spot which was familiar to his feet. Then the roads that lead from this spring! No one can be sure that they are the same; but it is likelier that they are than that they are not. For in a primitive country roads remain the same, the feet of men and animals wear them deep, and they become ruts in which the generations move. Then let these roads take you into the country and up the mountainsides! If Jesus the youth was anything like Jesus the man, he liked on occasion to be alone, and therefore must have frequently followed these paths into their quiet places. He knew these hills, and looked down upon this town, and gazed over the rolling country to the east and west, and to the south where was the city of his dreams. Houses have gone, and peoples passed; even the trees and foliage have been wasted and the land left bare. Into this scene have come invaders many—soldiers, priests, tourists—all equally destructive in their several ways. But the substance is left —the spirit is still abiding. I felt nearer to Jesus here than I had ever felt before.

Tel-Aviv

If Nazareth took us back into the past, Tel-Aviv held us within the present, save when it swept us fast and far into the future. Twenty years ago there were miles of sand dunes on the shores outside the ancient city of Jaffa. Now, on these same dunes, there stands a municipality of thirty-eight thousand souls, as thriving and busy as any typical American town. Tel-Aviv is nearer one hundred per cent Jewish than a much advertised soap is one hundred per cent pure. It is accurately described as the only one-hundred-per-cent Jewish city in the world. Its inhabitants, with a few scattered exceptions, are all Jews; its mayor, judges, police force, merchants, teachers, artisans, street cleaners, garbage collectors, all are Jews. Here is no segregation of Jews into a ghetto, into a few traditional trades, into circumscribed and traditional types of life. Jews in Tel-Aviv are occupying all the positions of society, and therewith proving their fitness for every type of leadership and labor. It is an amazing spectacle—this modern city of emancipated Jews.

Tel-Aviv, in its twenty years of life, has had its vicissitudes. During the Arab uprising in 1921,[5] its citizens suffered and endured the attack of enemies, and the city cherishes to-day the bodies of those who were killed in the riotings. Three years ago, in the familiar fashion of American "boom" towns, Tel-Aviv overreached itself, and underwent an economic collapse from which it is only now beginning to recover. The loss in population, suddenly sustained in this crisis, has not yet been made up again. Non-Jewish observers, particularly Englishmen, will tell you that the city is reared upon no secure foundations, and that its disintegration is as certain as the shifting of the sands on which it stands. But three days in Tel-Aviv filled me with its spirit. I caught the contagion of its enthusiasm and courage. These citizens of Tel-Aviv are not going to be beaten. First, they have the stiff-necked courage which "carries on," whatever the odds against it. Secondly, they know far better than their critics, and can make manifest to a sympathetic visitor, the resources which are at their disposal and upon which they are trusting. The new Pelestine must be largely agricultural, of course. But this new Palestine must have its industrial and cultural center as well. And here it is—brought into being by the determination and vision of a liberated people almost with the magic of Aladdin and his wonderful lamp.

I had extraordinary opportunity to see this vigorous young city of the Jewish renaissance. I had come under influential auspices, for my visit had been heralded in the name of Nathan Straus, beloved of all races and creeds in Palestine for his generous deeds for humankind, and espe-

[5] As also in the fiercer riotings this year (1929)!

cially beloved in Tel-Aviv for his gift of a public health center which is already one of the monuments of the place. So the mayor and his associates were determined to place all the resources of the city at my disposal.

On the day of my arrival, I was waited upon by the Mayor. On the morning of the next day I returned this official visit; and was duly placed in the good keeping of the general secretary of the municipality, a most accomplished and gracious gentleman, who took me for a personal tour of inspection of the city, placed at my disposal records and reports, and in general gave me every kind of information which I could desire. Under his guidance I saw the public buildings of Tel-Aviv—visited schools—inspected the great Rutenburg electric works—went through all the departments of a highly successful hosiery factory, pioneer of great industries yet to come—took a bird's-eye view of the city planning scheme laid out by Sir Patrick Geddes, to control the future growth of the city—motored through attractive residential sections, with houses covering by the law of the municipality not more than one-third of the area of each plot—and then through the crowded streets of retail business and trade—as a climax, surveyed the Nathan and Lina Straus Health Center, still in course of construction, with the new street to be laid out and named in honor of Mr. Straus. What I saw in this rapid visitation was a thriving center of population which promises to be that *rara avis*, a combined industrial and garden city. Tel-Aviv will have its factories and manufacturing plants; but also it will have its gardens and playgrounds and open spaces. It will be busy, but it will also be beautiful. Nothing but timidity and stupidity can defeat this project, and these are qualities seldom characteristic of the Jew.

In the late afternoon of this second day came the great event of the occasion, a public reception in the Mayor's rooms at the city hall. Invited guests thronged the chambers of His Worship, Mr. Dizengoff—the city officers, the judges of the courts, the heads of the great religious bodies, Jewish, Latin, Orthodox, Arab, Christian, Moslem, and Anglican, the editors of the local papers, distinguished citizens, etc. After an address of welcome in Hebrew by the Mayor, which was duly translated into Arabic and English, a speech was made by Mr. Bialik, the most famous and influential of contemporary Hebrew writers in Palestine; and then I was privileged to respond in an address brilliantly translated into Hebrew by the town clerk.

On my third day in Tel-Aviv, I was in private hands. The morning was spent in visiting Jewish agricultural colonies in the neighborhood—of which more later—and the afternoon with the leaders of the great trade union organization of Palestine. After luncheon with the head officials of the national union, I visited the attractive union headquarters—the Workers Bank, in which I saw what I never expected to see on this earth, a bank adorned with a picture of Karl Marx—the workers' library, a collection of seventy thousand volumes, at the disposal of all working men and women throughout the land—the workers' health center and free dispensary—the night club and school for working boys and girls, who, incidentally, have their own union—and a coöperative workers' printing plant. In the course of much talk, I learned amazing things about this workers' organization in Palestine. Its membership includes eighty per cent of the workers of the country; its ranks are crowded with unskilled and agricultural laborers; it seeks Arab workers as well as Jewish; it is not afraid to enter into politics, but on the contrary is one of the most militantly aggressive and potent political forces in the country. The whole situation can be summed up in the simple statement that the workers' organization in Palestine has character and intelligence. This is not to say that the workers are always wise. I heard serious criticism of certain of their ideas and policies. But it is to say that the workers have found their minds and mobilized their forces, and thus made themselves one of the mightiest factors in the making of the Jewish homeland.

An Adventure

My fourth day in Tel-Aviv was carefully planned. I was to go in the morning, under escort, some twenty miles or more along the coast, to the site of Nathanyah, newest of the Jewish colonies in Palestine, the only one organized during the last three years, and named in honor of Nathan Straus, under whose auspices I was traveling in the Holy Land. I desired to make this trip, first, in tribute to Mr. Straus, and, secondly, in satisfaction of my own desire to see a settlement in the very first stages of development. Scheduled to be back from this excursion at one o'clock, I was then to visit certain important colonies in the vicinity, and return to Jerusalem in time for dinner. An excellent plan! But the day was to bring me one more illustration of the truth of Burns's axiom, that "the best laid schemes of mice and men gang aft agley."

A group of five men, including an old American friend who was now a member of the Nathanyah colony, and a famous Palestinian journalist, Ittamar Ben-Avi, took me in charge at eight o'clock, and off we went on good roads to the north. An hour's riding, however, brought us to roads so bad that it was a relief, as well as a surprise, when we left the road and struck straight across the open fields. It was as though we were riding across New England pasture lands, save that here there were no fences, stone walls or trees—just the wild, bare, rolling country where we could move in any direction we pleased. But it had been raining in this part as in other parts of Palestine in recent weeks, and bogs must be avoided. So we struck across the high open fields, moved along the crests of ridges wherever they could be found, plunged into plowed lands whenever they could not be avoided, always at high speed, regardless of bumps and bruises, for it was dangerous to give the glue-like mud a chance to grip and hold the wheels. The sensation was not unlike that of being on shipboard in a heavy sea. How the car, swaying madly from side to side, managed to maintain its equilibrium, is a mystery which I have not yet solved.

Suddenly came disaster in the form of a slip and a sweeping slide into the mire at the bottom of a deep gully. In a trice the men were out, had seized spades, shovels, boards and ropes brought along for just such an emergency, and were hard at work. But nothing availed—the car would not move. "Never mind," cried our leader, "the other car will be along in a moment."

"The other car?" I queried. "Do you mean to say that another car is crazy enough to follow us over this trackless country?"

Then I learned that my hosts had carefully provided a second car, carrying six men, to dog our tracks, and lend a hand whenever needed. Even as we talked, this second car hove in sight with a merry tooting of its horn, six lusty "pioneers" jumped into view, and with a shout seized our car, and in no time had it free of the mud and on its way again.

Progress was now slower. Every hundred yards or so, two men would scout on ahead, to find some road over the empty waste which would be passable for the automobiles. Always they discovered what they were looking for—until suddenly with a quick sweep around an overhanging lift of land, we found ourselves on the bank of a brook, or "wadi," as it is called in this country. Ordinarily this brook was a shallow little stream, or, after the rainy season, a dry, stony river-bed. Now it had been swollen by the torrential rains into a river, forty feet or more wide, and flowing in midstream like a cataract. Waiting by the "wadi" was a pair of mules hitched to the crudest kind of wagon. "All out," was the cry. In a moment, we had left the machine, clambered into the wagon, and begun the fording of the river. Just how we got across I shall never know. To sit down was to be in danger of getting wet, to stand up was to be in danger of toppling over into the water. Half-sitting and half-standing, clutching fiercely at anything my hands could seize, I watched the foaming stream as it washed the wheels and lashed the legs of the mules. It was a wild passage, and I was not relishing the prospect of completing the trip to Nathanyah in this ramshackle conveyance, when I looked back and discovered to my vast astonishment that the automobiles were planning to ford the stream as well. Heavy layers of burlap were being bound fast to the radiators, the carburetors were being protected, and the gas tanks made tight. Even so, it seemed to me that I had never heard of a madder venture. But before I could exclaim, our machine gave a sudden roar, plunged into the rushing water, swayed and stalled and swayed again, and then, like a dripping bullock, came tearing up the bank. After such an exploit, I was ready for anything. Once more we went sweeping on across the waste.

But the going was now more hazardous. The terrain was more uneven, the gullies deeper and more treacherous, the mud more abundant. A new obstacle was encountered in sudden ditches, into which the car plunged madly, and out of which it struggled with an awful grinding of the engine. Scouting became now more frequent and prolonged. At last our explorers came back with the news that we had better walk on ahead; that they would find a way somewhere for the cars and catch up with us; if not, they would leave the cars, and pick them up again on our return. Nathanyah was not so far ahead—we could make it in an hour or more of brisk walking!

So off we strode in excellent spirits. It seemed good to be on one's feet again, and thus to enjoy a little stability and quiet. Our leader welcomed the sight of an approaching Arab astride a donkey. "He'll take us to his village," he said, "and give us donkeys for the rest of this trip." So we held up the Arab and told our need. Then the Arab held us up, and told *his* need. There followed a tumult of wild shouting and gesticulation, furious threats and recriminations. I backed away in fearful expectation of daggers, or at least of fists. Then, in a trice, everybody smiled; the price was agreed upon; I was astride the donkey; and we were headed for the village to get beasts for the other members of our troupe.

Fifteen minutes brought us to the Arab village. We were greeted by a wild attack of huge, ferocious-looking dogs, who lifted the hair on their backs like the quills of porcupines, and bared their ugly teeth like wolves. But this proved to be a salute, not an assault, and we went on unperturbed. Then came a crazier salute from a group of donkeys tethered at one end of the little settlement. "Hee-haw, hee-haw," rang out their lusty cries. My donkey responded with a call that seemed to rend my very spine. Then, kicking up his heels, he went galloping off to his companions, with a terrified rider grasping at mane, or tail, or any other thing which would keep him astride the fleeing beast. John Gilpin had no wilder ride than I, for those few minutes at least.

The village was a place of fascinating interest. I had

seen these rude encampments, with their long, black, goatskin tents, and huddling groups of dirty women and children, many a time from the train and automobile. These primitive people wander the Palestinian countryside to-day just as they did in the days of Abraham, pasturing their flocks, sometimes feebly tilling the soil, always moving on when the grass is cropped or the tillage done. The people now before me represented the lowest state of human culture that I had ever seen. The tents, raised only a few feet from the ground, were wide open to the south. They were crammed with dirty straw, and not infrequently occupied by goats and sheep. Before them stood the women, clad in long, black robes and headdresses, with faces partly veiled, the cheeks and brows painted in rude colors and hung with strings of beads and coins, amulets against the Evil One. The children, incredibly dirty and wretchedly clad, were at first timid. The sight of a few coins, however, cured them of their fears, and soon they were crowding about us more intimately than was altogether pleasant. Débris and filth were all over the place; animals were wandering everywhere; the smoke of smoldering fires poisoned the air. Yet the women smiled in welcome, even the dogs became friendly, and the donkeys were at our disposal for a beggarly price.

We were selecting our gallant steeds, when the wild tooting of horns told us that the automobiles had made their way through. We rejoined our caravan with all speed, and without further adventure reached the site of Nathanyah.

What I saw was a long, wide stretch of land, as fertile in appearance as any I had seen in Palestine. To the east rolled the long waste of open country to the hills of Galilee, now glowing in the blazing sun of noon. To the west rose a range of shore cliffs, giving shelter from the storms that sweep in here from the Mediterranean. Far to the north was a grove of trees, the boundary of the colony in that direction. Precisely in the center of the plain were two tents, where were living the first settlers of the colony. Near by was the well they had been digging—thirteen feet in diameter, thirty feet deep, and pure, sweet water at the bottom. We wandered about the place—followed a ravine through the cliffs to the seashore, saw the location of the first houses, marked out the range of the projected orange groves, noted where the first plow was to cut the soil this next week. High in the cloudless heavens rode the sun. Stout, bronzed, happy men stood about, and measured with eager eyes the acres which they were so soon to plant. The great sea roared in upon the shore, a steamer bound for Haifa went softly by. It was an auspicious moment, and every heart was light.

But it was after noontide. What about my one o'clock appointment at Tel-Aviv? With one accord we piled into our cars, and started on our journey back. But we must stop on the way to pay our respects to the sheik who had sold the land to the colonists! He was lord of all the domain for miles around—a kind of feudal chieftain who lived with his family and retainers in a village not far away, and expected to see visitors when they passed along. He was reputed to be a hundred and two years old; when I saw the venerable man, I placed him at not less than eighty. Accurate report had it that he consoled his aged bones each year with a brand-new wife, and no one knew how many children had claim upon his paternal care.

The sheik's village was a squalid collection of mud and stone huts. The only building of any size was a small mosque, in which we found some twenty-five little children strenuously chanting the Arabic alphabet in unison response to a young teacher well armed with a lengthy rod. Beside and beneath one wall of the mosque was an open latrine, a filthy place suggesting incredible things when fly time came. A winding and very muddy path took us down past the dirty houses to a kind of barnyard, where the old sheik held his court. In one corner was a motley collection of donkeys and camels; goats and sheep wandered freely about; poultry were abundant and omnipresent. Two industries were busily at work. On one side a rude mill ground into dusty flour the grain brought in by near-by Arab women. A group of these women, their faces carefully covered, were clustered shyly by the door of the mill. On the other side was a great pile of oranges, gathered from one of the sheik's groves; two or three men were making boxes, and filling them with the golden fruit. Litter and dirt were everywhere. I suppose the yard was sometimes cleaned, but the last time was long ago.

The sheik received us gladly. Quickly arranging a semicircle of orange boxes, he bade us be seated and partake of his hospitality. The old fellow sat nobly in the center, and placed the visitor from America at his right hand. In a few moments came steaming cups of thick Turkish coffee; these were succeeded by the offer of as many oranges as we could eat or take away; then, at the close, with gracious dignity, came a retainer bearing a curious vessel of water which he poured over our hands as we extended them for the bath. And all the while, encircling us in unbroken line, passed women bearing on their heads heavy baskets of oranges from the grove outside to the packers in the yard. Some of these women were old, some were girls; all of them were strong, and most of them superbly beautiful. Their bodies, unfettered by the harness of civilized women, were covered only by the loose robe of their tribe; their necks, as they poised the laden baskets, were like straight columns of bronze; their stride was the stride of Amazons, and their stature the stature of goddesses. They were dirty, judged by Western standards, but they were also magnificent. I could not keep my eyes off this unending line of marching caryatids.

It was now two o'clock, and my afternoon was disappearing. We leaped into the cars and resumed our journey. The way back was easily found, for we scrupulously followed the tracks made in the morning. We were stopped only twice in our speeding flight across the waste. Once our companion car, slipping into a ditch at too slow a pace, fell over flat on its side. Six merry men scrambled out of the upside, seized the prostrate vehicle, and promptly placed it erect upon its wheels. The second time we all dismounted, while our cars took a flying start, and leaped a four-foot ditch. By this time nothing surprised me. I had learned that an automobile could go anywhere and do anything. I was ready to "follow the leader" to the end.

My readiness was tested when we came again to the "wadi." The mule wagon was at hand, but this time our chauffeurs scorned to take it. They had passed the waters once; they knew the line of fording; and the flood must have subsided since morning. So in we plunged! Our companion car went first. It reeled and tossed like a derelict on a stormy sea, but it got across. Our car did as well —to midstream. Then, just as we reached the foaming crest of the river, our auto slipped into a hole, our engine roared and gasped, and suddenly was silent. We were marooned. Into the car poured the water, like Noah's flood. The machine, beautifully poised downward on my side, had completely immersed its rear wheel, and was sinking steadily inch by inch deeper into the stream. I freed my limbs, to be ready for the plunge. Meanwhile, our friends upon the farther shore had not been idle. The mule wagon, promptly summoned, was hitched to the car, and the mules lashed to strenuous exertions—but our machine did not budge. As its careening was now actually imminent, we were ordered to "abandon ship" and come ashore *via* the mule wagon. One by one we crawled out of the car, scaled the slippery sides of the hood, and leaped for the wagon. All were saved with little wetting and were soon on dry land again.

But the car! What to do with that? Just at this critical moment there came along an Arab who offered to do the job—for a price. Immediately the customary shouts, gesticulations, threats and oaths, then bright smiles. This man would pull out the car for fifty piastras ($2.50). Away he ran, shouting at the top of his lungs. A head appears over a near-by hill. Wild hallooings back and forth, and the head becomes a man. Another head over this other hill—more hallooing, and another man. More shouts, and more men! Till from somewhere, nowhere, everywhere, came a dozen sturdy fellows to lend a hand. A call from the leader—and as though by a single motion, tattered garments were rolled to the waistline, and sturdy limbs leaped into the stream. The men surrounded the flooded automobile like bees; they shouted together like college boys; then, dropping into a wild kind of song or chant, they began to push and heave.

"What are they singing?" I asked.

"They are calling on the Prophet," said one of my companions. "They want him to help."

But the Prophet did not hear. Or perhaps, like Baal, he was asleep. Time after time the men called, and sang, and lunged—and the automobile remained precisely where it was. Then suddenly, without warning, there came that curious moment when, as though by some divine intervention, mules and men all pulled together, and with a strength they had not had before. The car stirred, moved, leaped —and was on the shore!

"The Prophet has heard us," cried the Arabs, leaping about us in unashamed nudity. And he *had*, for nothing less than the Prophet could have supplied that final ounce of strength that at last released the car.

The afternoon was now late. I could do nothing more this day. We would stop in Herzlia, a Jewish colony on the way, and have some tea! Our car must in any case be dried out and resupplied with gasoline, before it could take us back to town. So we found our way to Herzlia, and ate. After this meal by famished men, we went out for a look at the prosperous homes of these Jewish farmers. We saw clean houses, beautiful gardens, and large, sweet stables. The men were coming in from their day's labor at the plow. Boys were driving in the cattle for the night's shelter. The village newsboy went by—an aged ghetto Jew, with gray beard sweeping his breast, papers tucked under his arm, sitting astride a diminutive donkey, with his loose legs dangling to the ground on either side. In the west, down into the glistening sea, the sun was dropping. Great pillars of cloud caught and lifted its flaming colors, and shone as a city of eternal fire. To the right, clear cut on the horizon, were two camels in coal-black silhouette. As the dark fell suddenly, our automobile appeared, and we drove back to the city. The blazing camp fires of the *Fellaheen* lit the gloom on either side. Afar, in the distance, gleamed the lights of Tel-Aviv. Above, the great stars burned with an unearthly luster. Quick, in the pathway of our piercing headlights, flashed a camel, a donkey, a lonely wayfarer. Palestine!—its toil and struggle all about us, and its golden promise shining in our hearts.

Jerusalem Again

Our automobile trip had taken us through Galilee and Syria, back to Judæa, a distance of more than nine hundred miles. We had been on the road for ten successive days in all kinds of weather, mostly stormy. We had traveled on paths as primitive as camel trails which outdate in time the span of recorded history, and had sped on highways as new and smooth as the latest speedways of the West. We had visited cities and villages, harbor mouths and mountain fastnesses, agricultural settlements and industrial centers, farms and factories, schools and hospitals. We had seen Jewish, Arabian and Syrian communities; talked with politicians and priests, teachers and toilers, native peoples and alien rulers. We had surveyed the land as it had existed for a thousand years under the croppings of wandering flocks and herds or the light scratchings of the primitive wooden plow, and we had studied it as, in chosen places, it was being restored by modern tools to modern civilized uses. We had discovered the Palestine of Abraham, and Moses, and David, and Jesus, and Saladin, and Abdul Hamid, and Lord Allenby, and Theodor Herzl—a land made holy at once by memory and by expectation. And now we were returning to Jerusalem which held all these elements of life within its ancient and modern walls. It seemed like home again as we climbed the swift ascent from Tel-Aviv, saw the domes and towers lift themselves above the hills, and suddenly looked once more upon the familiar pillars of the Jaffa Gate. Our stay was to last four days longer, and these days were to be spent in the City of David, mostly in conference with the leaders of Zion.

It seemed good to be on these streets again, and to gaze upon the most cosmopolitan population in the world. Surely in no other community is such variety of costumes, customs, races, creeds, and manners. So amazing is the phantasmagoria that no one is any longer surprised at anything. Within a single city block, in the space of five minutes or less, one may see a score of startling figures, any one of which would stop all traffic in New York City. But nobody pays any attention in Jerusalem. Here is a black Nubian gorgeously appareled in a great white robe with golden belt and buckle. In the street rides a magnificent Arab upon a gayly caparisoned charger. Along the sidewalk move a group of black-robed priests with handsome beards, and long, curly, thick-bound hair. In the gutter strolls a careless vagabond driving a flock of turkeys majestically before him. Youthful Jews, with fresh faces and long earlocks dangling by their cheeks, hasten in gladness along the sunny way. A woman passes, closely clad and thickly veiled. Here comes a train of camels, six in line, scornfully oblivious of the hurrying scene. A patient donkey canters by, a solemn old man astride its haunches. A superb woman, with a huge jar poised upon her head, walks with noble stride along the crowded road. A flock of sheep now suddenly blocks all the street. A group of English soldiers saunter by; Bedouin loaf in every corner; Egyptians offer wares or wait for bargains. What a scene is this! A dozen nations before our eyes, a half-score languages in our ears. Yet nobody looks or listens, save only the untutored American who never before has seen anything like this.

I never tired of the Jerusalem streets. Especially David Street—narrow as a back alley, steep as a Naples hillside, lined with shops, and thronged from morn till night with haggling traders from all the four quarters of the world. Only once did I see this street quiet—in a late evening stroll when my son and I set out to see the Mosque of Omar by moonlight. We saw the Mosque for a fleeting moment bathed in luster and crowned with stars, but this was "snooping," and an alert guard soon put us to flight. So we plunged again into the darkness of David Street. The closed shops gave everywhere the appearance of a dead city. Shut out from the sky by the low archways overhead, we found no light to guide our stumbling steps save an occasional lantern which only increased the surrounding blackness. Now and again we saw a candle gleam behind a latticed window up above, and here and there were pools of light from open taverns. We paused in such places to see old men ponderously smoking their water pipes, and eager gamesters bending over cards and counters. One little room leading direct from the street was crowded with silent figures listening to a turbaned man who stood behind a rude table reading passionately from a book. Was it the Koran —or some tale of Eastern adventure? Always these taverns were quiet, the guests absorbed and still, no drinking or carousing. The Moslem ban on liquor does its excellent work. Such places, however, were few. David Street was as empty by night as it was crowded by day. Its silence was almost uncanny—no baby's cry, no man's laugh, no woman's scream. Yet people were living in all these upper stories and hidden away in the walls in these side alleys. Jerusalem goes to bed early. By nine o'clock the city has fallen into slumber. As we walked along that night, we met a berobed old man thumping the pavement with his cane, a young man treading cat-like in the shadows, three or four officers on their beats, perhaps one or two others. But we saw no woman, and in block after block not a living soul. I envied the East its habit of living naturally and happily by the sun.

Bethlehem and Hebron

But I had little time for wandering in this idle fashion. These last precious days were crowded with interviews with important people, and there was one more excursion—this time southward to Bethlehem and Hebron.

Bethlehem was reached on an icy-cold, yet sunny Sunday, in a quick half-hour by automobile. I did my best to like the town, as I liked Nazareth. I thought of its old memories, running back to the time of David. I looked at its attractive setting in the lap of the barren hills. I even recited Phillips Brooks's lovely hymn——

> O, little town of Bethlehem,
> How still we see thee lie;
> Above thy deep and dreamless sleep
> The silent stars go by.

But it was all in vain! Bethlehem cast no spell on me. Perhaps it was because I saw it in the glaring light of noontime, and not, as Phillips Brooks did, in darkness and silence underneath the stars. Perhaps it was because I disliked its prosperity—its fat monasteries, its gaudy churches, and its long line of mansions of the rich. Perhaps it was because I have no faith at all that Jesus was born in this place, accepting rather Renan's verdict that he was born in Nazareth. More likely I was disgusted by the Church of the Nativity, with its preposterous shams of the stable and the manger, and its equally preposterous divisions of area between Latin, Greek, Coptic and other warring Christian sects. Every condition was favorable to appreciation. The sun was bright, and the sky a gorgeous blue. It was Sunday morning, and the streets were filled with Bethlehem women in their picturesquely distinctive headdresses. I even encountered a guide who refused to take a tip, and thus opened a new era in human history. But nothing served to move me to any joy or content in this old town. I might visit Palestine a dozen times, and never see it again.

But Hebron[°] was different. What a glorious old place! It was Sunday here, too, of course, but Hebron is a Jewish and Moslem, not a Christian center, and the place was seeth-

[°] The scene of the most terrible events in the August (1929) outbreak. Sixty-five Jewish men, women and children were massacred in this historic town.

ing with life. Everybody was out-of-doors seeking the warm sunlight, for the night had been bitter cold. Each sunny wall had its row of squatting old men, wrapped like mummies in swathe after swathe of their abundant robes. Women were clustered about their doorsteps, or hurrying busily along the streets, quickly covering their faces as we came in sight. Children were everywhere, playing with mangy dogs, or poking about in the filth of the gutters. The bazaars were as fascinating as those in Damascus, and were crowded with good-natured people who seemed more eager to find a place in the sun than to strike a bargain. We sauntered from shop to shop, chaffered with amiable merchants, priced chains and canes and gaudy scarfs, watched shoemakers making shoes out of automobile tires and inner tubes, marveled at the infinite variety of man's needs and desires even in this primitive country. We had to tread carefully, for the streets were dirty, and men and women were far from clean. But they seemed friendly, good-natured, happy, on this day at least, and it was pleasant to be with them.

Of course, we visited the ancient and very famous mosque containing the tombs of Abraham and Sarah, Isaac and Rebecca, Jacob and Leah. We had passed the tomb of Rachel by the roadside on the way down from Jerusalem. This mosque had for centuries been closed to all Jews and Christians. Even now it was difficult to secure admission, especially in this month of Ramadan. But we had letters from high officials, and after due delay the doors swung open. It was not an impressive or beautiful mosque, and yet there was something unusually attractive about its ancient and much dimmed splendor. Even the tombs were interesting, or they had imposing proportions, and nobody really seemed to expect us to believe that the bodies of the patriarchs and their wives were there. They were just memorials to great ancestors, and worth seeing as such. But I enjoyed more the richly robed old fellow sitting on his rug in the corner chanting the Koran in his high, clear voice; and that tired pilgrim in the outer court, arrived at last at the shrine of all his dreams; and the proud young scholar who took us about, himself some day to be a high priest of the Prophet. Yes, Hebron had more interest in one of its stones than Bethlehem in all of its walls. I shall go there again.

On the Mount of Olives

On our last night in Jerusalem, we decided to go to the Mount of Olives, and watch the sun set over the city. A little after five in the afternoon, our automobile took us up the long slope of the hill. We stopped for a little time at the British War Memorial where, row on row, known and unknown together, there sleep the dead from all the climes of the far-flung Empire who fell in the campaign against the Turk. Then we climbed to the University, so superbly located on the summit of Mt. Scopus. Still beyond lay the Mount, which we reached just as the sun was touching the western horizon.

The evening was like the one celebrated by Wordsworth in his immortal sonnet—

> It is a beauteous evening calm and free;
> The holy time is quiet as a nun,
> Breathless with adoration; the broad sun
> Is sinking down in its tranquillity. . . .

Behind us, to the east, lay the Jordan and the Dead Sea, now growing dark and drear beneath that rolling waste of desert hills. Before us, just over the ravine of Kedron, was the city, with every roof and spire aflame with light. It was not the city that Jesus knew—it was larger, nobler, more beautiful than Herod's town. But here upon this very Mount, perhaps where we were standing, a few feet from it at least, Jesus had paused on his last entry into the city, and had wept for her, that she should stone the prophets. Here, if nowhere else, we were following in the footsteps of the Nazarene. From this Mount of Olives, he had descended by this road here, and entered Jerusalem by that gate yonder. Just beyond must have stood the temple of Herod, where Jesus preached, and smote the money changers. Somewhere beyond the temple, outside the wall, not so far away, must have stood Golgotha. The whole vast drama of that last week—the greatest drama in history—had been enacted in the narrow area before me, shining and fading in the evening light. The sun was gone now, and darkness was creeping into house and street. The glittering gold over all the town was turned to dull, dun copper. Strange silence was everywhere. Was it possible that this Mount of Olives had not always looked on such loveliness as this? That it had seen, through smoke and flame, the sack of the city and the slaughter of its inhabitants by Titus—had echoed the Crusaders' clash of arms as they climbed the slope in helmet and mail, and smote the Saracen—had only recently shaken to the reverberation of Allenby's awful guns—and, on a day, had watched the sun sinking, not as to-night behind peaceful roofs and turrets, but behind three crosses, black as night and death and hell against the western splendor?

We turned away, for the city was now gone into the sudden dark. A last shimmer from the Dead Sea caught our gaze. An Arab was singing in his little house. Lights were shining. I wondered—where did Mary go on that last night, and where did the disciples hide themselves?

The Flight Into Egypt

The next morning saw us early on our train for Cairo. Within a few hours we began to approach the desert. At first came great stretches of arid land, and the disappearance of villages and people. Then came the sand. But in this sand appeared unexpected flushes, so to speak, of green —areas, large or small, where there seemed to be some hidden springs of nourishment. And here, invariably, were little groups of haggard men and women, with children, dogs, asses, sometimes camels, eking out some sort of a meager existence from these shallow oases. Then came the real desert, which swallowed up everything, like the vast flood of the sea. At first the sand rose and fell in great, far-reaching waves of empty desolation. Later these waves subsided, and there followed miles of flat and arid waste which might have served as the very floor of hell. The rolling sands behind had seemed to have some life in them, if only of the winds which caught up these myriad particles of dust, and tossed them as they tossed the waters of the sea. But here was only death—nay, worse than death! For in this unstirring silence, unchanged, unchanging, had never been anything that lived, or even moved.

The heat became intense. A mist of sand seemed to filter through the roof of our car and envelop our bodies like an atmosphere. We began to choke and cough, and wilt. We 'roused ourselves enough to gaze far to the south and east to catch a glimpse of Sinai, for this was the wilderness of the Exodus, but the ancient Summit of the Law was too far away to see. Only the waste—this hopeless waste! I marveled no longer at Moses's excitement over the quails and the manna, for how could his fugitives have lived without them? But that story of smiting the rock and making the water to gush forth was startling. It would take more than miracle to produce water in this arid waste. Even modern science could not do it, for when Allenby's army in the Great War marched along the line of this railway, they carried with them every drop in great pipe lines from

Kantara. What wonder that that march has become an epic!

I found it a fitting thing to end my adventure in Palestine in this Sinai desert, for it was here that the story of the Jews began. Through this wilderness of death had marched that host of men and women who were ready to endure all suffering, if only they could escape from slavery, and build in the land the Lord would give them a tabernacle of justice and of peace. And now, borne back to another and longer slavery, these Jews had escaped again, and were struggling anew, through the wilderness of a world's indifference or scorn, to rebuild the land which still was theirs by the Lord's hand. What centuries stretched between the old Zion and the new! This sand was still the same as when it was trod by Moses and his host. The same were human cruelty and lust and hate. And the same also the unconquered and unconquerable soul of Israel! Who could doubt what lies ahead, in the light of all that lies behind!

Suddenly, into the hot and dusty train there swept a breeze, and the salt smell of the sea. Bright and blue to our right was the Mediterranean, and just ahead was Suez. The world was once more with us.

"And the Redeemer shall come to Zion" . . .
                                                       Isaiah 59:20

CHAPTER II

ZIONISM

THE DIASPORA

IT was on the summit of Mt. Scopus, that commanding elevation to the east of Jerusalem where now stand the new buildings of the Hebrew University, that the legions of Titus were marshalled in 70 A.D. for the capture of the city It is on this hill, we imagine, that conquering armies have always gathered for their last and decisive attack upon this much beleaguered stronghold. General Allenby was only following the beaten path of an unending procession of soldiers before him, when he gained this height in 1917 and thus made Jerusalem untenable for the Turkish garrison. But that day in 70 had a finality about it which has made it a turning point in the history of the Jews—an ending of one era and the beginning of another. For when Titus's legionaries had swept down the slopes of the mountain, and seized and ravaged the Holy City, they destroyed that Jewish state which had existed amid vicissitudes innumerable since the time of Saul. One dreadful revival came sixty years later, when Bar Cochba led his fierce uprising against Rome—a lesser Maccabæus against a greater empire! But the end arrived in 134 A.D. when the revolt was overwhelmed after a four years' struggle, and the last smoldering embers of Jewish nationalism were extinguished.

Henceforth the Jews were a scattered people, "mingled among the heathen." This does not mean that there had never been any dispersion of the Jews before this date. On the contrary, long before the loss of Palestine, the Jews had established flourishing communities in various parts of the Roman Empire. It is estimated that, at the opening of the Christian era, there were some four million Jews living in these various centers of trade and culture in Egypt, Syria, Greece, Italy, even Spain, as compared with only some seven hundred thousand in Zion. Neither does this scattering of the Jews after the destruction of Jerusalem mean that all these seven hundred thousand were either massacred, or exiled to distant quarters of the globe. Just as there were Jews who miserably survived after 70 A.D., so there were others who survived even more miserably after 134 A.D. The Jews were never completely dislodged from Palestine. Cooped up in their four holy cities, of which Safed, safely hidden away in the inaccessible mountain fastnesses of Galilee, remains to-day the living monument, a remnant lived on, and maintained for centuries the tradition of Jewish learning and piety. How many they were, nobody knows—the number probably varied with economic and political conditions. But in 1770 the Jews in Palestine numbered not more than five thousand, and two generations later, in 1839, about eleven thousand.

Neither the Diaspora before the fall of Jerusalem, however, nor the survival in Palestine after this event, affects in any way the vast historical significance of the year 70 A.D. Whatever the dispersal of the Jewish community at the opening of the Christian era, that community was a single organism, and its beating heart was Zion. Here was the home of all this scattered multitude—and a home in no ordinary sentimental sense! Zion was at once a country and a church, a hearthstone and an altar. All that is now so passionately involved in patriotism on the one hand and in religious faith upon the other was bound together in the single attachment of the Jew to Palestine. There on Mt. Zion stood the Temple, the seat at once of domestic, social and spiritual law, and while that stood, Israel endured. But now the Temple was destroyed, and all the land of Jehovah given over to the conqueror. What mattered it if a few wretched men and women, wandering "in deserts and in mountains, and in dens and caves of the earth," still survived in Judah? There was no home any more to which the Jews could return, no country which they could call their own, no sacred place where they could bring their offerings to God. Suddenly, as by a single blow of the sword, they were cut off from the very earth on which they trod. And with a sense of shock, which marks one of the supreme psychological tragedies of history, they began that life of racial outlawry which has set them in ways apart from other men. For centuries the Jews came to alien lands unbidden, and lived within the borders of these lands unwelcome, guests. Denied association with their fellow beings, shut out from gainful occupations, robbed of culture, art and song, despised and spat upon, outraged, humiliated and plundered, fiendishly persecuted and always in the end hideously maimed and massacred, this miserable remnant of the tribes of Judah has reeled bruised and bleeding from one incredible horror to another. No people in all history has been so persistently abused and butchered over so long a period of time. And yet they survive! Like their ancestors of the Great Captivity,

> They wandered in the wilderness in a solitary way; they found no city to dwell in.
> Hungry and thirsty, their soul fainted in them.
> Then they cried unto the Lord in their trouble, and he delivered them out of their distresses.

Messianism

A miracle has been described as an event the causes of which are unknown. It is in this sense that the survival of the Jews, after nineteen hundred years of homelessness, during which has been endured every imaginable form of misery and oppression, may, indeed must, be described as a miracle. Not that the causes of this survival are unknown! But that none of them, nor all of them together, seem adequate to explain this supreme racial achievement of the ages. Central, of course, is Israel's loyalty to the Torah. This sacred Law has been the life of the Jew and the length of his days, as Moses repeatedly declared. The unifying influence of this great body of teachings, ceremonials and rules preserved the Jew as an undivided and indivisible entity in the welter of nations and races through which he had been scattered. To save and vindicate the Law was enough for enduring all. But this was for to-day only. What about to-morrow? What was the destiny of this Law, thus preserved at such bitter cost of suffering and death? There was more here, in this passion of the Jew for survival, than a mere "patriotism" of religious loyalty in the present. There was as well an exaltation of millenarian hope in the future. Through all Israel, in other words, there burned the mystic eschatological faith of the people in a recovery of the glories of Zion.

All ancient peoples have cherished memories of a Golden Age in the dim and distant past when men were innocent and the world was good. This Age was now lost, but not forever, for some day it would be restored. What once existed must somehow exist again. Having once been happy, it was incredible that men should not regain their former bliss. This universal hope of the restoration of a Golden Age took with the Jews a special form inwrought with the substance of their political life as a nation. Their Golden Age was not a shining haze upon the horizon of the past; it was a definite period in their history when a great king, David, was reigning over Israel. Their hope was not a vacuous dream of happiness; it was a profound faith in the coming of certain precise historical events in the not distant future. In the two centuries before the Diaspora this faith appeared as a conviction that the kingdom of David was soon to be set up again in their conquered land; in the centuries following it appeared as a dream of a return to that beloved land from which they had now been driven. Sprung partly from an actual previous experience of exile and restoration, quickened by an abiding faith in a deity peculiarly their own, clothed in the glowing and therefore glamorous imagery of that Messianic hope which deliberately transferred the greatness of David's age from the past to the future, the Jews everywhere, through all that dark night of the Middle Ages which lasted for them well into the eighteenth century, lived in the expectation of the return. They "might have lived for generations in Poland, or Russia, in Italy, Spain, or the Rhineland, but Palestine was still the Land of Israel. The exile might or might not be endurable; the life of the Dispersion was in any case but an episode."[1] Some day God would hear their cries, and deliver them out of the hands of their oppressors. At one marvelous moment, the Messiah, the Son of David, would descend out of heaven, and lead the faithful back to the old familiar places.

What and where these places were had long since become dim. Of the geographical location and character of Palestine, the Jews of the ghetto knew nothing. "They were not bound to it by ties of personal affection, nor haunted by memories of its sights and sounds. . . . The Palestine of

[1] "Zionism," by Leonard Stein, 1926. Page 19.

which they dreamed had for most of them long ceased to be the Palestine of concrete reality." ³ But it was there, somewhere, as this portion of the earth which still belonged to them, and which in God's good time would be returned to them again. As the centuries dragged their weary way through the darkness of the thousand and more years after Christ, this time must have seemed long. As the Jews suffered the recurring horrors of persecution, they must have wondered how much they must still endure, to be found worthy for the promised redemption of Israel. But nothing could discourage them, or break them down. Even the long succession of false Messiahs from Moses of Crete in the fifth century to Abulafia of Smyrna in the eighteenth, could not dampen their ardor, much less extinguish their flame. With a perseverance which remains one of the spiritual marvels of history, these Jews believed in God's deliverance.

As it is this Messianism, this abiding faith in a divine deliverance, which has kept the Jews alive from the hour of the Dispersion until now, so it is this same Messianism which has preserved their culture under conditions which have destroyed every other culture that man has ever known. By a kind of irony which reveals the essential justice of the universe, this divine hope made not only endurable but desirable to the Jews their exclusion from the life and love of their neighbors. For the former, quite as much as the latter, were opposed to any interweaving of their groups into a single and permanent social fabric. Whatever part they might be permitted to play in the societies in the midst of which they lived, was in any case temporary, and in every case dangerous. The Jews wanted to keep apart. How else could they be preserved from that amalgamation with the Gentiles which would make impossible the return to Zion? What more sure, and indeed necessary,

³ "Zionism," by Leonard Stein, 1926. Page 21.

than a policy of rigorous separation to keep them intact and pure for their great hour of salvation? These ghetto walls, in other words, had two sides—one which shut the Jew out from the world, and another which shut the world out from the Jew. Thus did the very cruelty of the Christian bring its own revenge and recompense; the very attempt to banish and destroy the Jew create the conditions under which his faith in his own survival could itself survive, and thus preserve him. The survival of the Jew must ever remain a miracle, and therefore a mystery, as I have said. But if there is any explanation it must be found in this combination of inward and outward circumstance which kept the Jew isolated through the ages for the fulfillment of his hope.

ZIONISM

And now, in this age, when the ghetto walls are down, and the Jew walks straight and tall among his fellows, deliverance has come. Not, as had been anticipated through the centuries of medievalism, by the hand of God reaching down out of heaven to seize and save his people; but by the labor, and thought, and sacrifice of men moved by the conviction that God was with them in their own endeavors! Not, as had been taught by the rabbis and seers of the synagogue, through a divine person, the Messiah, leading his people out of bondage; but by the people themselves undertaking their own deliverance, and thus making the race its own Messiah! For generations the Jews had sung, and prayed, and wept, and waited, for the return to Zion. Now they waited no longer, but got up and took the road. The return is at hand because men and women are returning.

The movement back to Palestine in our time may be divided into three waves, or impulses.

The first has no particular historical or social, but much human, significance. It is the flow of *pilgrims*—those who return to Palestine for reasons definitely personal. Thus, there is the scholar, young or old, who is seeking out the ancient haunts of Jewish learning in Jerusalem, Tiberias, Safed, or Hebron, that he may drink of the pure springs of the sacred Law. Then there is the holy man who craves the consolation of the Holy Cities. More numerous are the venerable and pious people who come back to Palestine to die, that their bones may be laid to rest in the sacred soil of their ancestors. Always there have been those who have sought to end their days in Zion. For generations they have trickled into the country, like drops of water into a desert, and quietly disappeared. With the growing freedom of the nineteenth century, however, these driblets of humanity have become something of a stream, and now constitute a charity problem of some proportions. For the ancient ghetto Jew, like the eager student, for that matter, is usually destitute; and pious offerings from abroad, which never cease, do not flow bountifully enough to care adequately for these helpless poor. Economically and socially they are an unrelieved burden upon the land.

It was partly to meet the needs of these Jews that Nathan Straus, most generous of benefactors, established his famous soup kitchens in Jerusalem. I visited the older of these, inside the walls, at the hour of food distribution in the morning. I shall not soon forget the scene. The rooms, leading off a squalid street, were already crowded, one with women, the other with men. In a third room, the kitchen proper, were great stacks of fresh-baked bread, and a huge vat of steaming soup. We watched the distribution of the food. The men took their soup and bread and went back, most of them, to the benches to eat their fare. The women, on the contrary, were obviously prepared to take their share away

They had children or aged parents at home, and these must be fed before they partook themselves. Characteristic of women the world around! It was an amazing sight to watch the faces of these hungry folk. Jews of every stock, from every clime; and some who were not Jews! Most of the men were pitiably old and weak, with faces haggard and drawn, yet hallowed by the ineffable dignity of long and patient endurance. The women varied more in age, and garb, and picturesqueness. They were friendly gossips, for the director had frequently to hush their eager talk, that the busy work might go on without confusion. Only the men were quiet, and obviously glad to get away. The system was superb—each applicant had his ticket, which represented sympathetic inquiry and knowledge as to his wants. Yet I saw hungry men and women who were fed without identification. It was a beautiful service of a pitiful human need.

The second tide of immigration into Palestine started suddenly, like a torrent, in the early '80s of the last century, from the ghetto wastes of southeastern Europe and Russia. This was a flow of *refugees*—Jews who had long lifted up their eyes to Palestine as the land of their ideals, and now turned there rather than elsewhere, under the lash of persecution and massacre. It was in 1881 that Czar Alexander III, following the assassination of his father, Alexander II, instituted the hideous pogroms which descended like a storm upon the Pale of Settlement. These horrors were followed in May, 1882, by the "Temporary Order Concerning the Jews" (still in force in 1914) designed to make the life of Israel in Russia unendurable. This started a flood of refugees which poured not merely from Russia, but also from neighboring countries which had fallen under the influence of the Russian madness. In the course of the next generation, something like two and a half million Jews moved out of eastern and southeastern Europe. Most of these directed their footsteps to America. Between two and three hundred thousand found their way to England, Canada, and South Africa. But a remnant, thinking in this hour of their agony of the ancient homeland of the tribe, turned to Palestine. They were idealists, of course, and in their hearts was matchless courage. For Palestine was poor and politically oppressed, and thus offered no such opportunity for security as the free and prosperous commonwealths of the West. But these Jews were seeking more than security. There was a question of dignity and self-respect here. And from this standpoint Palestine offered them far more than other lands of refuge, however hospitable. So these few turned south and east instead of west and north. Within a year after the promulgation of the May "Order," three thousand Jews had landed at Jaffa, and thereafter the stream flowed steadily.

These Jews, as I have said, were primarily refugees. They were fleeing from burdens too heavy and grievous to be borne. But they had chosen to come to Palestine, there to take up other burdens which they might easily have avoided by following the main stream of flight to England or the United States. For, destitute as they were, they had no intention of joining the pilgrims in the Holy Land and thus becoming dependent upon the charity of their more prosperous brethren in far places of the world. They proposed to work—first to maintain themselves, and secondly to redeem the soil of Palestine, and thus begin the vast undertaking of rebuilding the Jewish homeland. Immediately upon their arrival in the Holy Land, in other words, these Jewish refugees became transformed, by the clarity of their intention and the heroism of their spirit, into pioneers, or settlers, and thus joined that third wave of immigration into Palestine which had already begun to flow, and became suddenly and unexpectedly absorbed in this great new tide.

By this third wave I mean the real return—that definite, self-conscious movement back to Palestine which sprang from no other need and was quickened by no other desire than that of restoring Zion. Jews in various parts of the world had long been interested in various experiments in constructive philanthropy in Palestine, all directed toward the recovery of the country. As early as 1870 a School of Agriculture had been established near Jaffa. In Jerusalem and Safed the native Jews, encouraged from abroad, had crept outside their ancient walls, and attempted, though unsuccessfully, the planting of colonies upon the land. But there were no resources either of money or of men. Neither was there any real centering of interest upon a movement which must be sustained by the common will of an entire people if it is to succeed. It is doubtful if these feeble endeavors of scattered individuals or groups of individuals in the Jewish world would ever have come to anything, had it not been for the vast disasters of 1881-82. Suddenly there appeared these Russian refugees who sought to save themselves by saving Palestine. Asking no help of charity, all untrained and ill-equipped as they were, they straightway proceeded to settle upon the land, and there to labor and to die. The struggles of these first settlers were terrible, their sufferings incredible, their losses irreparable. Left to themselves, they would ultimately have perished, as many of them did perish, or at the best a few survived to eke out a miserable existence in the slums of Jerusalem and Jaffa. But their heroism became known. It stirred the compassion of Jewry. More than this, it made an irresistable appeal to the imagination of Jewry. All at once it was realized that the return to Palestine had begun. Without warning the footsteps of the Messiah were heard. Quickly organized support sprang up in various places. Societies and committees were established to foster interest and gather resources. Baron Edmond de Rothschild poured out his generous millions in succor of the struggling settlers upon the land. Best of all, hundreds of young Jews in Poland, Germany, Austria, felt themselves stirred to come to Palestine and join hands with these settlers, these dauntless brethren who were restoring Zion. Spontaneously from different parts of Europe came streams of men and women who, unlike the pilgrims, were not moved solely by pious or sentimental motives, and who, unlike the refugees, fled from no especial misery or oppression, but turned to Palestine with the single desire to rebuild the homeland of the Jew and thereby fulfill the Messianic dream. These were the *pioneers*. The third wave which swept to Zion, and turned the current of Jewish life from west to east!

This flow of pioneers to Palestine, thus begun, has not ceased to this day. Steadily, through the years, the Jews have come pouring in to their ancient homeland. At first a spontaneous impulse moving many hearts, an uncalculated and therefore undirected mass movement of racial idealism and devotion, it became in 1897, with the establishment of the Zionist Movement, under the leadership of that inspired prophet and statesman, Theodor Herzl, a carefully organized and deliberately sustained endeavor of the Jewish world to fulfill its destiny. In the face of difficulties innumerable and apparently insuperable, the work went triumphantly on. By 1914 there were one hundred thousand Jews in Palestine, of whom no less than thirteen thousand were settled on the land in forty-three agricultural colonies with an annual output valued at nearly a million dollars. "They were producing thirty per cent of the oranges, ninety per cent of the wine, and the bulk of the almonds, which together formed half the exports of Jaffa." [3] Land holdings, which had amounted to little or nothing in the old days, had risen to fifty thousand acres in 1898, and nearly one hundred thousand in 1914. The outbreak of the Great War, of course, brought a suspension of activity, which later found ample compensation in the acceleration of endeavor and achievement which followed upon the promulgation of the Balfour Declaration of December, 1917, and the establishment of the British Mandate over Palestine in July, 1922. During the past decade, the advance has been swift and sure. There have been discouragements many, and disasters not a few; but there have been no permanent setbacks anywhere, and progress everywhere. To-day not less than one hundred and fifty thousand Jews are in Palestine to stay. By their labors of hand and brain they are transforming a wrecked and wasted country into a center of industry and happy life. The return to the Holy Land is still an adventure, but it is also now an achievement. Messianism, transfigured by the changed status and changing temper of the modern Jew into Zionism, has become one of the great and central facts in the contemporary world.

Summary of a Movement

What this fact is, and what it means, should at this point be clearly understood. Messianism, in its origin and

---

[3] "Zionism," by Leonard Stein, 1926. Page 64.

[4] Lord Balfour in a letter to Lord Rothschild (November 2, 1917): ". . . His Majesty's Government view with favour the establishment in Palestine of a national home for the Jewish people, and will use their best endeavors to facilitate the achievement of this object, it being clearly understood that nothing shall be done which may prejudice the civil and religious rights of existing non-Jewish communities in Palestine or the rights and political status enjoyed by Jews in any other country."

deepest essence, was a vision of escape. In the days before the Diaspora, it was escape from the iron rule of Rome; in the days after the Diaspora, it was escape from the degradation and oppression visited upon the scattered host of Jewry in many lands. Incidental, also, was a thirst for vindication and vengeance—the human desire to see their enemies overthrown and destroyed, and themselves set proud and high in the seats of power. But the main idea was that of escape from the intolerable misery and shame of their lot. Linked up inextricably with this idea was the conviction that deliverance meant the return to Palestine. But this last was shadowy and vague. Escape was the immediate and pressing necessity. It is no accident that the first general movement into Palestine, apart from the casual drift of pious pilgrims, was a migration of refugees from Russian pogroms.

The unreality of Messianism, as a dream of escape, is manifest in its explicit terms of miracle and wonder. It is still more manifest in its incapacity to satisfy the soul of the Jews. For Messianism has been fulfilled in our time, in ways natural rather than supernatural, and the Jews are not content. The walls of the ghetto have been torn down, and its inhabitants restored to the world of other men; but more than ever do they feel themselves to be a lost people. For they have escaped only to find themselves scattered over the face of the earth, with no identity, no unity, no central consciousness of thought and life. They are immersed in floods of alien people, which threaten to engulf them. Physical deliverance has come, but with it the imminence of spiritual extinction. The leveling of the ghetto walls, which protected the Jews as well as imprisoned them, has brought to them for the first time a challenge to their survival. Hence the amazing fact, so poorly understood by the non-Jew, that the moment which brought the Jews emancipation and therefore an ending of many of their woes, has witnessed the rise of a new and greater Messianism, which is now called Zionism. Escape, which was formerly central to the dream of Israel, is now comparatively unimportant just because it is so largely attained. What was formerly incidental and very vague is now central and crystal clear—namely, the return to Palestine. The transformation of Messianism into Zionism has brought a complete reversal of values in the Jewish conception of his future. What was yesterday a merely negative idea of escaping from something behind, is to-day become the supremely positive idea of winning something before. The Jew, just because he is now free, would find himself again and thus make Zion once more a reality upon the earth. Not the refugee but the pioneer is henceforth the pilgrim to the ancient shrines.

It is from this standpoint that Zionism, or the return, may be said to express the aspirations of the modern Jew, free at last to live among his fellows, as Messianism, or the escape, expressed the aspirations of the medieval Jew, "cabin'd, cribb'd, confin'd" within his noisome ghetto. Palestine, as now being restored and redeemed by Zionists, means two things to Israel. First, and incidentally, a country; secondly, and primarily, an idea.

As a country. Palestine means a homeland returned to its people, as Ireland has been returned to the Irish and Poland to the Poles. Snatched from them by the sword and spear of the soldier, this land is now being recovered to them by the ploughshare and pruning hook of the pioneer. That the Jews, like other men, should want a country, seems strange to us only because they have been so long without a country. The centuries have multiplied since these Jews were first cast adrift upon the waters of affliction, and sought such havens of refuge as were open in the countries of other men. For nearly two thousand years, they have lived as a landless and homeless people, and thus, by force of time and circumstance, have seemed to take on the character of a people who are by nature landless and homeless. But the Jews, just because they are a people and not merely a religion, are quite like other people. They long to-day, as they have longed through all the centuries of their dispersion, for a home and country. They are not satisfied, as no people in any age has ever been satisfied, to be transplanted to an alien soil and climate, and there grow in the likeness of others and not of themselves. What they want is the soil and climate which is their own, and in which they can strike roots and spread branches of native health and beauty. So they turn to a Palestine wasted by centuries of neglect, wrecked by other centuries of devastation, and resolve to build it anew into the homeland of the ancient day.

This does not mean, be it said, that all the fifteen million Jews in the world will straightway go to Palestine and there begin life anew. Anti-Zionists are fond of ridiculing Zionists as Jews who are seeking to establish a country to which they themselves have no intention of returning, and never lose an opportunity of pointing out that, if any real "back to the homeland" movement should get started, Palestine could not begin to accommodate the flow. But all this is beside the point! A mass return of Jews to Palestine is no more to be desired or expected than a mass return of the Irish to the Irish Free State, or of the Poles to Poland. Palestine, when fully developed, may be able to take care of some two million Jews, and this is a total which will in all probability not be reached in any time now of interest to living persons. But a country of their own is still indispensable to Jews everywhere. It means to them forever a haven of refuge—a matter of importance to a people everywhere disliked if not persecuted, unwelcome and perpetually on the defensive. It means to them a country of their own, where their own distinctive life is in the ascendant, and from which they can draw spiritual sustenance, wherever they may be, for their own greater dignity and strength. Above all, it means to them a place in the great body of humanity—not a parasite on the organism, but a part of the organism—a Jewish people, with language, literature, culture, as well as religion. Zionism means a recovered, restored, regenerated Israel. Achad Ha-Am, the seer of Zionism, has summed it all up when he declares that Palestine must be "a natural spiritual center of Judaism, to which all Jews will turn with affection, and which will bind all Jews together; a center of study and learning, of language and literature, of bodily work and spiritual purification; a true miniature of the people of Israel as it ought to be." [5]

It is in such a statement as this that we see that Palestine is more than a country. It is also an idea—an idea of racial, even individual, self-expression and fulfillment. For what the Jew is seeking in Zion is not only his country but his soul. This soul is a peculiar thing in the sense that it is a distinctive thing. Alone among the peoples of mankind the Jews have had a destiny, or mission. Dominated by an unparalleled consciousness of God and of his holy will, they have felt themselves to be a people chosen, set apart, for the service of this holy will. Theirs has been the appointed task, as Moses Hess put it a half-century ago, of "translating religion into terms of a better social order." But this task has been frustrated by their experience of exile and servitude. No paradox of history is so tragic as this—the high mission of the Jews defeated by the Jew's own experience of helpless dependence upon alien and hos-

[5] "Summa Summarum," by Achad Ha-Am.

tile peoples! Unless this experience can be ended, the Jews must forever be frustrated in the one endeavor for which alone they desire to live. And how can this aim be won, save by such recovery of racial independence as is promised by the recovery of Zion? Here is the one chance which they have to be themselves—and the one chance which they have, therefore, to fulfill their mission. Just because Palestine is so wasted, they can in this, their own beloved land, begin their life anew. They can now, after the bitter experience of the ages, achieve what the prophets dreamed and the kings denied. They can build by their own labor and sacrifice what the Jews from the beginning of time have been appointed to build—an ideal society of free, healthy, happy, peaceful human beings. They can realize first among men what they themselves first among men dreamed:

... new heavens and a new earth. ...
There shall be no more thence an infant of days, nor an old man that hath not filled his days. ...
And they shall build houses, and inhabit them; and they shall plant vineyards, and eat the fruit of them.
They shall not build, and another inhabit; they shall not plant, and another eat. ...
They shall not labor in vain, nor bring forth for calamity.

And all this shall transpire in Jerusalem,

... Jerusalem a rejoicing, and her people a joy. ...

just as Isaiah prophesied and promised of old.

This is the idea, or rather ideal, that Palestine embodies to-day. What we have in Zionism, as conceived by its founders and now being achieved by its builders, is a great attempt to translate long-cherished spiritual values into concrete economic and social realities. It is the Jew seizing—nay, himself creating—his opportunity to fulfill at last that appointed mission so long frustrated by the tragic disaster of his historic experience. The Jew is seeking to redeem Palestine, his country, his home, his altar. But also, in redeeming Palestine, he is seeking to redeem himself. And therewith—who knows!—he may be redeeming this sick old world as well.

" . . . Neither is it in our power to redeem them, for other men have our lands and vineyards."

NEHEMIAH 5:5

CHAPTER III

PROBLEMS

First Impressions

It was with this idea of Zionism in my mind, but all ignorant of Palestine and its people, that I arrived in Jerusalem for my three weeks' tour of inspection and inquiry. One can do a great deal in Palestine in three weeks, especially under such conditions of careful and crowded preparation as I found awaiting me. The land itself is small—about the size of New Jersey. Its population is less than a million, and a considerable part of this total gathered in a few cities and towns located on the main arteries of travel. All the leaders of the Arab, Jewish, and English communities are easily accessible, and in my case were immediately and hospitably at my disposal. As I look back upon those three weeks of travel, sight-seeing, interviews, extended conferences, elaborate study, I can recall scarcely a lost moment or a wasted motion, not a single closed door, not a concealment, deception, or rebuff. How different was my experience in Palestine from my experience in Russia! In the Soviet Republic, I moved as in a daze—wandering in unfamiliar places, knocking at barred gates, groping uncertainly and even dangerously in darkness that seemed everywhere to envelop me. But in Palestine I moved with clear eye and mind, as in a blaze of light. In a few hours I felt at home; in a few days I knew just where I wanted to go, and whom and what it was important for me to see. Like a student not altogether unprepared and untrained, taken carefully through a laboratory by the scientific experts at work there, I seemed to learn what was being done, and why. Therefore in this case, as *not* in the case of Russia, I am willing to bear testimony.

Three first impressions—and last impressions, too, for that matter—linger in my mind.

First, the quiet confidence of the leaders of Zionism whom I met upon the ground—men like Arthur Ruppin, for twenty-three years the expert in charge of agricultural development through the colonies, and women like Henrietta Szold, founder and organizer of Hadassah, the great nursing and medical service of which for eighteen years she has been the head. In no one of these men and women did I find the easy optimism as to the future of Zionism which I have found so often in America. They live too near to the realities of the struggle, they have worked too long for results too meager, to be able at this late day to bask in any moonshine of delusion. These leaders blink no facts, evade no doubts, deny no defeats. But through their recognition of dark realities, like sunlight through a cloud, shines their basic confidence in the great adventure. They see a longer and harder road ahead than most long-distance Zionists have ever glimpsed. But they have traveled the longer and harder road behind them to where they are to-day, and in the light of this achievement they *know* that this road ahead can in time be covered. Not hope sustains these persons—not even faith! But knowledge—the hard, weatherbeaten, scarred and battered knowledge of the man who knows the worst, and is fitted therefore for anything that the future may bring. I came away from Palestine knowing a darker side of Zionism than I had ever dreamed before, but with an assurance as to its future as firm-rooted as the everlasting hills. These great leaders of the cause are not wasting their lives in foolish dreams, neither are they throwing them away in a reckless gamble. They know what they are doing, and that it is not in vain.

Secondly, I was impressed by the heroism of this vast undertaking. Especially the heroism of the pioneers, the *Chalutzim*, whom I met in the agricultural villages scattered widely and remotely over the land! These men and women, most of them young, many of them amply able to follow prosperous careers in the more highly developed societies from which they have come, are working at tasks which sap the utmost energy of fiber and nerve, and living under conditions primitive to the point of misery. And these conditions they can expect to see but little improved, and the tasks to which they have set their hands most certainly not completed, in their own time. They are living, laboring, suffering, dying, first, for the Zion of which their prophets dreamed, that it may be established on the earth, and, secondly, for their children and other successors, that these may receive a goodly heritage. As I met and talked with these toilers on the land, I could think of nothing but the early English settlers who came to the bleak shores of Massachusetts, and there amid winter's cold, in an untilled soil, among an unfriendly native population, laid firm and sure the foundations of our American Republic. For this reason I was not surprised later, when I read Josiah Wedgewood's "The Seventh Dominion," to find this distinguished Gentile Zionist of Britain speaking of these Jewish pioneers as "the Pilgrim Fathers of Palestine." Here is the same heroism dedicated to the same ends. And it is a heroism that stirs the heart.

Lastly, out of this sober confidence of the leaders of Zionism, and this steadfast, far-visioned heroism of the workers of Zionism, to say nothing of my own immediate observations and experiences, there came an indelible impression of the terrific problems which the Zionists to-day are facing. Problems which will not down! Not to see these problems is not to comprehend the nature of the Palestinian adventure; not to estimate these problems at their full weight of delay, discouragement, and defeat, is to miss altogether the challenge and the peril of the task to which modern Jewry has set its hand. The first duty of anybody who would understand Palestine to-day is to recognize the tremendous obstacles that stand in the way of any swift and sure accomplishment. As a mere matter of justice to those who are wrestling with these obstacles daily in sweat and tears, they must be confessed as frankly by the observer as they are faced by the worker. The job of Zionism is colossal. The problems involved seem many of them to be insuperable. Four of these problems are of immediate and momentous importance.

Land—Palestine

First, the land, which must be secured and occupied if the Jews are to live in Palestine, and profitably cultivated if they are to prosper!

When the first settlers came to America, they found the vast stretches of a continent waiting for their occupancy. Some of the forests and river banks were claimed in ownership by the Indians, but were easily and cheaply purchased by the new arrivals. The Jewish refugees from Russia and eastern Europe who fled to Canada and South Africa in the early '80s of the last century, had no difficulty in securing abundant land for settlement and tillage. In 1903, Mr. Joseph Chamberlain, on behalf of the British Government, offered to the Zionist Organization an area of six thousand square miles in the Guas Ngishu plateau in East Africa. To-day, in Russia, millions of acres of fertile territory in the Caucasus are being placed at the disposal of colonizing Jews by the Soviet authorities. But in Palestine there is no such available supply of land, and what there is is tightly held by private owners, mostly Arabs, in a kind of feudal tenure defined and guaranteed by old Turkish law. Some of these owners are lordly sheiks living in primitive affluence upon their estates; others are absentee landlords living in Jerusalem, Cairo, or even Paris. In the Holy City I met two highly cultivated Arab gentlemen who were described to me as belonging to ancient Arab families which were among the largest landowners of the country. To secure territory for colonization in Palestine there is no way except to buy it in the open market bit by bit, acre by acre, and this has not been, and is not to-day, an easy piece of business.

There have been owners, to be sure, who have sold their land to Jewish purchasers willingly and at a reasonable price. I found one such on my adventurous journey to Nathanyah—the ancient sheik, at whose village I was so hospitably entertained![1] The account of this man's sale of a portion of his land to the Nathanyah pioneers was like a tale from an Eastern story book, and showed this venerable chieftain to be a poet as well as a real estate speculator. Asked his price for the proposed site of the new colony, the sheik replied that he had no price. "This land belongs to you," he said, "and I shall be glad to give it to you, since you tell me that you want it."

"Give it to us," exclaimed the astounded pioneers. "Belongs to us!"

"Yes," said the shrewd old fellow, grinning with delight at the excitement of his Jewish friends. "This land, all of it, belonged to you Jews in the ancient days, didn't it? But you were driven away, and all these years have been wandering about in various parts of the earth. And all

[1] See Chapter I, pages 49-51.

these years we Arabs have been watching over this land for you, waiting for your return. And now you have come, and you want to settle down again on the soil of your fathers. The land is yours; it belongs to you; take what you want; I give it to you gladly."

"But," he went on—and the grin grew broader—"it is just that you should pay us something for our watching. We Arabs have been faithful guardians all these years, and our service is worth something. You can have this land, but I want payment for taking care of it while you were away."

It was on this basis that the bargain was struck; and with eager gratitude the pioneers told me of the fair price they had been asked to pay for the coveted site of their colony.

Such a story, however, is exceptional. Most of the landlords are none too willing to sell. The lands have been theirs for centuries; they are occupied by roving herdsmen who pay for their grazing rights and feel through generations of usage a sense of ownership; the Jews are alien invaders, who are come to drive out the Arabs and take possession of the country. To overcome such feeling nothing avails but the economic motive—the offering of a price for the land so high, so out of proportion to all essential value either now or in the future, that the owner cannot resist a temptation to wealth greater than he has ever dared to dream. So from the beginning the Jews have had to acquire land at inflated values. At first, to be sure, it was not so bad. The Jews were few and poor; the land they wanted, or would take, was empty, barren and malarial; the chance to turn such land into actual money was too good to be missed by the Arab proprietors. So prices were not altogether beyond reason. But soon the situation changed. Not scattered groups of wretched refugees were now seeking holdings, but a world-wide movement of colonization backed by the wealth of western Jewry. This movement became a bidder for land which it must have if its vast undertaking was to succeed. As its holdings grew from year to year, there came the ever-increasing demand for more land, and still more land, if the enormous capital of money and labor already invested was not to be lost. In Zionism from the beginning there was an urgency on this land question—a drive, a pressure, an inexorable necessity —which placed the whole situation in the hands of the Arab landlords who held the one commodity without which the whole vast undertaking must go to smash. So, like any possessors of a monopoly, these landlords asked their price —and are getting it! Every new area of land acquired to-day is purchased at a valuation which reminds one of the old story of covering the surface of a plot of ground with gold pieces. Nor is this the worst of it! For every such acre thus acquired pushes up by just that much more the sale value of the next acre to be acquired. In Palestine, exactly as on Manhattan island, there seems to be no limit to the price of land.

For a time it was believed that the establishment of the Jewish National Fund would solve the problem. This institution, organized for the express purpose of purchasing extensive tracts of land, and of holding this land as a perpetual trustee in the name of the Jewish people, had as its primary aim the establishment of a guarantee that the land of Zion, once purchased and dedicated to the cause, should not be lost or alienated, never even pass into private ownership. But incidental to this aim was the further aim of solving the problem of acquiring land by placing in the field a single operator powerful enough to cut his way through the tangle of haggling and bartering which was threatening to strangle the movement to death. It was an attempt, in other words, to gain the advantage of wholesale as compared with retail operation. But the appearance of so large a purchaser, equipped with such potentially enormous resources of capital, only served to aggravate the situation. Here were limitless funds— or so the Arabs thought! Why should not the land prices be limitless as well?

In the same way it was believed for a time that the transfer of Palestine from the Turk to the British, under the Mandate of the League of Nations, would solve, or at least greatly improve, this vexatious problem. Article VI of the Mandate expressly provides that the Mandatory shall "encourage the close settlement of Jews on the land, including State lands and waste lands acquired for public purposes." Here was a chance for Britain to step in, and, by throwing the extensive State lands on the market, or opening them for settlement, or condemning waste lands for occupancy by the Jews, to cut at one stroke the Gordian knot of extortionate land speculation. But up to the present, this Article of the Mandate has remained a dead letter. The English have done nothing. They have not even ended or mended the medieval land laws of the old Turkish régime, which are a constant source of difficulty and danger. On the contrary, the Mandatory authorities seem bent on sustaining the Arabs in exploiting to the full the dog-in-the-manger opportunity which is theirs.

So the problem lies! Enormous sums of money, raised by labor and sacrifice in America and elsewhere, are now being poured into the moneybags of Arab landlords, to be spent in luxury and idleness in the salons of Cairo and Paris. Unwilling or unable themselves to develop their land, these feudal barons propose that it shall be developed by the Jew only at a price which will give them wealth beyond the dreams of avarice, and the Zionist Movement the constant nightmare of bankruptcy. How, indeed, the land which must be had for Zion in the future can be acquired under the present system of exchange without ultimate bankruptcy, is something more than an academic question. Is there money enough in Jewry to meet the final exactions of the Arabs?

But the buying of the land is only a part of the land problem in Palestine, and, bad as it is, the less serious part. What kind of land is it which is thus purchased at so extravagant a price? What is its worth as an agricultural development, and "how firm a foundation" does it promise Zion?

Here we meet the inescapable fact that Palestine is a poor country. I doubt if it ever was a rich one. Much of it is a desert—the great stretch of the Wilderness of Benjamin, for example, between Jerusalem and Jericho. There is a beauty about these white, barren, burning hills, and even about that arid plain that bounds the waters of the Dead Sea. But there is a terror, also—the terror of desolation and death, of emptiness and waste and woe. As our automobile sped dustily through this endless area of chalk and sand, I looked in vain for any evidence of grass or shrub. There seemed to be nothing growing in this dead soil, not even the cactus plants that dot the deserts of Arizona and California. Yet once or twice, on the far brow of a hill, silhouetted black against the sky, we saw a shepherd. Had he found some hidden spot of green for his flock, or was he merely crossing the waste to the oasis of Jericho? This country could be cultivated, we were told. But at what expense of money and of toil?

The rest of Palestine is not so terrible as this, the fitting site of Sodom and Gomorrah. There is fertile soil on the Mediterranean coast-land between Jaffa and Haifa; the Emek is a valley of incomparable fatness and beauty; the upper reaches of the Jordan should yield rich tillage to the plow. But most of the country seems an unbroken stretch of rocky hills, interspersed with plains so bleak and barren as to furnish precarious pasturage even to the stunted sheep and goats of the vagrant *Fellaheen*, or with low, marshy valleys, pestilential with the poison of malarial fever. Like Browning's Childe Roland, as he passed through the desolate region to the Dark Tower,

> I think I never saw
> Such starved ignoble nature; . . .
> Penury, inertness, and grimace,
> In some strange sort, were the land's portion.

The lack of an abundant supply of clean, pure water is a conspicuous illustration of the calamitous nature of the country. It seemed absurd to me, floundering through the floods of the severest rainy season that Palestine had known in fifty years, that anybody should talk of a lack of water in this region. But these rains, the earlier and later rains, fall only during some six or eight weeks in the year, and, except for the sodden, poisonous pools in the low valleys, run off as fast as they fall. The "wadis," as they are called—foaming torrents in January and February, and dry, empty river beds through all the rest of the year—are the perfect picture of the country's plight. When the rains have disappeared, there is nothing left for the long, hot, parched months of the summer but the Sea of Galilee and the Jordan River, and a few historic springs, such as the Pool of Elijah at Jericho, the Well of Gideon in the Emek, and Mary's Well at Nazareth. Only huge reservoirs and vast systems of irrigation can keep this country alive.

There was a time, of course, when it was alive—and yet never, I believe, as richly and abundantly as we have been led to suppose. The Children of Israel, to be sure, found it "a land flowing with milk and honey," but we must remember that when they said this they were crossing the Jordan to the oasis of Jericho after forty years in the desert of Sinai. Later stories in the Old Testament of cities and kings, even the detailed narratives of the power of David and the splendor of Solomon, are similarly misleading. We read into these records the standards of our own time, or else the contemporary standards of great empires like Egypt and Chaldæa. More and more, as investigations are widened and deepened, it becomes evident that the kings of Israel and Judah were the chieftains of small tribes, whose standards of living were as poor as they were primitive. Certain it is that the archæological researches in our day are producing not the slightest indication of any wealth or splendor in ancient Palestine. As compared with the gorgeous remains of Egypt, for example, the relics of Palestine are not unlike the arrowheads and pottery of our North American Indians. Some archæologists—Professor Breasted is one—still insist that riches will yet be found in the soil of the Holy Land. The majority of scholars, however, seem agreed that the Bible has tempted us to lift the Israelites to a plane of wealth which they never at any time attained. There were simply no resources in Palestine ample enough to supply the inhabitants, or even the kings, with luxury. The land was poor, and the people were poor. Hard labor and intensive cultivation, coupled with a simple standard of living, made the soil fertile enough to support a much larger population than now exists, and beautiful enough to stir the heart of psalmist and poet. But the standard of living was always low, and the margin of comfort meager.

With the fall of Jerusalem, even this measure of civilization disappeared. The land was stripped of its inhabitants and lay open to the sky. There was nobody to drive a furrow, or prune a tree, or travel a highway. Cities were in ruins, and the landscape a wilderness. For centuries Palestine was empty, desolate, forsaken. Year after year torrential rains poured down in the brief winter season upon the hills, swept away the terraces with all their pleasant soil, and choked the valleys with débris and tainted the springs with poison. Then in the long, dry season of the summer, the cruel sun beat down upon the wasted scene, and blasted it to a desert. As though nature were not pitiless enough, there came at intervals into this neglected land huge armies of men, like swarms of locusts, to hasten with sword and spear the process of destruction. With the passing of each host came emptiness and silence again. Only the wandering tribesman of the Eastern world had courage to enter this waste, and seek a living from its soil. For a thousand years he has driven his sheep and goats to and fro across these barren hills. Occasionally weary of his pilgrimage, or tempted by some sheltered spot of green, he has settled down upon the land, and learned to sow and reap a scanty harvest. But the countryside has still decayed. These primitive herdsmen and farmers have not stayed the process of disintegration. What befell Sodom and Gomorrah in one fearful stroke of ruin, has befallen Palestine itself in the slow wastage of the years.

To-day we see on every hand this wastage of a land naturally poor and always inhospitable. Neglect, destruction, decay, meet one pitifully on every hand. I shall never forget the weight of depression that settled down upon my heart as, on my first morning in Palestine, all athrill with expectation, I watched the country through which our train climbed slowly the steep ascent from Ludd to Jerusalem. We seemed to be passing through a desert, not unlike the desert we had left behind us. Here and there were little groups of miserable people shivering in cave-like shelters in the earth, or working on rude terraces on the steep slopes of the hills. We saw an occasional shepherd who had found a stretch of pasturage for his sheep, or a plowman scratching the stubborn soil with his primitive wooden plow. But the scene was mostly dry, barren, desolate, shorn of verdure and empty of people.

Even at this first glimpse of the country I noticed what became to me in course of time a kind of horror—namely, the absence of trees. We know that, in the days of the kings, there were trees enough in Palestine. The battle in which Joab destroyed the armies of Absalom was fought in "the wood of Ephraim"; and we are told that "the wood devoured more people that day than the sword devoured," and have the interesting detail that Absalom, riding away from the field, "went under the thick boughs of a great oak, and his head caught hold of the oak, and he was taken up between the heaven and the earth."[1] There were also olive trees in the ancient days, and fig trees, and almond trees, scattered widely over the land. But now the trees are gone. I can recall a few palm trees in Jericho, some lordly cypresses in the gardens of the Bahaists in Haifa and Acre, a group of noble eucalyptus trees on the edge of Petah Tikvah, a few trees, or were they shrubs, on the foothills of Esdraelon, some lovely vineyards in the Jewish colonies, gnarled olive trees here and there, but otherwise I think of the land as naked. Mile after mile, and not a tree! The last growths, I was told, were cut away by the Germans and Turks as they retreated north from the pursuing army of Lord Allenby after the capture of Jerusalem in the Great War. But the land must long ago have been stripped, probably by the armies of the Crusaders and the Saracens, for not otherwise could the rains have swept the soil so clean from hill to vale.

Nature and man together have conspired this havoc, to make a wreck of Palestine. The country, like the Childe Roland country again, is

> now mere earth
> Desperate and done with . . .

As I looked upon its desolation, I thought of what Mark Twain had written of it sixty years before, in the spirit not of derision but of pity, in his "Innocents Abroad":

"Of all the lands there are for dismal scenery, I think Palestine must be the prince. The hills are barren, they are dull of color, they are unpicturesque in shape. The valleys are unsightly deserts fringed with a feeble vegetation that has an expression about it of being sorrowful and despondent. The Dead Sea and the Sea of Galilee sleep in the midst of a vast stretch of hill and plain wherein the eye rests upon no pleasant tint, no striking object, no soft picture dreaming in a purple haze or mottled with the shadows of the clouds. . . . It is a hopeless, dreary, heartbroken land.

"Small shreds and patches of it must be very beautiful in the full flush of spring, however, and all the more beautiful in contrast with the far-reaching desolation that surrounds them on every side. I would like much to see the fringes of the Jordan in springtime, and Shechem, Esdraelon, Ajalon, and the borders of Galilee—but even these spots would seem to be mere toy gardens set at wide intervals in the waste of a limitless desolation.

"Palestine sits in sackcloth and ashes. Over it spreads the spell of a curse that has withered its fields and fettered its energies. . . . The Sea of Galilee . . . was long ago deserted by the devotees of war and commerce, and its borders are a silent wilderness; Capernaum is a shapeless ruin; Magdala is the home of beggared Arabs; Bethsaida and Chorazin have vanished from the earth, and the desert places round about them . . . sleep in the hush of a solitude that is inhabited only by birds of prey and skulking foxes.

"Palestine is desolate and unlovely. And why should it be otherwise? . . ."

This is the country to which the Jews have come to rebuild their ancient homeland. Restoration means the driving of wells, the construction of huge reservoirs, the building far and wide over the land of permanent systems of irrigation, the draining of the marshes, the terracing of the hills, reforestration on a vast scale, the importation and breeding of cattle, sheep and poultry, and plowing, sowing, reaping season after unprofitable season. Money unreckoned, labor unstinted, years uncounted must go into this task. Not merely water, but sweat and tears and blood must fertilize this soil. What wonder that the English High Commissioner, as we talked together over this problem, held up his hands in despair, and, as though to divert his mind from the desolation of Palestine, described to me the rich lands of the African colony in which he had last served as a representative of the British crown! I sympathized with him, for as I had journeyed about this bleak and barren country, I had found myself thinking of the plains of Kansas and Iowa, of the forests of Wisconsin and Minnesota, and of the flowers and orchards of California. As a starving man dreams of a feast, so a sojourner in Palestine dreams of other and richer portions of the world. Why, if the Jews must have a homeland again, must they come here, where land can be acquired only with such difficulty and at such enormous expense, and is so poor and wasted when at last it is secured? Why not Africa, of which Sir John Chancellor spoke to me, or Canada, or South America, or even that great stretch of territory in Soviet Russia? In all these places land can be had for the asking, land which in a few years could be transformed into a garden of loveliness and plenty?

But as one may see in Palestine the wastage of the country and the vast labor of its restoration, so one may feel as well its hold upon the Jewish heart. Why talk of any other land for the Jewish homeland? This homeland must be a *home!* And on all the surface of this earth there is no home for the Jew save in the mountains and by the well-springs of his ancient kingdoms. Everywhere else the Jew is an exile—he lives by sufferance on land which is the heritage of others. In all other places he is an alien— he looks on scenes which stir no memories within his soul. But Palestine is his! For all the wanderings of these last two thousand years, this country belongs to him. Turks, Arabs, Christians, all lay claim to this thrice-sacred soil. But the old sheik was right—these are but guardians of the home from which the rightful owner has for a time, through no fault of his own, been absent.

Scratch a Russian, said Napoleon, and you find a Tartar. Scratch Palestine, anywhere, and you find Israel. In the vale of Esdraelon I passed a gushing spring, and was told by the Jewish colonist, who almost kneeled before it, that this was Gideon's Well. On the horizon I caught the outline of a mountain, and learned that this was Gilboa where Saul and Jonathan were slain in the great battle; and beyond was Beisan (Beth-Shan) where "they fastened his (Saul's) body to the wall." At Haifa I stood on a hilltop overlooking the town and the bright sea beyond— and this was Carmel where Elijah confounded the prophets of Baal. Far in the distance from Mt. Scopus I saw a little village nestling under the slope of a hill in Benjamin. This was Anathoth, the birthplace of Jeremiah; along that road, to the north and west, the prophet made his fateful way to the Holy City; there on the north wall he looked and saw the dust of the approaching hosts of Assyria. Bethlehem—the city of David! Hebron—where David was anointed king of Judah after the death of Saul! Jerusalem—the stronghold which David built, its very foundations the flesh and blood of Israel! And Jordan—where

John baptized Jesus, but also where Joshua entered the Promised Land! Everywhere in Palestine are these historic places. There is not a spot which is not stamped with the footprint of some ancient tribesman. Not a road, a spring, a mountain, a village, which does not awaken the name of some great king, or echo with the voice of some greater prophet. There may be other countries more hospitable to the Jew than this, but none which can give such shelter to his soul. There may be more fertile dust upon this planet, but none so sacred to his tread. Surely this is his homeland, if ever again he is to have a home.

"Man does not live by bread alone," said the greatest of all Jewish prophets. In the lives of men there are imponderables—mysterious inner essences of the spirit which cannot be weighed or measured, touched or handled, defined or seen, but which move the heart, and turn the tides of destiny. Such an imponderable is the appeal of Palestine to the Jew. Against it all the tangible realities of ease and wealth and power weigh as nothing. For centuries the Jew has dreamed not merely of an escape from his misery and oppression, but of an escape in terms of a return to the land which once was his. In a dozen countries he could enjoy a prosperity and perhaps a larger liberty which Palestine could never yield. In his present far from happy places of abode he could with patience in this modern age make his way to free and ample life. But it is not for this that the Jew has survived these centuries of bitter pain. He has a higher, nobler motive in Palestine than the economic. "Why on earth did you come here?" cried Dr. Lee K. Frankel, to a pioneer worn and broken by labor which had brought him no return. "I *had* to come," replied the Jew, with quiet fervor. "I am a Zionist." The Jews, in other words, are still a people with a mission; this mission is to restore Zion; and Zion is Palestine—Palestine taken over once again by her children, and built at last into the substance of their dreams.

For Zion's sake will I not hold my peace, and for Jerusalem's sake I will not rest, until the righteousness thereof go forth as brightness, and the salvation thereof as a lamp that burneth.

In Palestine, and not elsewhere, must the new Zion be established. And there to-day it is being established. Forty years of labor on desert lands have made some stretches of them at last to blossom as the rose. Hundreds of acres of fertile soil, reclaimed, rebuilt, now yield their abundant harvest of oranges and olives, almonds, grapes, and corn. Thousands of eager toilers, with cruel labor and slow but sure success, like an army of invaders push steadily forward their reconquest of this ancient soil. What has been done on a small scale will soon be done on a large scale. What two generations have achieved will be achieved again a thousandfold in generations that are to be.

"Look at those mountains," I said one day to a Jewish companion, pointing to a barren range of hills to our left. "There's nothing you can do with those."

"Those hills," he replied, "were once beautiful with figs and olives. We shall make them beautiful again."

"How will you do it?" I asked.

"We shall terrace them," he said, "as they were terraced in the old days. Those slopes are not mere sand and rock. There's soil there still. And the soil that has been washed away into these valleys, we'll carry it back, basket by basket, shovelful by shovelful, until the hills are green again."

"You can't do that," I cried, "not in a hundred years!"

Then came the bravest words I heard in Palestine:

"What's a hundred years to a Jew?"

PEOPLE—THE ARABS

A second problem in Palestine is that of the people who own or live upon the land. Palestine is not an unoccupied country. From the standpoint of its immediately available resources, it is not even sparsely occupied. It has an old, highly self-conscious, native population, which feels a sense of ownership in Palestine, and does not propose to see itself dispossessed by the Jewish pioneers, as the Indians of North America for example were dispossessed by the English, French, and Spanish settlers.

The variety of people in Palestine, as I have pointed out, is amazing. To walk on the streets of the cities, to travel through the open stretches of the country, is to see a panorama of the East and of a considerable portion of the West. Here are native Jews, survivors of the remnant never completely extirpated from the ancient homeland, Syrians from the north, Egyptians and Bedouin from the south, Turks, Armenians, Persians, Nubians, a group of German Protestant colonists, an American commercial colony, the English official colony which came in during the War, and innumerable varieties of eastern and western Christians. Predominant among all these people are the Arabs, who drifted into the empty and wasted country in the wake of the great Moslem renaissance, and, living there more or less precariously for thirteen centuries, have long since become the native population of the region. How many Arabs there are in Palestine has long been doubtful. The Turks took no accurate census, and the British have been slow to organize this branch of civic administration. But as I write, there comes to me from Palestine an official communique of the British administration on the number of inhabitants in the country as of March, 1929. This estimate shows a total of 794,331, of which 557,649 are Moslems, 149,555 Jews,

78,463 Christians, and 8850 others. It will be noted that this official report shows a smaller total than that usually reported hitherto from unofficial sources. Of the Jews the smaller proportion, some thirty thousand, are on the land; the rest in the cities, fifty thousand in Jerusalem, thirty-eight thousand in Tel-Aviv. With the Moslems, or Arabs, the situation is exactly the reverse; the overwhelming majority of these are on the land.

A survey of the Arab, or native, population shows that this may be roughly divided, like Cæsar's Gaul, into three parts.

First, and most numerous, are the Bedouin. The mountaineers and shepherds who, with their families and flocks, wander from place to place over a circumscribed but nevertheless wide area of country, and subsist as best they can upon what they find! Their standard of living is the lowest I have ever seen—the simple standard of primitive pastoral life, surviving almost unchanged into our time from periods too remote in history to be recorded. Driving over the main highways of the country, or riding along devious paths through the mountains, I would discern every now and then a lonely shepherd, out on the plain, or up on the lower slopes of the hill, surrounded by his sheep and goats. There he stood, the only human figure in the landscape, leaning motionless upon his staff, wrapped voluminously in his heavy robes against the cold and rain, usually silent, but now and then calling his shrill, weird cry to his scattered animals. So Isaac and Jacob must have stood, and so they must have called, in the ancient Bible days! These shepherds, even in the severe weather of the rainy season, are frequently out on the hillsides in this fashion, all alone, for days, even weeks, at a time. But somewhere, frequently miles away, is their family, or tribe, camping out in some sheltered spot, a dozen, a score, never more than a hundred men, women, and children. I saw one such family which numbered only one man, one woman, one child, and a camel. I saw others which must have numbered eighty or ninety persons.

The encampments are always identical with the one I visited on my trip to Nathanyah, and have described above [2]—little groups of long, black, low-hanging, flat-roofed goatskin tents, with the side to the south wide open to the weather. These tents are floored with grass or stubble, damp, dirty, foul-smelling, and give shelter to men, women, children, sheep, goats, asses, and savage dogs. All bunk in comfortably together, and in the cold weather as close as possible for the sake of warmth. An encampment never remains in one place for more than a few weeks, at the longest in the rainy season for two or three months, at a time. I saw one such encampment being moved—the tents struck and folded and laid on the asses, the sheep and dogs herded in a confused and huddled mass, the women and children stumbling along under heavy burdens in a wet and sodden procession. The men, as I met them, are large, strong, not infrequently handsome, and uniformly hospitable. The women also are tall and powerful. All are illiterate, superstitious, cruel, dirty. They represent the most primitive type of social life. Some have learned to drive the plow; and occasionally they stay long enough in one place to scratch the soil a few inches deep and grow a quick and scanty harvest. But the Bedouin as a class must be said still to be living in the pastoral stage of civilization. They are frankly wanderers, seeking pasturage for the flocks which are the stable substance of their lives.

Secondly, among the Arabs, are the *Fellaheen*, or villagers. These are the people who have crossed the thresh-

[2] See Chapter I, pages 47-48.

old from the pastoral to the agricultural stage of civilization, and thus have settled down into permanent abodes upon the land. The villages in which these people live are conspicuous as one journeys about the country—groups of low, mud houses, rounded into domes which look for all the world, as I have said, like the igloos of the Eskimos. Entered by little doorways pointing to the south, these houses, or huts, are utterly dark and unventilated save for tiny apertures at the top which, as I passed by, were all tight closed against the weather. In the dry, hot months of the year, of course, the people live in the open, using their houses more for storage purposes than anything else. But in the rainy season they seem to bury themselves, like animals that hibernate from the cold. On more than one occasion I passed these villages in the middle of the day, and looked in vain for any sign of life. Even the dogs were gone, and the great camels out of sight. Yet in many of these villages there are anywhere from three to five hundred people. Some of them might be regarded as towns, except for the fact that there are no streets, no public buildings, no industries, no arts, none of the things that make up the structure of community life as we understand it in the West.

These villagers, like the Bedouin, have their flocks, for Palestine is still predominantly a grazing country. But they are distinctive in the fact that they till the soil. Their plowing, to be sure, is as unchanged from the habits of ancient times as the shepherding upon the hills. The plow is the same sharpened wooden stake, with wooden handles and braces, that has been used in this part of the world for centuries unnumbered. By such an instrument, the soil is but lightly turned. On our adventurous trip to Nathanyah, we drove our automobiles straight across a field which was being freshly plowed by one of these wooden plows drawn by a camel, and we were no more conscious of the furrows than of sticks or straws upon the road. From such a field the harvest of course is poor, and the people therefore poor. How they eke out a living is one of the unsolved mysteries of the country. Indeed, apart from their settled life, and, if their villages be located near the cities, their contact with established civilization, they subsist upon a social and economic level scarcely higher than that of the Bedouin. Their habits are as primitive, their illiteracy as general, their superstitions as deep and dark. But they have definitely crossed the line from the pastoral to the agricultural stage of social development. Many of them have left the country and gone to the towns, where, as laborers and tradesmen, they comprise the Arab population of these places. They thus represent a definite upward step in the progress of civilization.

Lastly, among the Arabs, are the well-to-do, even rich, merchants and landowners who, with the small group of professional men—lawyers, journalists, teachers, priests—constitute the aristocracy of the country. Some of these feudal lords, like the aged sheik whom I visited on my trip to Nathanyah, live in genuine if somewhat primitive feudal splendor upon the land.. So Abraham must have lived when he "sojourned in Gerar." More frequently these barons abide in the cities, sometimes in Egypt and Europe as absentee landlords, and there maintain such wealth and culture as Palestine affords. The glory of the country in this regard, however, has long since passed away. Jerusalem was never a center of Moslem power and learning in the sense that Cairo and Bagdad and certain cities of India, for example, have been for centuries. There were no resources in the land adequate to produce and sustain a real flowering of civilization. But there was formerly a society of moderate light and leading which now has disappeared.

I remember the Sunday morning I spent in the Mosque of Omar and the surrounding plaza, formerly the seat of Herod's temple. I was shown some of the treasures of the place by one of the most scholarly of present-day Mohammedans. On turning back toward David Street, I noticed long rows of upper chambers on top of the great wall, through the portal of which we were about to pass, and I asked what they were used for.

"Nothing," replied my Moslem friend. "All empty! There was a time, and not so long ago, when they were occupied by eager students sitting at the feet of the teachers of the Koran. But these students are all gone now," he continued, shaking his head in melancholy fashion. "The schools are dead."

Much else is dead, or has never come to life, in Palestine. Poverty, illiteracy, superstition, a savage religion, a feeble press, these are the depressing features of Arab life. Yet is there a society in this ancient country which represents the very essence of culture and fine breeding. I remember with something of a thrill the evening I called alone, by appointment, at the home of one of the most influential Arab gentlemen of Palestine, a somewhat important government official. It was late in the evening as I made my way through the empty streets, guided by the light of a cold but brilliant moon. On wall and pavement and distant tower the radiance glowed like silver, and seemed by some witchery to make Jerusalem a fairy city. I knocked at the appointed door, and was straightway admitted to the central hall-like room, which is the characteristic feature of Arab houses, and received kindly by my host, whose quiet voice and careful English were like music to the ear. The light from the hanging lamps was dim, and cast into mysterious shadows the rich hangings upon the walls. In one corner, beside low smoking tables, were deep, couch-like

PROBLEMS 111

chairs, in which we sat for our conference together. My host was clothed in loose garments, with Oriental slippers upon his feet, and the familiar tarboosh upon his head. As we talked a servant, moving as lithe and silent as a cat, came and went to fill our coffee cups and pass the little cakes and wafers. Here was the essence of comfort, charm, cultivated and gracious hospitality. I was seeing the use of wealth without its display, and of power without its pride and pretension. In this home and in its master was a heritage of culture so ancient and so refined as to have become a second nature to the spirit. Suddenly I knew the beauty of old families and of cherished ways. And their exclusiveness, as well! For there was something not seen within this house—something hidden, undescribed. My host was guarded in his speech; careful and prudent in his answers to my questions. I could not see into his mind, as I could not see into the corners of his room.

Memorable in a different way was my visit to the Mayor of Jerusalem, a member of the great Nashashibi family, a landowner of much wealth, and a man long prominent in the public affairs of the country. Here was a home made beautiful by works of art, and a man remarkable not so much for that noble breeding which I had found in my Arab host the other night, as for a certain sophistication characteristic of a man of the world of high intelligence and realistic temper. He was dressed in European fashion, and seemed Western rather than Eastern in his bearing. I seemed to note, however, that his general philosophy was a refined type of Oriental fatalism, founded on the instinctive rather than trained conviction that things happen, and men must learn to act accordingly. It was easy to understand the quick and effectual way in which he had transferred his loyalty from the Turkish to the English rulers of the land. The Turks had gone, the English had come!

It was his business, was it not, to be as useful under the one régime as the other? As a Moslem, and the first citizen of his community, he was faithful to the outward practices of his church. But I could not see that he took his religion overseriously, or was much concerned with problems of piety. Was it an accident that the five of us gathered together that afternoon within his home represented five different faiths—the Mayor a Mohammedan, his wife a Roman Catholic, the Vice-Mayor a Greek Orthodox, my escort a Jew, and I, if I was anything, a Protestant? His Honor knew enough to see into the hearts of men, was honest enough to confess frankly to himself and others what he saw, and because, or in spite, of what he saw, or seemed to see, he had become somewhat cynical and disillusioned. He understood his world, had mastered its forces, and was serving its interests. It seemed fitting that I should meet this distinguished Arab in the bright, hard light of a cold, yet sunny afternoon, amid the gorgeousness of elegant decoration, just as it had seemed fitting that I should meet that other Arab amid the semi-darkness of soft lights and heavy hangings. The glitter of this Eastern world is matched by its mystery.

These two gentlemen were both of them, in their way, typical representatives of the Arab aristocracy of Palestine. Between such men and their families upon the one hand, and the Bedouin and the village tribesmen (*Fellaheen*) and their families upon the other, is the span of centuries. In the latter we see the beginnings, as in the former the completion, of a social process. And all three groups are inescapable factors in the situation which confronts the Jew as he plants his feet upon the soil of Palestine to possess and use it. For whatever the gulf that yawns between the Bedouin who wanders upon the land, the villager who occupies and tills it, and the landlord who owns and profits from it, all are united in a common distrust and fear of this newcomer. These three divisions of the Arab world, in other words, are no longer three but one when they look upon this alien who would dispute with them their own.

The problem of the relation between Jew and Arab in Palestine is very simple. I guessed the general nature of it as rooted deep in the constant elements of human nature; I learned the specific nature of it as inextricably interwoven with the peculiar circumstances and conditions of Palestinian life. In answer to my express request, I was privileged to meet alone with Arab leaders—lawyers, editors, teachers, merchants, politicians—and hear their side of the story. These men were frank with me; they stated their case with a fullness and a fervor that were impressive. These men were resolute as well as frank; they voiced not merely opinion but conviction, and a stern and rigorous purpose. It did not take me long to understand these Arabs, even to sympathize with them. I know I got their minds, for I had the feeling, as I listened to them, that my mind would be theirs were I an Arab.

The problem can all be summed up in the statement that the Arabs believe that Palestine belongs to them, and that the Jews are undertaking deliberately to take it away from them. They have lived upon this land for thirteen hundred years—a thousand years longer than Americans, even of the colonial stock, have lived in America. It is true that, before this time, the Jews lived and flourished in Palestine for an even longer period, but in this prolonged interim the Arabs have possessed the land, and thus won it for their own by right of occupancy. Why should they be asked at this late date to vacate and surrender it? If Palestine were a large country, with thousands of acres of virgin territory, or if it were a fertile country, capable of supporting an abundant population, it would be a different story. But the land is as small as Wales, and has a soil more stubborn than that of the Welsh highlands, and is thus no more able to sustain large numbers of people than the little mountainous country to the west of England. As a matter of fact, argue the Arabs, Palestine has as large a population to-day as it can hope reasonably to support, even upon the low level of life that now prevails. The entrance of the Jews into their ancient home, therefore, means inevitably the expulsion of the Arabs from their present home. Every Jew who comes into Palestine to-day, said an Arab editor to me, forces the expulsion of an Arab. There is food enough for one of them, but not for both of them. If the settler stays, the native inhabitant must go. Even if he finds it possible to stay, he will be driven from the land, and thus made permanently landless and helpless.

How would you like it, I was asked, if millions of aliens suddenly appeared upon the shores of America, and insisted upon taking over the land and settling upon it as their own? You have already answered this question, I was quickly told, by your immigration policy. So long as there were millions of acres of free territory to be cultivated in America, you were glad to have the labor of strong hands and stout hearts. But the moment you began to feel that pressure of population which is acute with us, you closed your gates. Look at what you did to the Japanese in California, said an Arab lawyer, pushing the immigration argument through from the general to the particular.

"But the Japanese," I objected, not in defense of our American policy, but in explanation of it, "the Japanese had no claim upon America. California had never been their homeland. And it is only fair to remember," I continued, astonished and ashamed to find myself extenuating the Japanese exclusion policy of my country, "that these Orientals represent a type of life utterly alien to ours."

"So do the Jews represent a type of life utterly alien to *ours*," was the sharp retort. "The West is as alien to the East, as the East is to the West. And suppose the Japanese *had* lived in America in some remote period—hundreds of years, let us say, before Lief Ericson landed in Labrador! Would that have made any difference in your policy? When the Japanese became numerous enough to occupy your land, crowd your people, and threaten your culture, would you not have done just what you *have* done —banned them from your ports of entry, and denied to those already within your borders the right to own the land? If America, with all her prosperous millions, and all her enormous stretch of territory, cannot stand a few thousand Japanese, why should we, in this little country, be asked to receive these Jews, who in numbers and resources can outmatch us in a generation?"

This was the Arab case as presented to me more than once by the intelligent and highly trained leaders of the Arab community in Jerusalem and elsewhere. It is not to be imagined that the masses of the Arabs in Palestine argue in any such fashion as this. The *Fellaheen* know nothing about the Japanese in America, and have little idea as to whether their country is underpopulated or overpopulated. But what the cultivated landowner or professional man thinks, the lonely shepherd or wretched villager feels. What expresses itself among the educated classes as a deliberate agitation directed to the end of specific political and social reforms, is fomented among the illiterate hordes upon the land as a smoldering sense of outrage and peril. The *Fellaheen* react when they are driven from their ancestral soil by people whose faces are strange and language unfamiliar. Who are these sudden invaders whose plows devour more land in an hour than their plows can cover in a day; whose orchards creep like a flood over the land and chase the flocks to the barren hills; who send inspectors into the villages and order things done differently from what they have been done since the days of the fathers; whose women dress like men, and whose gods are alien? They seem friendly, these newcomers, and their friendliness in due time, as we shall see, works the perpetual miracle of peace. But meanwhile the Arab, undisturbed in his primitive ways for centuries gone by, is afraid for himself and his possessions. And his fear is tinder which catches fire at the casual spark struck by the friction of contact between strange races, and leaps into flame at the breath of agitation. Ignorant, superstitious, fanatical, these Arab hordes are as dry fuel for any conflagration which the leaders of the race may desire for any reason, at any time, to kindle.

The situation thus revealed in Palestine may be said to have passed through three somewhat definite stages of development since the first appearance of Jewish settlers in the Holy Land. In the beginning, the Arabs were not particularly disturbed. The Jews came in small numbers; their early settlements were failures; the later and more successful undertakings seemed to promise no serious development and growth. With the organization of the Zionist Movement, of course, the tide of immigration began to flow with increasing volume and force; by 1914, as we have seen, there were one hundred thousand Jews in Palestine. Interest was now aroused among the Arabs. Suspicion, even hostility, were becoming rife. But the feeling was latent rather than active. The volcano was rumbling, but not in eruption.

The war period (1914-1918) brought a twofold change in the situation. On the one hand, as regards the Arabs, there came the English invasion, and the defeat and overthrow of the Turkish rule. Added, in other words, to the excitement of war and fighting—with all its disastrous psychological consequences—was the vast upheaval as by an earthquake of the established order of society. The Arabs were in the hands of the victorious Allies. What was going to happen to them?

What their ambitious leaders wanted to happen was the creation in Asia Minor of a great confederation of Arab states, which should include Arabia, Syria, Mesopotamia, and also Palestine. They insisted that, in return for their assistance during the War, the Allies had promised to establish such a confederation by declaring their purposes to be "the final liberation of the peoples so long oppressed by the Turks and the establishment of national governments and administrations deriving their authority from the initiative and free choice of the native populations." But this all-Arab autonomy was not granted at Versailles. On the contrary, the whole region of the Near East was subjected, rent apart—Syria to France, Palestine to Britain—and Arab power thus dissipated, and high-wrought nationalistic Arab ambitions frustrated and defied. Immediately a storm of resentment swept the Arab world—a storm which, though quieted, rages still in the hearts of millions. The Arabs felt themselves, and still feel themselves, betrayed. A situation was arbitrarily created by the Allied peacemakers which will vex the East for years.[3]

On top of this defeat of Arab nationalism came the establishment of the British Empire in Palestine under the Mandate of the League of Nations, with the definite committal of the Empire to the task of "placing the country under such political, administrative and economic conditions as will secure the establishment of the Jewish national home."

---

[3] No one can understand the August (1929) riots in Palestine who does not understand this chapter of history. Nationalistic ideals, far more than religious fanaticism, was at the bottom of the disturbances which swept the land with death and ruin.

Here was the Balfour Declaration of 1917, which had already stirred the Palestinian Arabs to excitement and unrest, written right over into the terms of the Mandate. This meant—what else could it mean?—that the British Empire was committed to the support of the Zionist Movement, and would henceforth put its might behind the Jews in their endeavor to recapture the ancient homeland. It was true, to be sure, that Lord Balfour's statement declared that in this endeavor "nothing shall be done which may prejudice the civil and religious rights of existing non-Jewish communities in Palestine"; and that the Mandate echoed this pledge in words which promised the "safeguarding" of "the civil and religious rights of all the inhabitants of Palestine, irrespective of race and religion." This seemed to promise a protection of the Arab population against the Jews. But what were promises in war time? How often were the rights of a subject people respected by their rulers? What the Balfour Declaration and the Mandate obviously meant was that the British were going to take this country which they had seized by force of arms, and by the same force of arms pass it over to the Jews of England, America, and eastern Europe. The Arabs, who had pastured their flocks upon these hills for a thousand years, were now to be driven away, and their land surrendered to the ruthless invaders who had already bought or stolen their foothold upon the soil as though in anticipation of this moment. A native people, in other words, were to be dispossessed of their country. What wonder that there swept over this people a tempest of terror, which followed, like a tornado after a thunder storm, the wrath over the frustration of the Arab state!

It may well be discovered, before the tale is done, that the English conquest of Palestine, and the English government of Palestine under the Mandate, constitute together the greatest tragedy that ever befell the Zionist Movement.[4] They certainly created an actively hostile Arab mind which had not existed before, and might never have existed but for these events which followed upon the upheavals of the War. But the Jews saw nothing of this. On their side, for the time at least, there followed an exultation which matched perfectly, and disastrously, the alarm and anger of the Arabs. For the Jews also read the Balfour Declaration and the Mandate as the promise of Britain to redeem Israel. In its solemn pledge to "favor the establishment in Palestine of a national home for the Jewish people," they saw Palestine handed over to themselves, to occupy and use as they saw fit. The Jews took it for granted, in other words, that the British Empire looked upon Zionism exactly as the Zionists did themselves, and that the promise "to establish such conditions as will secure the establishment of the Jewish national home," meant that the Empire would do what the Zionists on their own behalf would have them do. They were convinced that suddenly, as though by the hand of God, their struggles were over, and their hour come. Palestine was from this time forth a Jewish country, and all the Jews had to do was to enter it. The result was a profound and excited stirring of Jews throughout the world. A kind of fever seemed to possess the Movement. Not a few Zionist leaders began to talk extravagantly, even arrogantly. Wild words were cast abroad as to what was going to be done in Palestine, and done at once. It was a type of chauvinism —very unusual with the Jew, but natural enough when the Jew was marching in the wake of armies, and reaping the blood-fruit of the sword.

The alarm of the Arab in this situation was as ill-founded, of course, as the exultation of the Jew. But it was natural, and led to uprisings which were in essence the strug-

[4] See Chapter V, page 254.

gle of an outraged colonial people for liberty. The Arabs had seen themselves balked and betrayed in nationalistic ambitions as dear to them as the Zionist ambitions to the Jews. Now they saw, or thought they saw, the loss to them of Palestine. The Arabs were suddenly convinced that a great incursion of Jews, the protégés of England, was imminent. They were certain that they were about to be driven from their lands at the point of the sword. Among illiterate people, scattered far and wide over a bleak countryside, it was easy to spread abroad wild rumors; and in the confusion and madness of the post-War period there were those who had good reason to make sure that such rumors traveled fast and far. The result was local uprisings of the Arabs, and the outbreak of what is called rioting, but what in actuality was a foretaste of war. Individuals in Jerusalem were attacked, small Jewish settlements were threatened, and in Petah Tikvah Jewish settlers, fighting in defense of their homes and families, were slain. Tel-Aviv was threatened by an Arab mob of five thousand men. In the center of this city to-day may be seen the honored ground in which lie buried the bodies of citizens who were struck down in Jaffa, on the seashore, or in orchards outside of Tel-Aviv. In many places in the land I heard the tale of Trumpeldor, a Jewish patriot, whose death in battle against the Arabs seems to have become a kind of symbol of sacrifice for Zion. How far this warfare would have gone, had it not been for the English soldiers in occupation of the country, nobody knows. The Jews are inclined to minimize its hazard. On the other hand, the English Bishop gave it to me as his opinion that, had it not been for the troops, the Jews would have been wiped out to a man. It is foolish to speculate, perhaps, about possibilities in a chaotic situation of this kind. The fact is enough that, in this hour of excited feeling, the Arabs declared war upon the

Jews, that for a few weeks after violence was suppressed and order restored by the English military authorities there was much local uneasiness and readiness of embers to burst into flame, and that in the end the Arabs sank back in sullen anger—a frightened, frustrated people resolved to husband their strength and bide their time for a later and more successful revolt against their enemies.

To-day, as in recent years, the situation is one of tension, with lines drawn taut and thus liable to break at any time.[5] For the moment English policy has subdued both Jews and Arabs. Thus, the exultation and arrogance of the Jews are largely gone. Their hopes have been disappointed, and are now changed to a resigned acceptance of the slower progress of pre-War days. In the same way, the hysterical fears of the Arabs have been quieted, though by no means extinguished. The rigorous restrictions imposed upon immigration by the government have convinced them that they are not to be inundated by floods of Jewish settlers, and they are satisfied that danger of Jewish supremacy is for the present at least passed. The Arab leaders seemed to me to be well content on this point. More than one of them told me with calm assurance that Palestine was an Arab country, and would remain so. But the Jews, if no longer exultant, are bitterly aggrieved that their glowing hopes are dead. The Arabs, if no longer terrified, still nurture with their brethren in other Moslem states the dream of nationalism—so curiously the same kind of a dream the Jews are dreaming!—and in Palestine set themselves in grim resolve to hold their own. The volcano is now sleeping, but deep down in hidden caverns the fires burn hot, and seem to await the hour of fresh

[5] One week after this paragraph was written came the news of the August (1929) riots which swept Palestine with more dire consequences than the earlier outbreaks.

eruption. Whatever the changes in recent years, tension remains as the constant factor in the situation. At three points of contact between the races, the strain is serious.

First and foremost are the racial and religious differences which divide Arabs and Jews. These constitute the most dangerous point of strain, since they stir the fiercest passions, and lead to the most sudden and ghastly outbreaks of violence. Yet they are in no way peculiar to Palestine, have no essential connection with the problem of Zionism, and, except as they serve as a cloak under which to hide other and deeper problems of dissension, cannot be regarded as important. For race prejudice is nothing new. It is an ever-present element in human life, and society everywhere has had to find a way of getting on with it rather than without it. When complicated with religious fanaticism, as in Palestine, prejudice takes on an added bitterness, which leads not infrequently to dreadful happenings. But this bitterness is as old as time. In Palestine, undoubtedly, it has an intensity which is unusual. Three religions regard this country as a holy land, and for centuries have struggled for its possession. Jew, Christian, Moslem, all walk in the same tradition, and for this reason have savagely contended for an inheritance which they would make exclusively their own. The result has been the discord of ages, which has run the gamut of tragedy from the sordid spectacle of street brawls and riots to the grim epic of holy wars. But in all this, as I have said, there is not so much a unique as a universal fragment of experience. It is matched, bit by bit, by the furious and fratricidal religious massacres of the Middle Ages. In modern times we find its parallel in the fierce racial and religious feud between north and south Ireland, in the persecution of racial and religious minorities in contemporary Europe, in the Hindu and Moslem outrages in India, and in the race riots, lynchings, and Ku Klux Klan horrors which have stained the history of Negro and white America. Mankind has always been afflicted with manias of this kind. Country after country, age after age, has had to reconcile its life with prejudices, bigotries and fanaticisms which could no more be obliterated than the heat of the tropics or the cold of the arctic. These passions, unhappily, are a part of life, and will remain so until all men are educated and thus redeemed from superstition. Palestine will suffer from them long, and pay, as other lands have paid, the bitter price of tears and blood. But she will also survive them, as mankind itself has always survived the woes that waste its strength and wreck its beauty.

A second point of tension between the races is the economic struggle for the land. Here the problem is complicated by three factors—the Arab owners, the Jewish purchasers, and the Arab *Fellaheen* or villagers. If it were a question simply of Arab and Jew, the Arab who sells and the Jew who buys, there would be no trouble. But under the feudal system which prevails in the East to-day exactly as it prevailed in Europe in the Middle Ages, there is this inevitable third factor—the shepherd or farmer who lives upon the land which the absentee landlord does not use and perhaps has never seen. Glad to dispose of this land which he never expected to sell, certainly never at such a price, the rich Arab owner takes his money, and spends it lavishly in Jerusalem, Cairo, or Paris. Meanwhile, upon this land which he has thus sold to a group of Jewish settlers, or to the Jewish National Fund, there live hundreds of primitive, illiterate, poverty-stricken men and women, who know nothing of what has happened until they are asked to move on. To them this land is theirs, as of course for all practical purposes it is. They have pastured their flocks upon these hills and plains for years unnumbered. They have driven their rude plows through this stubborn soil, father and son, for more generations than can be remembered. So old and fixed is their tenancy of these acres, that they have "bounds to their habitation"; one tribe must not cross the unseen borders of a tract of land which belongs by ancient usage to another tribe. And now they are asked to move on by people whom they do not know, whose language they cannot speak, whose rights they cannot understand.

The complications and the occasions of grievance in such a situation as this, are obvious. So serious did the situation become after the war, when large purchases of land were made by the Zionists, that the English Mandatory had to step in, and establish formal conditions for the transfer of property which would guarantee some degree of protection to the helpless *Fellaheen*. Thus it was provided that the people upon the land must be given due notice of its sale, and adequate time to arrange for removal from their ancient home. Further, it was provided that no tribesmen should be finally dispossessed of their land, until other land in some other part of the country had been provided for their occupancy. The English themselves were able to help here a good deal through their use of the State lands which fell into their hands upon the departure of the Turk.

Action of this kind eased the situation. But the tension continues, as it will long continue, at this point of contact between the races. At just the time when I was in Palestine, for example, there broke out a furious dispute in one of the oldest of the Jewish colonies. Years ago this colony had purchased large tracts of land between Jaffa and Haifa. The original pioneers, however, had not been able to work more than two-thirds of the land which they had bought. The remaining third they left in the possession of the Arabs on definite lease agreements. As the colony grew, of course, it gradually extended its borders, and thus from time to time took over portions of the ground which had in the beginning been left to the original inhabitants. At last came the hour for the occupancy of all the property. The Arabs were asked to leave on a certain date, and they refused. The Jews, in assertion of their legal rights, went out to take possession of their land, and were resisted. Blows were struck, blood drawn. The efficient English police promptly stopped the brawling. Then the Jews called upon the police to drive away the Arabs and thus secure them the possession of their land. Whereupon they were informed that it was the business of the police to keep order, not to settle disputes. The trouble must be adjudicated in the courts. But why in the courts, where the case would be heard by Arab judges and determined by Turkish law? Here are our deeds, cried the Jews. Let the government enforce them! As I went away, Jewish deputations were waiting upon the High Commissioner, who was stubborn in his contention that this was a question not of administration but of law, and that the courts must give the verdict. Meanwhile, English police were keeping Jews and Arabs from open violence, and anger was sweeping through the land. This episode is typical. It is the tragedy of the dispossession of a primitive and weak people by a civilized and strong people. And all the while the Arab landowners, the responsible factors in the situation, are far away, snug and secure from the storm.

But the most serious point of strain between the two races has yet to be mentioned. I refer to the political situation, which centers in the question of who is to run things —that is, in the question of nationalism, or self-government. The Arabs, who outnumber the Jews some four or five to one, want self-government in Palestine, and want it *now*. This desire for autonomy, wholly natural and right in itself, is undoubtedly intensified and embittered to-day by the fact that there was a time, shortly after the close of the War, when they could have secured a considerable degree of independent political control. But at this time the Arabs were engulfed in the full tide of wrath against the Allies, more particularly against France in Syria and Britain in Palestine, for their failure to realize the dream of an Arab state. Their spirit was revolt, and not submission. They organized a policy of non-coöperation, and for several years would do nothing with, and accept nothing from, their enemies. But to-day the mood of the Arabs, at least for the moment in Palestine, is changed. The hope of Arab autonomy, to be sure, still flames within their hearts, waiting, like hidden fires of earth, to break forth in conflagration. But meanwhile they discover the British administration established and stabilized in Palestine, and by no means hostile to their interests as over against the interests of the Jews. For an indefinite period, long or short, they must live under this régime; and have reason to believe that they can live with some degree of happiness and safety. But at this same time they see their racial and religious brethren in other portions of the severed Arab world suddenly enjoying, or about to enjoy, self-government. Thus, the British Government has treated with the Hedjaz tribes and agreed to the establishment of an independent Hedjaz kingdom under the rule of a native prince. It has granted sovereignty to Egypt, and, more recently, to Irak. Even upon the semi-civilized tribesmen of Trans-Jordania the English have conferred a large degree of political autonomy, and with the Syrians the French are negotiating a constitution. All this moves the Palestinian Arabs to wonder why a friendly English administration should not grant similar privileges to them—why they should not at least exercise to-day that somewhat considerable degree of self-government which they enjoyed even under the tyranny of the Sultan. But the fateful moment has passed. Their change of mood has come too late. What was offered yesterday is now denied. The Jews are now the ones who will not coöperate, and the Mandatory, without agreement between the two races, will not, as indeed it cannot, act.

It is this refusal of self-government to the Arabs of Palestine which helps to explain the fury of these Arabs not only against the Jews but also against the English. This fury—I know of no other word to describe it—was a complete surprise to me. I remember how I first met it in a conference of Arab leaders where I had expected to find only strong feeling against the Jews. This anti-Jewish sentiment was present, no doubt about that. But to my vast astonishment it was all but swallowed up in the sweeping tide of feeling against England. The articles of the indictment were numerous. The country was overridden with English officials—four hundred in the senior ranks alone!—who drew high salaries and lived in luxury; the taxation levied upon a poverty-stricken people was extortionate—a tithe of an income averaging not more than four pounds a year; the law of the land was no law, only the arbitrary edicts of a single man, the High Commissioner; the courts, administering this law to the people, were all in the hands of the English through the control of the chief justices who were invariably Englishmen. So the charges ran! But they all centered about, and could all be summed up in, the single grievance of a denial of autonomous political control. The Arabs were living in utter and abject subjection to the British crown. They were to-day, what

* Reference here is to the state. In local matters there is representative government not at all unfavorable to Arab interests, as witness an Arab mayor in Jerusalem, in which city the majority of the population is Jewish.

they had never been in all their centuries of history, a slave people. Pride could not endure, and would not long accept, such servitude.

Resentment against the English on this score is instant to-day within the Arab heart. But this resentment is coincident with an equal resentment against the Jew. For it is the Jew whom the Arab regards as responsible for the present political *impasse*. And in this opinion the Arab is correct. If there is any one thing that the Jew will not, and cannot in his judgment concede to-day, it is self-government for a country which is dominated by a race bitterly hostile to everything that is vital to the cause of Zion. In this attitude the Jew is sincere to the point of terror. In any grant of political control of Palestine to the Arab, he sees, or seems to see, the immediate and permanent closing of all ports of entry to Jewish immigrants, the denial to Jewish settlers of all rights to ownership and use of the land, in general the repression and ultimate extinction of a helpless minority by an ignorant, ruthless and fanatical majority. Self-government, says the Zionist, must be indefinitely delayed in the interest of both the peoples concerned. It can come safely and happily only when the Jews in Palestine are numerous enough to balance the Arabs; or, better still, to outnumber them, and thus to guarantee a Jewish state which may administer justice and right to all.

This situation, of course, involves a deadlock, with the key in the hands of the English who will not use it. To the outsider, who is neither Jew nor Arab, the case of the Jews is unanswerable. One has only to talk frankly with the Arabs to understand that the Jews have much to fear from them, and that the cause of Zion cannot, for the present at least, be committed to their mercies. On the other hand, to this outsider the case of the Arabs is similarly unanswerable. My heart leaped to them as they argued the justice of their equal claim with the Zionists to a national state, and of their appeal in Palestine for the same degree of self-determination granted freely to other peoples. Why should they be asked to live indefinitely in a condition of political subjection for the sake of a minority who had not been asked to come to the country, and were not wanted? And why should they be expected to wait patiently and subserviently through the years, until this minority, by reason of outside and alien help, had become a majority, and then itself took over the government of the country? This was slavery forever for the Arab—the old, familiar, colonial slavery—slavery to Britain to-day, to Zion to-morrow. Other peoples have risen up against less sinister tyrannies than this, and fought for liberty. Why should not the Arabs do the same, and be honored for so doing?

There is no answer to this plea, at least apart from the special interests of the Zionist Movement. It is this fact which throws the Jews into the unhappy position of depriving another people of their rights for the sake of their own larger happiness and progress. I know the Jewish argument that the rights of the Arabs are more than amply protected by the British, and will, under the rule of Zion, be amply protected by the Jews. But rights are not rights when they are bestowed by some one else. Liberty has always been an original and not a derivative blessing. I think to-day, as I thought in Palestine, that the Zionists are in no one other position so unfortunate as in their willing conspiracy against the Arabs in the latter's larger hopes for a nationalistic state, and their particular demands in Palestine under the Mandate for a constitution and laws. Nor can I believe that the problem is quite so impossible of solution as the Jews would have others believe because they believe this so sincerely themselves.

The Jews are right in insisting under any circumstances

that the ports of entry into Palestine shall not be closed to their immigrant settlers, that their freedom to purchase and hold land shall not be denied or in any way curtailed, that their security in property and life shall not be placed in jeopardy, that all the safeguards and supports specified in the Mandate and thus pledged to Zion by Britain and the world shall not be withdrawn. But protection of such minority rights and privileges as these are in no way inconsistent with self-government. Nor is there evidence that the Arabs would reject an autonomy subject to reservations covering these points so essential to Israel's future in Palestine.

As an American, I remember that there was an apparently impossible problem which stood in the way of the writing of the Constitution and the establishment of the American nation in 1787. The small states among the thirteen original colonies were there pitted against the large states, as the Jews are pitted against the Arabs in Palestine; and the small states were opposed to the Constitution because of their fear that they would be overborne, absorbed, and at last destroyed by the large states, just as the Jews are opposed to a constitution in Palestine, because of their fear, and justified fear, that they will be wiped out by the Arabs. But what remained a deadlock in Philadelphia for months was suddenly released by the infinitely ingenious and justly famous compromise, which established a national legislature of two houses of equal and coördinate power, one of which was controlled by the large states and the other by the small. What genius conceived, experience has fulfilled. Why not a similar conception, and a similar reliance upon experience in Palestine? Is it impossible to write a constitution in that land which shall create a political balance of power between the two contending interests, which in turn shall give secur-

PROBLEMS

ity to both sides, as the American Constitution gave security to states small as well as large? Should it not be easy to establish guarantees for the protection of the Jewish minority to-day which shall hold, as similar guarantees held in America until there was no need of guarantees? Especially with Britain fixed for an indefinite period in the seats of power, to furnish an ultimate guarantee that there shall be no injustice nor reign of terror, but that the people shall rule "with malice toward none, with charity for all" should it not be possible to arrange an adjustment which should satisfy the Arab and protect the Jew.

Whatever our opinion on such matters, one thing would seem to be certain, and that is that the indefinite continuance of the present situation is impossible. Nothing in the relations between Jews and Arabs seems to me to be quite so hazardous, so fraught with peril of the future, as the policy of drift which is now in the ascendant. It was the ending of this policy of drift in America, by the acceptance on faith of a workable compromise in the Federal Convention, which saved this nation from the chaos which would have destroyed it in that "critical period of American history" from 1783 to 1787. It was the refusal, or the inability, to stop a similar policy of drift on the slavery issue, after the first "critical period" was passed, which plunged the nation into a second "critical period," which all but drowned its life in the blood of the Civil War. The present drift in Palestine can go on, perhaps, for generations. It can go on the more safely since England is on the bridge to give such guidance to the ship as may be possible. But where is this drifting going to take the craft in the end? At present the Jews are in the unhappy position of a minority, deliberately denying to a majority, from motives of selfish advantage, their basic rights as a proud and independent people. This is wrong in principle, and fatal as a matter of policy. For what chance is there that the Arab will allow the Jew, when or if the latter is in the majority, to take over that power of self-government which he himself was denied by the Jew when he (the Arab) was in the majority? From such a situation of mutual *impasse* there can come nothing but civil war. From the fires of anger kindled by such a situation there can spring nothing but conflagration. I urge that this problem be taken in hand by Jew, Arab and English, working generously and wisely together, before it is too late for any generosity or any wisdom to settle it.

The problem of Jew and Arab seems dark. And it *is* dark when the world in which these two races live side by side is looked at from the standpoint of its two poles. The tragedy of the situation is the dominance on both sides of extremist programs which allow of no adjustment or reconciliation. Thus, there are Arabs who would stop all Jewish immigration, kill or expel all Jews now inside the borders of Palestine, destroy Zionism, and then, if possible, overthrow the Mandate, establish their own government, and join hands with their brethren throughout the Moslem world in the formation of an Arab state. In the same way there are Jews who would open wide the ports of entry, overwhelm the present Arab majority by a sudden flood of immigrants, set up their own constitution and laws, and bend the English sword to subdue the native population to the rule of the Jewish state. From extremists of this type nothing is to be gained. The only hope is from moderates who can see that both races may live together in a land which is their mutual heritage, and can coöperate in working out a relationship of peace. Among both races, fortunately, such moderates can be found. These moderates see facts which are encouraging, and trust to forces which are healing and beneficent. Already, on the darkness of their

PROBLEMS 133

Eastern horizon, they discern a glow which they dare to believe may be the dawn of a new and better day.

There is no basis, for example, to the idea that in Palestine it is necessary for one race to oust the other that either may survive. The Arabs need have no fear that the logic of Zionism is their expulsion from their soil, and thus from the borders of their native land. The situation is not that of two drowning men fighting for possession of a raft which can keep only one of them above the waves. Palestine is a wasted country, and must ever be a poor country; but, for all its waste and poverty, it can support many more people than live to-day within its borders. It is not true, in other words, that the present population of less than a million people is the maximum of possible density, and that for every Jew, therefore, who comes into the country, an Arab must leave. Already, in their older colonies, the Jews are demonstrating the possibility of sustaining large groups of people upon comparatively small areas of ground. Intensive methods of agriculture, scientific study of soil and seeds, modern machinery and tools, hard labor by healthy and happy toilers, a constructive development of industry and culture, these are certain to produce relatively the same results in Palestine that they have produced in other portions of the globe. What the population of this country was in its ancient days, before the waste and ruin of the last two thousand years, is a disputed question. It is agreed, however, that this population was far in excess of the present total. Certainly another million could be accommodated without hazard; and when irrigation has been far extended, water power developed, the hills terraced, and the plains made beautiful with flocks and herds, this million could be doubled, and then trebled. So far from driving out the Arabs, or even cutting down their present number, the incoming of the colonists of Zion will enable more Arabs to live in Palestine, in peace and comfort, than have ever lived there before. It is no accident, but rather an inevitable development of the situation, that the Arab population has steadily increased since the Jewish occupation.

Again, there are economic forces at work for the healing of the differences between the two races in Palestine, which are stronger than all the personal agitations and passions on either side. One need not be a materialist to understand that, in the long run, it is money and not men, food and not feelings, which determine the destiny of nations. There is an economic determinism at work in the world, in other words, which is more potent than all statesmanship and philosophy, certainly than all prejudice and ill-will. And this economic determinism in this case is working steadily to unite and not divide the interests of Jew and Arab.

Thus, the development of the Zionist Movement has brought more wealth into Palestine than this country has known in all its history. For a half-century now, from all parts of the world, but more particularly from the British Empire (Canada and South Africa), France, and America, a tide of money has steadily been pouring into this wasted land; and, if Zion is allowed to grow, this tide will continue for years to pour in in greater volume and swifter flow. Much of this money, unfortunately, has gone into the hands of a few rich landowners; and, of this, a considerable portion has been taken and spent out of the country. But this is nothing new or strange. It is only one more illustration of the inequitable distribution of wealth which prevails everywhere to-day under our capitalistic organization of society. But these rich have not been able to gather all, nor even most, of this new money into their reservoirs of private treasure. Inevitably this tide of wealth has spread, slowly but surely, over the land, and thus is bringing to the people a prospect of ease and comfort such as never shone before upon the horizon of their lives. The result, of course, is an inevitable easing of tension between the two races. If the coming of the Jew means more food and better food, more clothing and better clothing, work and the income that work produces, the *Fellaheen* are not going to hate this Jew very long or very hard. The Jew may be an alien, and he may seem to be wanting more than he should properly have, but incidentally he is bringing wealth into the country which he is sharing with the inhabitants. He is opening up, in other words, a common source of supply; and a common interest in this source of supply is bound to hold the people of the land together. I found an impressive illustration of this fact in Haifa, where enormous harbor improvements, incidental to the development of Zion, promise to make this Arab city the largest and most prosperous port in the eastern Mediterranean. Is it remarkable that the Jews in Haifa enjoy a large influence in civic affairs, that relations between the two races in the community seem to be excellent, and that the Mayor, an intelligent and highly cultured Moslem, is the friendliest Arab with whom I met and talked in Palestine? Economic interests are binding the races together in this city in a way that makes dissension and hostility increasingly difficult. Both groups have too much at stake, from the monetary point of view, not to weld themselves by common effort into a single community. And Haifa is only one particularly interesting and important illustration of what is going on to a greater or less degree, all over Palestine.

But the Zionist Movement has done, and is doing, more than bring mere wealth into the country. It is also, and inevitably, along with this influx of material resources, bringing a higher level of life for the entire native population. The Jews, in a word, are deliberately undertaking to lift the Arabs out of the depths of degradation in which they have languished for centuries, and carry them up on to that plane of comfort and culture upon which they are steadfastly determined themselves to live. The Jews were under no obligation to do this. They might well have regarded these primitive folk upon the land as barbarians, and exploited them as serfs. Certain of the English, long used to colonial ways, have definitely suggested that the proper solution of the economic problem of Zion is for the Jews to do the skilled work, and leave the unskilled work to the Arabs. "But this would be a violation of Israel's ideal," cried a Zionist leader to me in Jerusalem. "We are here to establish justice and brotherhood, and this means that we shall enjoy nothing which is not enjoyed by everybody. There must be one family in Palestine, and therefore, one burden of toil, one standard of life, one level of culture and enlightenment, for all the people."

The Jews are sincere in this fraternal attitude toward the Arab. But they are also wise, and not completely unselfish. For they know, after all, that there can only be one level of life for the people of Palestine, and that if the Jew, therefore, does not pull up the Arab, this Arab will sooner or later pull down the Jew. There is a common center of gravity in these matters, and if this center is not held high, it is certain to fall low. "No real progress in ameliorating the conditions of labor can be helpful, except by international agreement," said Lord Robert Cecil in 1919, arguing for the labor clauses in the Covenant of the League of Nations. "Although, in a sense," he continued, "the conditions of labor in a country are a matter of internal concern, yet, under the conditions under which we now live, that is not so in truth, and bad conditions of labor in one country operate with fatal effect in depressing conditions of labor in another." If this is true as regards the laboring classes in two different countries, how much truer as regards the laboring classes in the same country! No, the Arab must be kept up to the standard of the Jew, else is the Jew certain to fall to the standard of the Arab. So the Jew has undertaken deliberately and heroically to share his life with his Arab neighbor. In the Jewish colonies, the Arab laborer must be paid the same wages as the Jewish laborer—there must be no distinction between the two. In the Jewish trade unions, membership must be open to Arabs as well as to Jews, and every endeavor made to educate the Arab to the advantages and benefits of the union. When I was in Palestine, a strenuous campaign was on to induce the Arab railroad workers to join the Jewish railroad union. There is wisdom, as well as justice in all this. "There are many members, yet but one body. . . . And whether one member suffer, all the members suffer with it, or one member be honored, all the members rejoice with it. (Therefore) the members should have the same care one for another." These are Christian words, but in Palestine they are Jewish practice. The pioneers of Zion are making common economic cause with the Arabs, and thus creating for both races a common economic and social life.

To many of the Arab leaders, both political and religious, this raising of the level of the life and culture of the common people by Jewish influence, is an unwelcome phenomenon, and therefore a fresh occasion for suspicion and hostility. Better wages, better standards of living, better education, wider contacts with the world of men and things, these mean inevitably that the Arab population will be released from that subjection to their feudal lords which has so long been to the latter so abundant a source of profit and power. These leaders therefore fear the liberating and uplifting influence of the Jews—resent it and resist it. But nothing can long impede this movement of mutual economic and social advantage between the masses of Jews and Arabs. Already one sees in the common life of Palestine the knitting of the two races together into a single fabric of experience and achievement. Wherever work is being done and foundations laid, a sure and steady interweaving of the racial strands is going on. But unfortunately this interweaving process takes time—not days, nor even years, but decades! In cities, like Haifa, in agricultural settlements, like Kfar Aaron, where Jews and Arabs are working happily together, the strands are joined, but not yet are they bound and tied. Accident, or effort, might tear them apart. Over the larger portion of the country, these strands of contact and coöperation have not even been joined, much less secured. The Jews are working inland from the shore, out from the cities, slowly like pack trains along the highways, and the remoter hordes of Arabs, the wild nomads of the· hills and the Bedouin horsemen of the desert, know them only as invaders whose coming imperils the country, even the faith of the one God, Allah. Years must pass before these tribes are touched by the friendly contacts of the Jewish settlers. A generation must succeed before the larger wealth and higher economic and social life of Zion work the transformation of understanding and good will already wrought where Israel is strong. The more reason for pushing these forces to the uttermost and relying upon them to work the vast achievement of understanding and good will between the races! "We'd get along all right," said an Arab farmer to me, "if the fellows at the top would just leave us alone." The fellows at the top—and at the bottom, too! Down among the workers and out among the tribesmen I found Communists, whose only business it seemed to be to make mischief among two peoples striving painfully and dangerously to live together. During my

PROBLEMS 139

own stay in Palestine, these children of chaos were appealing to the Arabs, in a deliberate campaign of agitation, not to sell or vacate land to the Jews. These Communists are balanced at the top by Jewish agitators and especially by Arab politicians, religious leaders, and fanatics generally, who find it profitable, and in some instances what they regard as a patriotic and pious duty, to stir up trouble between the two races. Thus do "the heathen rage, and the people imagine a vain thing." But these elements of agitation are like froth at the top, and a foul growth at the bottom. In between are the workers who comprise the deeps of life. From this vast sea of human toil flow the tides that move the world. The future of Palestine is in the hands and hearts of those who labor. If Jews and Arabs learn to dig and delve together, this future is secure.

Economic forces are thus already uniting the two races. Are not political forces destined eventually to do the same? At the moment, of course, these forces are operating to divide and not to unite. Every aspect of the present situation tends to make the Jews and Arabs fierce and contentious rivals. But it cannot always, nor even long, be so. A rivalry against one another for the political control of Palestine must soon or late be transformed into a common rivalry against England for that control. For England, under the Mandate of the League of Nations, is master of the land, and, to the Jews as well as to the Arabs, an alien master. Already, for special reasons of immediate self-interest, as we have seen, the Arab leaders are arrayed in furious opposition to the British Crown. The Jews, for equal reasons of self-interest, are seeking the protection of the Crown, but are more and more, as we shall see, finding its shelter irksome and its power dangerous. It cannot be long before these two groups, now engaged in such bitter political contention, will find that their common grievances against the government outweigh in importance their grievances against one another.

England, in other words, with her alien rule and her alien imperial interests, must sooner or later become the focal point of opposition to all the inhabitants of Palestine. In this opposition these inhabitants will discover a sense of possession of a common country, and of citizenship in a common state, which now is dim and distant in their minds. The Arab to-day is still thinking of himself primarily as an Arab, and if he thinks of his country at all, finds his consciousness wandering away to Syria, Arabia, Trans-Jordania and his dream of an Arab state. The Jew in much the same way is thinking of himself primarily as a Jew, and his primal loyalty goes out to his dream of Zion and its restoration. If there were no other factor present in the situation, these two races might well remain hopelessly divided forever. They might never find a common center of interest and devotion in their common land. But there *is* another factor present—a government, alien to them both, which was established and is now maintained not by the consent of the people from within, but by the imposition of military and political authority from without. The presence of this government creates at once for Jew and Arab a common grievance, and by the same token a common cause. Already the movement of self-determination against Britain is under way. Slowly but surely all the inhabitants of Palestine will be joined together in this movement, and find in its exactions the rallying center of their lives. As they serve it, they will forget their domestic differences, as the Hindus and Moslems of India who have caught the vision of *Swaraj* are forgetting their ancient feuds. As they sacrifice for it, they will discover their common interests and loyalties in a country which is their own, and of which they are the citizens together. The Arab will no longer be an Arab; the Jew will no longer be a Jew. Both will be Palestinians, as members of many races and religions in the United States are now Americans.

In nothing was I more interested in Palestine than the organization to-day of what is significantly called the "Palestine Party." This is a political organization, sponsored largely by Jews, for the purpose of bringing Jews and Arabs together in a common recognition of the existence of a common country, and in common service of the interests of this country. In this "Party" we see a vivid dramatization of those basic political forces in the life of Palestine which are destined eventually to end the division between the rival races. It is a sign of the times—and a prophecy of the future.

The forces making for unity among the people of Palestine are strong. But none so strong, in the last analysis, as the temper of the Jew, if only that temper is not betrayed by impatience, selfishness, stupidity, or fear. At the bottom of all hope in Palestine, as the firm foundation of the future, is the determination of the Zionist to do justice to the Arab, and to live with him in relations of good will. This determination has itself a twofold basis.

Deep down is the social idealism of the Jew which is the spiritual substance of his life. His one vast achievement in the world, his one unique contribution to humanity, is his prophets' dream of righteousness and peace upon the earth. This dream, defeated in political Israel, was born again in the heart of a scattered and despised race, and for ages was cherished as a light in the dark misery of the ghetto. Some day this light would be lifted up again in Zion; and this time it would not be quenched, but kindled into a pure and golden flame for all the nations of the earth to see. And now the day has come! The Jews are again in Israel, to make true the prophets' dream. And right here, in the problem of the Arab, is a challenge to the dream's reality. The Zionists understand this challenge. They know that in this problem is a distillation of all the problems which they are likely to encounter in their great adventure. If they fail here, they fail everywhere. So to this task of reconciliation with an alien, suspicious and hostile people are they setting themselves with an heroic determination, a divine fervor. Here at the start shall the ideals of Zion be shown to be no vain and futile faith.

But there is more than sheer idealism in this matter. There is also common sense. The Jews know perfectly well that the future of Zionism, not only as a prophetic dream but also as a practical piece of statesmanship, is at stake here in this problem of the relations between themselves and the Arabs. For Zion can never prosper, nor even long survive, in the midst of a hostile population. This population must either be exterminated, as Americans exterminated the North American Indians, or it must be befriended and fostered as partners in an undertaking which is to be regarded as a joint enterprise. As the former alternative is impossible, so the latter is difficult. But from the beginning the Jews have adopted it as a policy which must be carried through to success, if Zion itself is to endure.

There is an epic quality in the story of what the Jew has done for the Palestinian Arab. When violence and bloodshed broke over him like a storm in the hectic days following upon the early riots, he sought no vengeance upon his enemy, and attempted no retaliation. If he fought, it was upon his own land, to resist invasion and devastation; if he fired and killed, it was in defense of his home and family. And when the smoke of battle cleared away, he was the first to rush upon the field and bring succor to his

PROBLEMS 143

foe. Thus, when detachments of Hadassah nurses and physicians went to the actual scenes of the fighting, they cared for wounded Jews and Arabs alike, without discrimination. What was true in the cruel days of war, is still more true in the kindlier days of peace. The great medical organization of Hadassah, for example, is as freely at the disposal of the Arab as of the Jew. Its physicians bring Arab children safely and cleanly into the world; its nurses teach Arab mothers the best methods of feeding and caring for infants; its health officers establish in Arab villages sanitary conditions of living; its hospitals and laboratories serve the ills of Arabs as quickly and efficiently as those of Jews. And as rain falls equally upon the just and upon the unjust, so the bounty of Jewish philanthropy falls equally upon the two races of this wasted land. Here the great American philanthropist, Nathan Straus, is a conspicuous example. His soup kitchens serve all who are hungry, be they Arab or Jew. His child-welfare stations minister to the needs of children, those who prattle in Arabic as well as those who prattle in Hebrew. His pasteurized milk goes freely to Arab, Christian, and Jewish homes. Over the doors of his Public Health Centers in Jerusalem and Tel-Aviv are inscriptions in three languages, Hebrew, Arabic, and English, inviting all to enter and be healed in body and in spirit. His Nathan Straus Fund is established for the service of any human need. When the earthquake shook the country in 1927, and a homeless people trembled upon a trembling earth, his $25,000 contribution toward relief, the first received, was specifically donated for Arab as well as Jewish sufferers. As it happened, it was predominantly the Arabs who were stricken by this disaster, so that this bounteous benefaction of a great Jew was expended almost exclusively for the native Arab population.

Work like this is not in vain. Such spirit can heal all

wounds, still all fears, remove all hates. It can even ease, as—if trusted wholly—it would surely end, tension such as now distracts and imperils all the land.

It was a late afternoon, and the coffee cups had long been drained. Yet nobody seemed to want to go away. The talk was too exciting, the subject too important. I had come to this hospitable Arab home, especially to meet the leaders of the Arab people. And here they were—a dozen of them—lawyers, editors, teachers, merchants, politicians. What I wanted was the Arab point of view on the question of the Jews, the Zionist crusade, the English Mandate. And I was getting it! Thanks to some happy chance, this was one of those occasions when barriers drop, when reserves are scattered to the winds, and each man speaks his mind. I sat in tense silence, as these men clustered about me, and bared the convictions of their minds. It was illuminating—but also terrifying; for here was the problem of races, of nationalities, of majority and minority groups, which had wrecked many a country and blasted many a human hope. I wondered how this problem could be solved. I sought an answer in these intelligent, intent, nerve-drawn faces, and found none. Perhaps it was because I saw so clearly their point of view, and sympathized so inevitably with so many of their contentions. Then, by some chance, there was spoken the name of Nathan Straus. For a moment, at least, the spell was broken. Nothing seemed impossible as a common smile lit every countenance, and a common love warmed every heart.

Government—The English

The government in Palestine is the British Empire, established as the Mandatory by the League of Nations, as

France was established by the League as the Mandatory in Syria. This government, in fact if not in spirit, is absolute. All power is centered in the British High Commissioner and his deputies. The edicts or ordinances from Government House are the law of the land without appeal. There is no constitution except the Mandate, and no local autonomy save that established by grant of the government to certain Jewish and Arab agencies. As in all countries controlled by England, there is a large degree of civil liberty enjoyed by the people, and little use of arbitrary power.

The advent of England in Palestine, in succession to "the unspeakable Turk," was hailed by Zionists throughout the world as the greatest and most beneficent event which had transpired in the history of their Movement. No Jew anywhere, I imagine, was able after the War to foresee that, in less than a decade, the Crown in Jerusalem would rank with the land, and with the people upon the land, as one of the most serious problems of Zion. Yet a shrewd Jew, familiar with the motives at work in the Great War and with the history of the nations engaged in the War, might well have anticipated some such *denoument* as this, especially after the compromises and repudiations of Versailles. For the central fact about the Balfour Declaration, upon which Jewish hopes were based, is that it was a war measure, issued not to help the Jews to Zion but the English and their Allies to victory. This Declaration, says Karl Friedrich Nowak, in his great history of the Peace Conference,[7] was a promise "given by the (British) Cabinet to Lord Rothschild and the great and wealthy Jewish families in Britain in return for their financial assistance." This explanation seems superficial as compared with the deeper truth that England had to defeat the Turk, secure com-

[7] "Versailles," published by Payson & Clarke, Ltd., New York 1929. See page 90.

plete control of the Near East, and thus swing every influence in that region to her side. Whatever the precise motives at work, it still remains a fact that when the Declaration was issued, on one of the darkest days of the War, England was thinking primarily of herself and her military needs, and only secondarily of Zion and its spiritual aspirations. The very name, Balfour, should have been enough to stir doubts and conjure fears within the Jewish heart. This distinguished English nobleman never had an unselfish emotion in his life, and never anywhere served any great humanitarian cause. He has been as consistently cynical in his statesmanship as he is agnostic in his philosophy. The common people, Gentile or Jew, have never existed in his world, save as a nuisance and occasionally a danger. He would harry the Jews of Palestine to-day as ruthlessly as he harried the patriots of Ireland yesterday, if they disturbed the interests or threatened the peace of British rule. To think of this man sharing the hopes of the Jews for Zion, or serving these hopes except as incidentally they served the Empire, is utterly fantastic. Nothing of all I saw in Zion so disturbed me, so disquieted me, as the elevation of "Bloody Balfour" as one of the patron-saints of Zion. In his face, as pictured on the walls of many Jewish homes and public buildings, I seemed to see the fitting sign and seal of the disappointment that has engulfed the heart of Zion, as darkness engulfs the day, after seven years of British rule. The honeymoon was sweet, especially in the days of Sir Herbert Samuel, the Jewish High Commissioner. Yet even before the retirement of this great administrator, who sought so exactly to do justice to the Jews, the Arabs, and the Empire, that he did injustice to the Jews lest he seem to favor them, disillusion had set in. And now this disillusion is passing into a kind of despair—a reaction exactly proportionate to the enthusiasm that followed the adoption of the Mandate. I found Jews who wished that the Turk were back again.

This last state of mind, of course, is as exaggerated as the first. The substitution of English for Turkish rule has wrought much good for Palestine, and incidentally for Zion.

Thus, the English have built an excellent system of modern highways along the main arteries of travel. Instead of rough dirt roads for carts and carriages, or ancient trails for camels and other beasts of burden, there now run between all the great centers of population automobile roads as wide and smooth as those with which we are familiar in the West. Many of these roads were expensive and difficult to build, as, for example, the superb highway which plunges precipitately through the mountain passes running down from Jerusalem, twenty-seven hundred feet above the level of the sea, to Jericho and the Dead Sea, fourteen hundred feet below this level, and that thrilling ascent which winds and twists around the mountainsides and along the edges of towering cliffs from Tiberias to ancient Safed. All these roads are carefully rated, according to fixed standards of construction, as first class, second class, third class, so that the nature of every journey may be known beforehand. What the roads mean is demonstrated whenever one leaves the main highway, and, penetrating into the remoter regions of the country, finds oneself following a desert of dust in summer and a sea of mud in winter. Automobiles in these places yield at once, and gladly, to more ancient and primitive methods of transportation. The difference is also seen as one passes out of Palestine—into Syria, for example. In the dreadful conditions of storm and flood which I encountered in my ten days of travel through the country north of Jerusalem, I met no serious trouble until we crossed the frontier of the Jordan and started for Damascus. Here in Syria we found the road in many places under water.

Other roads in this region were described as impassable. In verification of these reports we encountered travelers in Damascus who had lost their automobiles, been marooned in Arab villages, and suffered other discomforts and disasters. To a very considerable extent, and almost alone among Eastern countries, the roads of Palestine have been modernized. Native money paid the cost and native labor did the work, but English rulers and English engineers conceived and achieved the undertaking.

In addition to good roads, the English are responsible for vastly improved conditions of sanitation in Palestine. The streets of Jerusalem and other cities are as clean as those of any European or American town. In the houses, especially in the slum quarters of Jerusalem and Jaffa, sanitary arrangements are crude in the extreme, but organized instruction and careful inspection have established standards never known before to any Eastern population. English health officials, however, have not confined their activities to the cities. They have gone out into the country, even to the remote Arab villages, and there taught the people how to live. British rule has made Palestine a clean and healthy country. I traveled far through many regions; I entered intimately into homes in city and in field. I found much that was primitive, but little either to offend or to alarm.

The greatest achievement of the English, perhaps, is the establishment throughout all the land of general conditions of law and order. It seemed curious to me, as I traveled through the country in exactly the same way I have traveled through the countryside of England and America, to hear stories of conditions that prevailed in the days before the English occupation. Brigandage was at that time rife. It was not safe to journey from place to place without arms, or, if inexperienced oneself in the use of arms, without an escort At any moment from the hills the robbers might

PROBLEMS

descend, and relieve the traveler of property or even life. But now all this is at an end. Brigandage in Palestine is no longer a profitable occupation. The English authorities have discouraged lawless and violent depredations upon unoffending people, and thus established conditions of order hitherto unknown. And they have done this with a minimum display and use of force. There seemed to be no soldiers in Palestine—I was told there were some five or six hundred. There seemed to be no police—certainly not as many in Jerusalem, relatively speaking, as in New York or Chicago! On the roads through the open countryside, one could drive for hours and see no armed patrol. Then suddenly, once or twice a day, perhaps, one would meet a horseman, superbly mounted, clad neatly and inconspicuously in a dark blue uniform, with a cartridge belt and a rifle slung from the shoulder. This was the Palestinian police—or constabulary, as we would call it in America. Several times, as we drove along, I can recall seeing a small building some distance from the road—on the side of the hill, perhaps—which seemed to be different from other buildings. This I was told in each case was a guardhouse. A group of mounted police were located here, and from this place as a center rode out through the country upon their lines of patrol. It was amazing that such conditions of security, in regions where brigandage has for so long been a tradition of the countryside, could be maintained by so small and scattered an armed force. I could not help contrasting conditions in Palestine with the conditions I found in Syria, where the French maintain a standing army of occupation of some fifty thousand men, and patrol the roads with an unending procession of soldiery. It seemed to me in Syria as though we were never out of sight of sentinels and patrols. In Palestine, *per contra*, it seemed as though we encountered officers of the law only by chance.

Of course, the situation in the two countries was very different. In Syria great masses of the population had been, and to a certain extent still were, in open revolt against the government. In Palestine, whatever the bitter feeling toward the government in Arab circles, there was no armed movement against it. The Mandatory was safe from all assault. Brigandage was dead. The only trouble was the bitter contention between local and hostile native groups. As the English had long met this situation in India with a minimum of force, so they were doing it now in Palestine. There were times, I confess, when I felt nervous, and perplexed. I had not been in the country a week before I found the awful strain of tension between Arabs and Jews. In Beth Alpha I saw the night watchman, with his rifle, guarding the settlement against wild beasts, and *men!* In this colony, as in other remote colonies, I suppose, there was a store of arms, granted by the government under seal for use in emergencies. What if the "emergencies" came! But the English, like the ancient Romans, know how to rule. They had the situation in hand. In answer to my direct inquiries, they expressed not only no alarm, but the utmost confidence in their control.[*]

These are achievements which must be placed to the credit of British rule in Palestine. But they seem superfi-

[*] I let this paragraph stand as I wrote it before the outbreak of the August (1929) riots. The achievement of the administration in policing the country, and thus ridding it of the disorder and violence of brigandage, is as real to-day as ever. But it is now tragically obvious that the administration did not have "the situation in hand." From the policing standpoint, the Jews have just complaint, and the English an awful responsibility, for what transpired. On the other hand, the situation as revealed by the Arab outbreak cannot be ended—not even ameliorated, but only aggravated—by the use of extensive force by the Mandatory. There is no solution, not for the Jews, in the Syrian precedent. If Palestine is to be garrisoned by the English as Syria has been garrisoned by the French, then Zion is a failure, and its work had better be ended now than later.

cial to the Jew. The ardent Zionist at least weighs them lightly as over against certain other matters of central importance to his heart, in which this rule, he feels, has failed. His indictment of Britain is long, often confused, not seldom passionate. But its main items became clear to me as I talked with the Jews, and also with the English.

First of all, the English manifest that Western prejudice against the Jew, which in Palestine is harder to bear than even the open and fierce hostility of the Arab. This prejudice, be it said, is offensive enough in the home countries, from which the Jewish pioneers have come, but there, like the climate and the soil, it is something which is a part of life and therefore to be borne. But here in Palestine, where the Jews are free and happy in the homeland of their dreams, this traditional prejudice of the Gentile suddenly becomes intolerable. It is like a foul smell, or a hideous noise—a source of irritation, outrage and disgust. Yet it is all about them in their relations with the English. The soldiers of Allenby showed this prejudice in a form of crude contempt which went far in the case of individual Jews to take the bloom off the English conquest of their Holy Land. The same prejudice, in forms much more refined, and frequently unconscious, now shows itself in the day-to-day life of English officialdom. I encountered it in the case of an English under-secretary, a university man, who was one of the most insufferable snobs I have ever met in my life. If he stirred me, a casual Gentile visitor, to anger and disgust, what must he have done to a Jew who had to live with him, and submit to him as a ruler of the land! We were speaking of the perennial question of the relations between Arabs and Jews, and this English youth was expressing his strong sympathy with the natives. "These Arabs, you know," was his final remark, spoken in his best English accent, "well, they are gentlemen, and one can invite them to his table. But the *Jews!*"—and his hands took up the burden of expressing the contempt which his tongue was unable to convey.

Secondly, the English, as the governing authorities of Palestine, do not like the Jews as a subject population. In fact, they do not know what to make of them, as in all their imperial experience they have never had to deal with people of just this kind before. As comprising a part, and a large part, of the inhabitants of the country, the Jews must of course be classified as natives. But they do not seem like natives. They are acquainted with Western culture; they are themselves cultured, in the true English sense of the word; many of them speak the English language, and are familiar with English ways. What is more, these Jews do not act like natives. They are not submissive, and obedient, and grateful for benefits received. On the contrary, they are independent and proud—as "stiff-necked" as their progenitors of whom we read in the Bible. They send delegations to Government House not to suggest boons but to exact rights. They do not petition that a certain thing may be done—they demand that this certain thing shall be done. The Jews are trouble makers—for the English—and thus are regarded by the English not only with the traditional prejudice of the Gentile for the Jew, but also with the active dislike of a superior class for an inferior class which does not know and keep its place.

But this dislike is more than mere dislike. In certain instances I seemed to find it developing into suspicion and a kind of fear. It was disturbing, for example, to find a distinguished Englishman, of high authority in Palestine, confusing the work of the communal colonies upon the land with the political agitations of the little group of Bolshevik Communists in the cities. These latter are a pestiferous lot, bent deliberately upon making all the trouble that can be made for the British Empire. It was not surprising that the authorities were arresting and deporting members of the group as fast as they could lay their hands upon them. But these political Communists are as hateful to the Jews as to the English. I have already referred to their attempt to stir up trouble between Jews and Arabs by intruding upon the delicate entanglements of the land question. Yet I found in the minds of English officials, some of them in high places, an utter confusion of these idle and irresponsible agitators with the hard-working, idealistic settlers in the communal colonies, and a conviction that these colonies must be watched as possible centers of sedition against the British Crown. Nothing could be farther from the truth *—yet there are English officials who believe it! These men dislike the Jews; they do not understand the Jews; they are mystified by what the Jews are trying to do in Palestine; and therefore they are suspicious, even afraid. Here, as everywhere, fear is the offspring of ignorance and despite.

The dislike of the English for the Jew finds its natural counterpart in a definite liking for the Arab, and, in matters of administration, in a growing partiality for Arab interests. The Arab, in his fever of outrage against the political *impasse*, would deny this. "If the English care for us," he cries, "why don't they grant us the self-government we want?" The English, also, would deny it, and point to this very matter of self-government as evidence of their insistence upon being fair to all parties beneath their rule. And in this they would be sincere. The English want to be just, and try to be just, in Palestine. But they feel at home with the Arabs as they do not, and probably never can, feel at home with the Jews. These Arabs are natives in the real sense of the word. They behave as the English have found natives behaving in other parts of

* See Chapter IV, pages 183-184.

the earth. They are indigenous to their own strange soil. Therefore the English know what to do with them and how to treat them. They can play their pipes as they have played them in a hundred lands. Furthermore, the English regard the Arabs, and the older Jews—as in Safed, for example—as the real native population of the country, and have a fixed idea that these Arabs and Jews, particularly the Arabs, must be protected as residents from the Zionist Jews who are intruders. It is not too much to say that the Mandatory authorities feel that they are in Palestine, among other things, to stand between the Arabs and these Western Jews who would steal their country. This is a part, and an important part, of the duty which they are pledged to the League of Nations to fulfill. But with this conviction are mixed up selfish motives as well. For England is in Palestine primarily not to "secure the establishment of the Jewish national home," as the Mandate puts it, but to secure the safety of the British Empire. The imperial interests in the Near East are enormous. All through this region—north, south, and east to India—are peoples who by blood and faith are brothers to the Palestine Arabs. To win the favor of these Arabs is to win the favor of the Moslem world; to alienate these Arabs would be to alienate this world. It is not only advantageous but necessary for Britain to live on good terms with the native population of the Holy Land. And this the demands of the Jew will not allow. The Jews, living in Palestine under the Mandate, exact a protection which the Arabs insist upon interpreting as hostile to themselves. The Zionist Movement is therefore an embarrassment, an obstruction, to what the government regards as wise British policy. It is therefore a constant source of irritation to the British mind. Hence a resentment against the Jew which easily transforms itself into favor for the Arab!

PROBLEMS 155

Various forces, as one can see, are here at work; and all tend to persuade the English to do what they can to help the Arabs. Some things they cannot do. Thus, under present conditions, they cannot grant them self-government under a national constitution and with officers of their own choosing. In a matter of such vital concern, of such awful menace, not only to Palestine but to the Empire, the Mandatory must hold the balances rigorously even as between the two contending races. But there are other matters in which they can and do favor the Arabs. Thus, in the vexed land situation, the English find it easy to use the State lands in their control for the benefit of the Arabs, while refusing their use for the equal benefit of the Jews. In the same way, they find it convenient to have petty magistracies, the police, and other local offices in Arab hands, even in places where the Jews comprise the larger element of the population, and thus to subdue the Jews to local laws and customs as interpreted and enforced by unenlightened and frequently corrupt Oriental tribesmen. Especially grievous is the policy of England in the matter of money grants for education. Owing to linguistic, religious and other difficulties, separate schools are provided for the children of the two races. In spite of the fact that the Jews have many more children in school than the Arabs, the English insist upon distributing budget funds for public education on the basis of population (the number of Jews and Arabs respectively in the country) rather than on the basis of registration (the number of Jewish and Arab children respectively in the schools). This means that the Arabs have more money than they can use, and the Jews much less. With the net result that the Arab schools are all public schools, built and maintained by public funds raised by taxation of all the people, whereas the Jewish schools are predominantly private schools, built and maintained out of the general funds raised abroad in the interest of the Zionist Movement! The situation is not at all unlike the situation in the southern states of the United States as regards schools for whites and blacks. It is in such matters that the government, consciously or unconsciously, is favoring the Arabs. Injustice to the Jews is an all too frequent feature of British administration in Palestine to-day.

Much more serious is the attitude of the English toward the Zionist Movement and its work. This attitude is at the best distrustful and unsympathetic, at the worst contemptuous and derisive. The typical Englishman has no faith in Palestine; he regards it as a poor, miserable country which can never be made to support a flourishing population. He has little faith in Zionism, which he regards as fundamentally unscientific and, from the business point of view, unsound. "It has no economic basis," said one influential Englishman to me. "It is supported, and will continue to be supported as long as it lasts, in the same way that the Christian churches and holy orders in the country are supported—by charitable contributions from abroad." "Tel-Aviv," said an important official to me, referring to the Jewish city which has been created out of nothing in twenty years, "Tel-Aviv is a boom-town. The people live by taking in one another's washing. It has no basis of industry or civic life. It has had one collapse. The next one will end it." "The agricultural colonies," said another official to me, "are all sentimental nonsense. The Jews naturally belong in cities; they can't maintain themselves upon the land." "The Zionist Movement," said still another official to me, "is in the hands of paid officials, who go to Zionist Congresses and bargain for their own support. A few years more, and the bottom will drop out from under them. The second generation of settlers here in Palestine will get tired, and refuse to work any more; the Jews abroad will get tired, and refuse to give any more. And that will be the end."

These men talked of the Zionist Movement with impatience, frequently with contempt, and always with a suggestion that they would be ineffably relieved, if not actually pleased, if the whole thing could only blow up and disappear. That there are ideals in this Zionist Movement precious to millions of people and of great significance to humanity, ideals rooted deep in the genius of the Jewish race and deeper still in the suffering and high resolve of this race through centuries of persecution, this the English do not see, or, seeing, cannot understand. They think upon this question as practical men, deeply versed in the ways, and utterly dedicated to the interests, of empire; and thus, in all honesty, they can find in their hearts no sympathy for Zion, and no faith in its future. Like the Romans in their first encounters with Christianity, the English in their contacts with Zion are on the one hand not impressed and therefore contemptuous, and on the other hand, are irritated and therefore hostile.

This attitude toward the Zionist Movement goes far toward explaining, and also vindicating, the chief grievance of the Jews against the English in Palestine, which is that the government, in disregard of its pledges to the world of Jewry and to the larger world of good men everywhere, has done and is doing nothing to advance the cause of Zion. The Balfour Declaration announced that "His Majesty's Government view with favor the establishment in Palestine of a national home for the Jewish people," and committed this government to the task of using "their best endeavors to facilitate the achievement of this object." Article 2 of the Mandate charged the same Government with definite responsibility "for placing the country under such political, administrative and economic conditions as will secure the establishment of the Jewish national home (in Palestine)." These phrases, according to the Jews, are contracts, and thus mean something positive and constructive. Not the political capture of the land for Zion! The Jews are not insisting that these pledges mean, for the present at least, the organization of a Jewish state. They are thinking rather of those basic equities of administration and services of good will which any people has a right to expect of any government organized to protect and advance their interests. On the basis of such pledges, the Zionists have invested thousands of lives and millions of dollars. Yet during the years that have passed since the Declaration was given to the world, and more especially in the ten years since the Empire assumed the Mandate of the League of Nations, the English authorities have done little to advance the cause of Zion. In the matter of the land, for example, which threatens as we have seen to bankrupt the Zionist Movement, and in any case to hinder its progress and embarrass its normal and right development, the Mandatory has been consistently indifferent, in spite of instructions in the Mandate itself for the use of State lands to help the Jews.[10] By a wise use of these State lands, and a frank refusal to tolerate exploitation and extortion in the sale of private lands, it could quickly end a condition which is a disgrace to the government and a serious menace to the "achievement" which it has promised its "best endeavors to facilitate." In contrast with this inaction is the vigorous action of the Mandatory in establishing drastic restrictions on immigration, and thus cutting off Zionism from that source of supply from which for years it has drawn its increasing strength. Undoubtedly in the days immediately following the establishment of English rule, when the hopes of Zion were higher than they had ever been before, or

[10] See page 94.

have been since, the immigration of Jewish settlers into the country was excessive. The Zionist organizations in Palestine could not absorb, nor even properly take care of, the flood of men and women that came pouring into the country. The Movement at this time, unquestionably "o'erleaped itself," and thus was itself responsible for the collapse of 1926-27. From this point of view the action taken by the government in admitting Jewish settlers only if they have capital in hand or jobs in prospect, was wise and wholesome. But restriction of the inflowing tide is one thing, and stoppage is another. At the present time, immigration into Palestine is practically at a standstill. The few hundred men and women who are now able to pass the gates each year are insufficient to supply the leakage from the colonies through death and other natural causes. An administration eager to use its "best endeavors to facilitate the achievement" of Zion, would see this situation and relieve it. Such an administration would be quick, also, to do many other things in friendly coöperation with the Jews. But the English administration is not friendly. Why should it be, when it does not believe in the Zionist adventure, nor even understand it? In Palestine, to-day, the English are no longer counted among the influences helpful to the advancement of Zion. If the Movement gets ahead, it is not because of but rather in spite of England's presence in the land.

What explains all these difficulties between the English and the Jews, in the last analysis, has already been hinted at above in my passing reference to the imperial interests of Great Britain in the Near East. At bottom, these two groups, the Mandatory and Zion, are not interested at all in the same things. Whatever may be the words of the Balfour Declaration, or the Jewish interpretation of these words, it remains a fact that the English did not go to Palestine, and are not now remaining there, for the purpose, even incidentally, of establishing "a national home for the Jewish people." On the contrary, the English went to Palestine, as they have gone to many other remote places, and they are staying in Palestine, as they will stay there for a long time, simply and solely to safeguard the interests of British power throughout the world. When disputes arise between the Zionists and the Mandatory authority, the Jews think at once and exclusively of solutions in terms of their own interests as rooted in the cause to which they are giving their very lives. But the English neither think of nor seek such solutions. Their concern is not with Zion but with the Empire. "Beyond the Alps lies Italy." Beyond Palestine lies India. The highway to India from Europe runs, as it has always run, through Asia Minor and the East. In the old days, when Turkey ruled this region, it was necessary for England to keep this highway open and secure by diplomatic strategy, military intervention, and occasionally war. Thus, Egypt was held in suzerainty to the British Crown; Constantinople protected from Russia; Bagdad denied to Germany. When the war came in 1914, there must be an immediate conquest of these regions. Hence the hurrying of British soldiers to the East! In Palestine, so close to the Canal, there must be a permanent predominance of British power. Hence the Balfour Declaration in 1917, and the Mandate in 1921! To-day Suez, Palestine, Trans-Jordania, Mesopotamia, are all lying safely beneath the British flag. And in all these places, the interests of this flag are of first importance. If in the Holy Land these interests can be made consistent with the interests of Zion, well and good. Then, incidentally, since it will do no harm to the Empire, these interests may be served. But if these interests are dangerous to the Empire, or are an obstacle however small within its path to power, then in one way or another they must be brushed aside. Now that Britain is in Palestine, she intends to stay there. Staying there, she intends to rule the country in the interest of the vast, far-flung Empire of which now this desert area is so small and insignificant a part. Let the Jews understand this fact! Let them know that no final trust in the Empire, even for protection against the Arabs, can serve the cause they love! The Empire, with its power, its pride, its high self-interest, is a disturbing element in the life of Zion. It is this which lies at the heart of the baffling problem of England in the Holy Land.

I pondered these things as I met and talked with Englishmen in Palestine. I had never before encountered the representatives of empire—these modern successors to the proconsuls of ancient Rome. The High Commissioner, trained and tried in the imperial service, the gracious embodiment of culture, hospitality, and high personal distinction; the Secretary to the Commissioner, dark, inscrutable, firm; the Deputy Commissioner in Jerusalem, polished man of the world, elegant against the background of his Arab home all shadowy with Eastern hangings and dimly-burning lights; the Anglican Bishop, splendidly clad in purple robe and golden cross, a fascinating talker, filled to the brim with curious and erudite information about the lands and peoples in which he had served the church of Christ, a proconsul not of the sword but of the spirit; these and other Englishmen, official and non-official! In meeting them I had the feeling not that I was meeting so many different men, trained in different schools, stored with different knowledge and experience, equipped with different ideas, outlooks, visions, but on the contrary that I was meeting in every office, in every home, in every person, a single mind that looked, thought, believed, and dreamed always the same. This mind had been cast in the mold and geared to the machine of empire and for this reason was not fitted nor prepared to understand the mind of the Jew in his great adventure in the homeland. The Englishman has had wide experience in imperial administration—a man of the type of the High Commissioner is the rarest and finest product of its kind that the world has ever known. Suavity and grace, backed by that calm assurance which springs from the sense of power in England and in England's cause, represent a combination to stir the blood in admiration—and also in terror. Here is a force which has mastered the world for three hundred years, and shows to this day no sign of diminished vigor and authority. But in Palestine for the first time it has met a force which has endured longer than itself, and outridden storms and perils it has never known. England is to-day attempting to rule the Jew—and that is a new thing under the English flag. Whether the English proconsuls know this or not, is one of the pressing questions of the hour. They gave to me, of course, no slightest intimation of worry or concern. But I felt, and wondered if they did not feel, that all that they had learned the world around must be unlearned in this strange land of Israel.

ZION—THE JEWS

These are serious problems [11]—a stubborn land from which to wrest support, a hostile people with whom to live, an alien and unsympathetic government to which to yield obedience! But these problems, while more immediate and even terrifying, are yet not more serious than one remaining problem which concerns the Jews themselves, in isolated relation to their own great adventure of the return to Zion.

[11] Never more so than now (August, 1929), when Palestine is swept anew with destruction, and seething with fresh hatreds and alarms. Are the woes of Israel never to end?

In undertaking what the Balfour Declaration defines as "the establishment in Palestine of a national home," the Jews are seeking the recovery of what they lost when they were first subdued and then destroyed by Roman arms—namely, their separate existence as a nation. In all history there is no parallel to these Jews, who were scattered by their conquerors over the face of the world, and yet refused to disappear. Through all the centuries they have lived as no other people have ever lived. Other people have had a country, a home, a language, a law, a separate political and cultural experience. Even when subjected to alien rule, like the Irish, they have had a land which they could call their own, and within its borders have been able to maintain the precious traditions of their race, and on occasion to rise up in heroic rebellion against their enemy. Even when torn, like the Poles, into fragments, and divided among different countries and under hostile flags, they have still remained in their ancient homes and villages, have felt beneath their feet the sacred soil of the fathers, and in a language and literature of their own have sustained their life. But the Jews have been denied all this. They have lost everything which could tie them to the earth. No country, save the inhospitable countries of other men; no home, save the prison chambers of the ghetto; no language, save the corrupted dialects of alien speech; no law, save the law of exile and persecution. Now that the hour of their liberation has come, they propose to have what other men have had—a land, a law, a language of their own, and an identity which will give them again a place within the sun.

What this means to the Jew we have already seen.[12] For him there can be no final dignity, no ultimate self-respect, until he has some spot upon the earth which he can call his

[12] See back (Chapter II).

own. Furthermore, he must have a larger liberty than the grudged tolerance of other men, a liberty which is his own by right of birth and use, if he is to achieve his distinctive destiny. But is this the only way in which the Jew can comfort his soul, and regain his standing among his fellows? Must he travel backward to old times and places, in order to fulfill his mission to mankind? What is the world trying desperately to do at this very moment but escape from that very status of nationalistic life to which the Jew is seeking to return in his quest of Zion?

To many an observer of the Zionist Movement, inside as well as outside of Jewry, the whole undertaking marks a reversion to the past. It is the turning of the face of a whole people back toward a condition and ideal of social life which has no abiding place in our civilization. If the Jew can have any compensation for his centuries of suffering, it must be found in the fact that, thanks to his outlawry from society and his consequent removal from the line of social evolution, he has escaped that experience of nationalism which, with its parochial pride and prejudice, its trade rivalries and armament competitions, its alliances and *ententes* and balances of power, its traditions of war and violence and vainglory, is leading our Western world through blood and horror to its death. To be sure, the way of the Jew has been the way of blood and horror. But it has led him not to death but to nobler, freer life. To-day, in the hour of his emancipation, he is a universal man. Because he belongs nowhere, he belongs everywhere. Passing all frontiers, he knows all nations and makes the world his home. The Jew is the true internationalist. He is the one man who may think and live in terms not of a nation but of humanity. Why now should he seek to restore his nation, and thus crawl back again behind the barriers of separation? Why vex his soul with the hatreds and divisions from which, as from the ghetto, he has through irony of circumstance been happily delivered? If the Jew has a mission, here it is—to leaven by his presence the spirit of the peoples whose life he shares, and therewith lift them to his own high plane of universal vision. For the Jew carries Zion in his heart. Wherever he is, there may be the reign of righteousness and peace. Not in Palestine alone, but in the world, shall the prophets' dream of brotherhood come true.

There is a beauty to this plea, but to the Jew an unreality. He knows too well the refusals of men, to cherish any hope that he can fulfill his mission in the countries of his present sojourn. If the leaven would "leaven the whole lump," it must first be accepted by the "lump," and this acceptance humanity has never yet been willing to give to Israel. But even if this plea were not unreal, would it be true? Does the return to Palestine necessarily mean a reversion to nationalism? Must the Jew forego a home and altar, that he may retain the spiritual virtue of that discipline which has been laid upon him as a rod of chastening? Is it the further discipline of the internationalist, in other words, that he shall have no nation of his own—the perpetual penalty of the universal man that he shall be "a man without a country?"

I cannot believe so. Yet is there just enough truth in this suggestion to reveal the danger which now besets the Zionist, and thus creates the final problem not of Arab nor of Englishman, but of himself? The problem of his inner life! The Jew is now deliberately undertaking to build himself a nation. What assurance is there that he will not at the same time, and as the inevitable result of his endeavors, make himself a nationalist? The Jew, for all the uniqueness of his experience, is still a man like other men. The substance of his nature is the human nature which compacts us all. Warped and maimed through stress of suffering, he is still in essence like ourselves, and will react, as we react, to the same influences and conditions. "Hath not a Jew eyes?" cries Shylock, in the play. "Hath not a Jew hands, organs, dimensions, senses, affections, passions? Fed with the same food, hurt with the same weapons, subject to the same diseases, healed by the same means, warmed and cooled by the same winter and summer? . . . If you prick us, do we not bleed? if you tickle us, do we not laugh? if you poison us, do we not die? if you wrong us, shall we not revenge?" And if you give us a country, a government, a flag, Shylock might well have continued, shall we not become patriots, nationalists, chauvinists, jingoes, with all the sins of these unholy folk upon our heads? "If we are like you in the rest, we will resemble you in that!"

It is the testimony of Henry Adams, in his "Education," that he did not enter upon a political career because he dreaded the power of public office and its corrupting influence upon men's souls. In the same way, may we not dread the entrance of the Jews, or any other tribe, upon a nationalistic career, for fear of the corrupting influences of power upon their lives? What people have ever remained unspoiled in this experience? Not the Jews in ancient times, when they had their state and were ruled by their kings? The history of Israel involves the same elements of exploitation and cruelty, violence and bloodshed, wars and rumors of wars, that make up the life story of all nations. If there was a difference between Israel on the one hand and Egypt, Assyria, Babylonia on the other, it was a difference in power, and not in the uses of that power for selfish ends. It is true that Israel produced its prophets, with their higher vision and loftier faith. But these prophets were overborne by the truculence, arrogance, lust of power and delusion of grandeur of kings and warriors;

they came into their own only when these politicians and soldiers had been destroyed, and Israel herself reduced to centuries of weakness and utter woe; they may well be overborne again in this latter day when Israel grasps once more the rod and sword. Already the Zionist Movement has shown symptoms of the nationalistic disease. Long since it developed its patriots and chauvinists, with their policies of arrogance, aggression, and racial pride. Thus we have already seen how, in the exultant days following the war and the granting of the British Mandate, the Jews gave way to outbursts of nationalistic fervor comparable to the manias of pride and power which swept Europe in 1914. In our time there are agitations among Zionists for a "Jewish Palestine," loud talk by irresponsible youths about driving out the Arabs and establishing a "Jewish nation." In this is no hope for Israel, nor for mankind. By 'such endeavors the Jews are neither redeeming themselves, nor restoring Zion. Rather are they deliberately abandoning what has been their strength for ages—the capacity to suffer and endure, and therewith conquer their enemies through pity and not through force. The world has no need of one more nation, made in the pattern and infused with the spirit of other nations; it can give no welcome to another center of struggle and discord among men who perish for lack of peace. But for a people who will be stricken and not strike back, who will be hurt and yet forgive, who will seek conquest through love and not through force, as it will exult in culture and not in power, for such a people the world has long been, and is still, waiting.

In this peril of a reversion to the corruptions and indecencies of nationalism is Zion's greatest problem to-day. Lying at the heart of the whole question of Zion's future, and of the future of the Jewish race itself, its discussion must wait upon and be absorbed in the larger discussion of this future and its promise.[13] Meanwhile, we may see in it the ancient drama, restaged in this late day, of the prophets and the kings. In the earlier time Israel made choice between these two, when she demanded of the prophet Samuel, a ruler.

"We will have a king over us," they cried, "that we also may be like all the nations."

And the prophet protested against this demand, and warned the people, saying, "This will be the manner of the king that shall reign over you: He will take your sons, and appoint them for himself, for his chariots, and to be his horsemen; . . . and he will set them to ear his ground, and to reap his harvest, and to make instruments of war."

But the people demanded again a king, that they might be "like all the nations." And the Lord instructed Samuel to heed them, "for they have not rejected thee, but they have rejected me, that I should not reign over them."

From this day of fatal choice, the history of the kings began. And this history was like the history of all kings. Now comes another day, and another occasion, of choice. Again, as in the day of Samuel, Israel must decide whether she shall be a people, winnowed out of all other peoples as "a suffering servant" of God for his work of justice and peace upon the earth, or a nation "like all the nations."

[13] See Chapter V.

"And they shall build the old wastes, they shall raise up the former desolations, and they shall repair the waste cities, the desolations of many generations."

Isaiah 61:4

CHAPTER IV

ACHIEVEMENTS

BACKGROUND

THE problems of Jewish Palestine present in many ways a depressing picture. Its features are sordid, its colors dark.

Here is a land which was never rich, and is now neglected, wasted and wretchedly poor.

This land is sparsely populated by Arabs, denizens of the most primitive type of civilization, illiterate, ignorant, superstitious, savage.

In this land are a few Moslem trading centers (Jaffa, Haifa), a few Christian towns (Nazareth, Bethelehem), a few Jewish cities (Safed, Hebron), and Jerusalem, the ancient stronghold of David, now the holy city of Jew, Christian and Moslem. But otherwise Palestine is an empty and desolate country, through which pass the ancient camel trails, and wander the *Fellaheen* shepherds and the Bedouin hillsmen.

Over this land before the War ruled the Turk, indifferent, inefficient, corrupt, cruel. Since the war has come the rule of the English, honest, able, but consistently in the interest not so much of the inhabitants of Palestine, either Arab or Jew, as of the Empire of many peoples in many far-flung quarters of the world.

Into this land have come the Jews, through a long succession of years. Always there were pilgrims—young men, to visit the ancient shrines and seats of learning, old men and women, to lay their bones in the sacred soil of the fathers. In 1881, and succeeding years, came streams of refugees from Russia and eastern Europe, in search of a home in the ancient shelters of their race. In 1897 began the Zionist Movement, with its deliberate purpose and endeavor to take over the land and make it again the national homeland of the Jewish people. From this time on, until comparatively recent years, a flood of youthful pioneers has poured itself into the country, glad in the vision of the new Zion, the new society of Israel, which leaps like a fountain within their hearts.

It is this new society, now built and building, which constitutes the achievement of Zionism. It seems a wonderful achievement, especially as set and seen against the background of this wasted land and savage people. What will come of it in the end may still be doubtful. The Jews may never become, or desire to become, a nation in the technical sense of the word; they may never recover or control the territory which once yielded sway to the sceptre of David; they may never gather more than a meager fraction of world-Jewry within the ancient bounds. But already in Palestine these Jews have become a people; they have reclaimed their lost hearthstones and raised anew their ruined altars; and they are laying deep and sure, in their own high spirit and devoted labor, the foundations of a new civilization comparable alike in achievement and promise to nothing that humanity has known since the founding of America.

Agriculture

At the bottom of this whole vast undertaking of Zion lies the reclamation of the land, for the possession of mother earth and the production of the fruits of her womb are to-day, as in the days of Moses, the only possible basis of an enduring social order. It was not enough to come to Palestine and try to develop some system of economic life in the cities. That way led either to utter disaster, or, at the best, to charity. If the national home were to live at all, it must be self-sustaining—and this means that the pioneers must live upon the land, and, by cultivating its soil, develop the only stable wealth upon which any society can feed and prosper.

To get Jews out onto the land, however, and make of them a tribe of farmers, is no easy task. For two thousand years these Jews have been, from hard necessity, a city folk. They know little about agriculture; and if they ever had any love for the soil, have long since lost it. For this reason, also, is there no assurance, if they are taken to the land, that they will stay there. In Argentina, for example, where Jewish families have been settled in rich soil at great expense, these families have grown prosperous, only to lease their land and flock to the cities to spend their income. Nothing has saved, or perhaps could save, the Palestinian situation, where the permanent development of the soil is the *sine qua non* of the whole experiment, but the call of Zion. The settlers who come to Palestine come not for money, nor for a refuge, but from a conviction which stirs their souls. They are held to their task upon the land not by wages, nor economic necessity, nor authority, but by the urge of an ideal which has mastered their lives. Not to make any living for themselves or their families, not to win any position of ease and comfort in the world, not to escape from any hardships or persecutions, but to redeem Israel! This is the vision which they see; and this vision binds them to the soil by fetters faster than the chains which bound the galley slave to bench and oar. The men and women who catch this vision, and are faithful to it, are of course as rare in quality as their vision is high. Few loafers come to Palestine, fewer fortune hunters, no cowards. Comparison is interesting with the Russian colonies in the Caucasus, where richer land, an easier life, and a surer promise of success bring inferior human material. If ever there were "a chosen people," it is these pioneers of Zion. City-born, city-bred, they seek a soil which can bring them nothing at last but graves in which to lie, and there through years they dig and delve that the foundations of the Jewish homeland may be firmly laid.

And it is being laid! Where yesterday were barren hillsides and fetid marshes are to-day the homesteads and farmlands of more than one hundred Jewish colonies, old and new. Where for generations the Arab farmer scratched the surface of a rough and stony soil with the wooden plow of his remotest ancestor, the Jewish peasant to-day drives deep the steel blade wrought in the foundries of Britain and America. What for centuries furnished scant pasturage to the sheep and goats of the *Fellaheen*, now feeds fat the sleek cattle of the Jewish herdsmen. Orange groves cover with fragrance and beauty what was formerly the waste and desolate sand dunes of the Mediterranean shore. Wheat and barley yield their abundant harvest in lowlands drained of those stagnant pools which smote even the wandering horseman with disease and death. New-planted forests dot a land which was long since stripped of trees; factories and power plants break the ancient silences with the modern clash of the machine; towns with schools and libraries and cultured citizens cover a country given over to the mud hut of the illiterate villager or the goatskin tent of the primitive nomad. From Russia, Roumania, Poland, Czecho-Slovakia, Germany, Britain, America, come the healthy, hearty, idealistic pioneers of Jewry who have left all to settle this lost land and restore it, a paradise of plenty, as Israel's home. The world has seen nothing like

ACHIEVEMENTS 175

this since English pioneers crossed the ocean westward in the early seventeenth century, and dotted the Atlantic seaboard with their settlements.

THE COLONIES—THREE TYPES

I must see these colonies, was my first and last resolve on my visit to the Jewish homeland. These, if nothing else! They are at once the foundation and the beating heart of Zion. Here is the organism of the whole movement actually at work; and here its life, therefore, is to be seen and understood. But I encountered extraordinary difficulties in carrying out this highly important object of my trip to the East. For I had come to Palestine in the winter season, as I have said, and was in the midst of storm and flood. Sober folk, not given to exaggeration, agreed that the violence of weather was unprecedented. This sounded to me at first like talk I heard once in California in the midst of a furious February hurricane. But when I saw the roads under water, railroads at a standstill, the great Rutenberg Works devastated by the raging torrent of the Jordan, I realized that something extraordinary had broken loose.

Now the colonies, with few exceptions, are located in remote sections of the land. They are "in the country," off the main highways, and therefore in such weather as I encountered extremely difficult of access and approach. Certain of the more important colonies were actually inaccessible, as for example those located along the road between Haifa and Jaffa, which was closed to traffic. Others, reached by automobile, could not be penetrated except by wading processes for which I was not at the time equipped. Only my horseback ride, under conditions already described, enabled me to reach Ain Harod and Beth Alpha. Centers of the greatest interest I missed on the day of my adventurous drive to Nathanyah. Nevertheless, in a period of three weeks crowded with activities, I visited in all *ten* colonies which represented every period of Zionist history, every type of organization and theory, and all ranges of wealth and dearth. I saw colonies as old as Petah Tikvah (founded, 1882), and as young as Nathanyah (founded this very year, 1929); as individualistic as Herzlia and Kfar Aaron, and as communistic as Beth Alpha; as prosperous as Rishon le Zion, and as poor as Kirjeah Anavim, or "Dilb," as it was familiarly called. In general I was able to classify these colonies, largely on the basis of inward organization, into three distinct classes. First, the extreme individualistic or bourgeois colonies, which may be said to occupy the right wing of the pioneering army; secondly, the modified individualistic or coöperative colonies, in the center; and, lastly, the various kinds of communistic, or, more accurately, communal colonies, on the left.

The individualistic colonies are predominantly the older colonies, founded in the early days before the advent of organized Zionism, and, because of the generous aid given in critical times by the Baron, not infrequently called the "Rothschild Colonies." These settlements have put their early pioneer days well behind them. Rough evidences of early struggle and privation are disappearing, and signs of an established, ordered, settled-down kind of existence are everywhere apparent. Economic stability and comfort, if not actual wealth, have been secured, and are bringing along the usual social phenomena.

Petah Tikvah, located some miles outside of Jaffa, is an excellent example of what I mean. The early history of this settlement is an epic in itself. Fighting heroically against impossible odds, the first pioneers lost more than half their number the first year from starvation, exposure and malarial fever, and were obliged to abandon their project. But they were not to be beaten! Coming back in

1882 with reënforcements, they battled through triumphantly, and laid the foundations of the present busy and happy town. Petah Tikvah to-day has a population of more than ten thousand souls. These subsist predominantly upon the products of the far-flung orange groves which stretch about the city like an enveloping forest. Streets, sidewalks, public squares have been laid out; and are bordered by attractive houses and thriving stores. Our party partook of an elaborate luncheon on the day of our visit at the local hotel, inspected the synagogue, and attended sessions at two public schools. Going and coming we traveled over a smoothly macadamized road, and admired large and thriving groves of eucalyptus trees. Petah Tikvah has arrived—an attractive, comfortable, conservative bourgeois town.

Rishon le Zion is very different, and yet the same. Different, because its major industry is grapes, and not oranges; the same, because the industry is flourishing and its people prosperous! Its present population, three thousand in number, sprang from an original ten, who came here over forty-seven years ago and began the cultivation of the vine. One of these ten, Menesah Mayerowitz, the only surviving member of the original group, was our host on the occasion of our visit. With what relish did he sit us down, revive old tales, and then regale us with rare specimens from his wine cellars. Then the veteran took us into his subterranean vaults, built years before by Baron Rothschild, and ranking to-day as the third largest cellars in the world. I was startled, as we moved along, to hear Mr. Mayerowitz declare that the atmosphere of these cellars was so rich that persons had been known to become intoxicated just from walking through. I began at once to sniff, and, dropping behind our party, to walk straight lines in the pavement to see if I could keep an even course. Time after time I tried, and time after time I moved as straight and sure as an arrow. It was a relief to my Puritan conscience, none the less, to regain the upper air. Mounting our automobiles, we drove away through the attractive stretches of the town. Here were long streets of pretty houses, with bright gardens and lofty trees. We saw well-laden shops, a synagogue, and schools. Like Petah Tikvah, the place looked established, respectable, prosperous and contented.

Colonies of this type are of the ordinary Western variety of town. That is to say, they are of the strictly individualistic and capitalistic order. The land is owned, as it was purchased, in individual holdings, most of them so large as to be plantations rather than farms. Each owner works his land as he sees fit; owns his own house, buildings, tools and equipment, and makes as much money as he can. His labor is mostly hired labor—Arab men and women employed on a regular basis of day wages. The original settlers and their successors are now landed proprietors. The colonies enjoy certain features of coöperative life, of which we know little in America—coöperative buying of basic supplies, and coöperative marketing of produce. But they rest upon the twin pillars of the capitalistic order—private ownership in land and the wage system of labor. In this sense they are nothing new, and, to quote Josiah Wedgewood, "nothing very exciting."

Colonies of this individualistic type, as I have said, are the old colonies. I must now modify this statement by pointing out that the four latest colonies to be started in Palestine are of this kind. These colonies are all the work of a new society, called Bne Binyamin [1] ("Sons of Benjamin"), which was founded expressly with the idea of leading the second generation of Jewish youth in Palestine to stay on the land, found new colonies, and thus keep the

[1] Hebrew name of Baron Edmond de Rothschild.

ACHIEVEMENTS 179

homeland growing. Bne Binyamin boasts two thousand members, of whom eighty-five per cent are sons of pioneers. The society is a movement of enormous importance, as representing the first extension of Zionism by native forces within instead of alien forces without.

The colonies founded by this group are all strictly individualistic, in true fidelity to the faith and practice of the fathers. But there are certain important modifications in the system. Thus, the land, bought by the group, is resold to the individual members of the group *in equal parcels only*. Such parcels, if resold, must be sold back to the group. Water development, roads, schools, etc., are owned and conducted in common. Land in these colonies may be sold to outside membership investors on a regular investment basis. I could have bought an orange grove, had I the money. Labor, of course, is hired, usually from Arab sources.

Kfar Aaron was the one of these colonies which I visited and inspected most carefully. Founded three years ago, it has to-day a population of twenty-five families, or about one hundred persons in all. Ten of these families have erected attractive individual homes—the rest are living in temporary barracks. There is also a common building, a sort of community center, used for synagogue, school, and general social purposes. A splendid water system is in operation, and lovely orange groves stretch far away on every side. This colony, and its sister colony, Herzlia, which I also visited, showed remarkable signs of growth and prosperity.

The second of the three groups into which the colonies of Palestine divide themselves is well illustrated by Nahalal, a colony near Nazareth, which I visited during my stay in this latter town. No visit could have been less propitious. The rains descended and the floods came and the winds blew as the very climax of the storms in which I had been plunged now for over a week. I got into the settlement, located well off the main highway, because of an excellently constructed road which had been recently laid by the colonists. But once arrived, I faced conditions worse than those which I had found in Ain Harod and Beth Alpha. Situated on low land, Nahalal looked like a Mississippi valley town after the flood had gone through. Days of uninterrupted and heavy rain had simply drowned the place. To get about was literally impossible, unless one was dressed and trained for the job. So I contented myself with settling down in the main building of the Girls' Agricultural School, located at the front door of this colony; and, after inspecting this building, talked with a delegation of the colonists who had gathered there to meet me. In rooms damp and cold from unprecedented exposure, we kept ourselves warm with delicious cups of steaming tea, and discussed from all angles the philosophy, methods, and practical achievements of a colony organized and conducted like Nahalal.

The land of this colony was purchased and is now owned in perpetuity by the Jewish National Fund. This is in accordance with the fixed policy of the Zionists to-day that the land of Palestine shall henceforth be acquired and held in the name of the Jewish people, and never under any circumstances alienated. A blow at the first pillar of the capitalistic system—private ownership in land! The soil, thus held in perpetual ownership by the Fund, was then leased, on forty-nine year terms, with right of renewal, to the individual colonists, in individual holdings for individual development. This is a system which is based on common ownership, but which works out in terms of individual control.

ACHIEVEMENTS

The land holdings have one remarkable characteristic. As compared with those which I saw in Petah Tikvah and Kfar Aaron, for example, they are extraordinarily small— like a New England farm rather than like a southern plantation or California orange grove. This is strictly according to plan or rule, in order to enable each individual leaseholder to work his land with his own labor. For no hired labor is allowed. A blow at the second pillar of the capitalistic system—wage labor! No man must own, or rather lease, more soil than he can cultivate with his own hands and those of his family. For it is believed by the Zionists to-day that the foundation of the state must rest not only upon public ownership of the land, but also upon private, or personal, labor upon the land. Not the proprietor who hires another to work his acres, but the peasant who produces with the sweat of his own brow, must be the center of the social order.

This principle leads to curious adjustments. In Nahalal, for example, if a colonist falls ill, and his family is unable to keep up the work upon his place, the other colonists take turns in lending a hand. If the colonist continues ill for more than three months, a laborer is hired at the expense of the colony as a whole. If the colonist is ill for an indefinite period, or becomes permanently incapacitated, he must give up his holding in the settlement, and thus surrender his place to another. In cases of emergency, the labor or disaster of one is met by the coöperative activity of all the colonists. "Bear ye one another's burdens." The coöperative principle is also recognized in Nahalal, as in Petah Tikvah and Rishon le Zion, by joint buying and selling, and by a centralized system of general management in which all participate. There are also public schools for the children, and a common house for the common life of the colony. Unable to inspect the settlement by direct observation, I gained from the colonists whom I met—quite as much from their general manner as from their specific statements—a distinct impression of happiness and confidence. There did not seem to be the same atmosphere of established and substantial prosperity as in the older colonies. The spirit of adventure and experiment was still abroad. But Nahalal is succeeding.

It was in this colony that I met Nathan Hofshi, a humble man, who is living his life in consistent fidelity to the extremist type of Tolstoyan non-resistance. The rigor of this man's gospel is thoroughgoing. He applies it not only to men but to animals. Such reverence has he for life and its essential sanctity, that he not only will not slay animals, but will not even enslave them to his use. He will not work a horse, or drink the milk of a cow, or eat the honey of the bees. He must live by his own labor, and exclusively of the fruits of his toil upon the land! Love is of course his law, and the practice of this love a discipline which must extend to the whole animal creation. Like every man of the kind whom I have ever met, Nathan Hofshi was all sweetness and light. There was a certain pathos in his countenance—a shadow of seriousness which seemed to show that the way in which he had set his feet was no easy path. But there was not a trace of pride or censoriousness —he lived in peace and harmony with a group of persons no one of whom accepted his far-reaching creed. In place of hardness there was gentleness, and over all a touch of patience and humility which was sublime. Here was a lovely soul! Right or wrong, wise or foolish, his presence was like an angel's among men. Perhaps it was the beauty of this presence that made him a welcome resident at Nahalal. As a worker, he could not be very helpful to the group. Extreme individualism of this Tolstoyan type is difficult to reconcile with a form of social life essentially coöperative in character, and moving constantly close to the margin of subsistence. But "man does not live by bread alone!" Nathan Hofshi contributed in his gentle spirit more perhaps than his due debt to the common life.

By all odds the most interesting and certainly the most unusual of the Palestinian colonies comprise the third group—the voluntary communes known as the *Kvutzoth*. These are commonly called "communist" colonies, since the members are in all cases professed Communists. But these Communists themselves earnestly object to being called such, on the ground that it mixes them up with Bolshevism, with which they have no connection and in which they have little interest. For these *Chalutzim* are not political Communists at all—or most of them are not! On the contrary, much nearer to Tolstoyanism than to Leninism in their general attitude toward the problem of reform, they put political opinion aside as of no concern to them, and give themselves utterly to the specific practical endeavor to organize and maintain by personal labor an ideal coöperative society. So, in order properly to differentiate the economic from the political, the practical from the theoretical, they drop the word "communist," and ask to be described rather as *communal* groups.

Furthermore, as it happens, there is a special reason at this moment for this distinctive emphasis, which pertains to the activities in Palestine of that small but busy group of political Communists, to whom I have already referred. These Communists, as I have pointed out, are doing everything in their power to harass and embarrass the Zionists. This attack on Zionism, however, is only an indirect and convenient means of striking at the British Empire. The English authorities know this and with drastic rigor are combating what they regard as a serious menace to British rule. Now the *Kvutzoth* have no desire, and certainly no purpose, to become confused with these Bolshevist agitators. On the one hand they seek the good will of the English authorities for Zion; on the other hand they have real reason for suspecting that a government none too intelligent upon this question may eventually attack them as centers of subversive influence. Wholly interested in a momentous undertaking which drains their utmost strength, they insist upon being distinguished from those who are idle and malicious agitators against all they hold most dear in the rebuilding of the homeland.

I was so happy as to visit four of these communal colonies—Kirjath Anavim, or "Dilb," a suburb of Jerusalem, Ain Harod and Beth Alpha, located in the great plain of Esdraelon, and the Girls' Settlement on the outskirts of Petah Tikvah. Of these, Ain Harod is the largest, boasting a population of one hundred and twenty families. Beth Alpha has about seventy-five families, and "Dilb" thirty-five families. The Girls' Settlement is one of twenty settlements organized exclusively for women. This colony is composed of eighteen girls who live by themselves, and do all their own work on the farm, in the stockyard, and in the poultry run. These girls' settlements, I may say, serve largely as training schools for girls who later go to other established colonies as wives or regular workers; but in this settlement which I visited, I found several members who had been in the colony from the beginning.

Each of these four colonies has distinctive characteristics, but in all essential things they are the same. That is to say, they are frankly communistic in organization and life. Like the early Christians, the members "hold all things in common." Thus the land, whether purchased outright or leased from the Jewish National Fund, is undivided, and is worked as a single unit by all together. The houses, the barns, the stock, the equipment, the supplies, the produce, the clothes, the food, all belong to all. There is a common treasury, out of which all expenses are paid, and into which all income is poured. No man owns anything —not even the actual clothes upon his back. Coats, hats, trousers, dresses are bought in bulk, and distributed like army uniforms. Soiled linen is gathered each week into a common pile, and, when laundered, is redistributed without any attempt at personal identification. Books are purchased from the common fund and held in the common library. In Beth Alpha I saw a member passing about cigarettes after dinner, and learned, upon inquiry, that cigarettes are provided from the common stores on a ratio of half-a-box per person per day. Those who smoke little, or not at all, gladly pass over their rations to those who smoke a good deal. The night watchman, on his lonely rounds, is allowed to smoke as many cigarettes as he pleases.

The center of these colonies is a common house, in which the members eat their meals together at great long tables, and assemble at evening for transaction of business, discussion of problems, and general social entertainment. This house, of course, has the common kitchen, supply rooms, etc. The members sleep in small houses scattered about the premises. These houses contain three or four rooms, each one of which is assigned to a married couple, or to a couple of roommates. These rooms are utterly simple, containing no adornments and only the barest necessities in the way of furniture. The best building, invariably, is the children's building; and no activity of the colonies is more carefully thought out or more zealously pursued than that of the care and upbringing of these children. And here the colonies differ from one another in their programs of procedure.

All, be it said, recognize the marriage relation, and the precious tie of parentage. In "Dilb," more conservative than the other communal colonies which I visited, the children sleep at home with their parents. Thus, after the working hours are done, the traditional family is established. Each family has only a single room, and there in each case we saw the little cribs for the children side by side with the parents' bed. During the day, in this colony, the children are placed under the care of women members of the community who are assigned to and duly trained for this specific work. During their first year, the children are kept in the "nursery"; from their first to their second year, in the "playhouse"; and after their second year, in the "kindergarten." These children have their own vegetable gardens and flower plots apart from those belonging to the general community, and these they cultivate together on an out-and-out coöperative basis.

In Ain Harod, we took refuge from the storm in the nursery of the colony, and thus saw this better than any other institution in the community. Here in this nursery the children are placed just as soon as they are born, and are cared for by women trained to this particular task. When we entered the room where the infants were kept, some of these women, or nurses, were flitting about the little white iron beds in which the children lay. One or two others were passing to and from the kitchen where food was being prepared according to the best dietary standards. Another had an errand in another room, where some older children were playing happily inside their kindergarten "pens." Some of these women are themselves the mothers; other mothers, however, prefer the fields to the nursery, and their places are taken by young women members of the colony who find their chiefest joy in caring for children. The children are held together from the beginning as a group, and are of course tended and reared as a group. Parents are free to come and see their children whenever they please, but they may not take them to their own rooms, or keep them by themselves. Day and night the children must live together in their own house—at least, in the early, formative, and therefore critical years. Later on, after their sixth or seventh year, if the parents so desire, the children may be taken home. I was greatly impressed, I may add, by this nursery—and by the children, who were a hale, healthy, happy lot.

Beth Alpha goes to the logical extreme in this matter of the communal upbringing of children, by separating them permanently from their parents into a group or community of their own. The children's building was the one outstanding structure in the settlement. Here the children are placed when they are born, and here they live with their contemporaries until they are man and woman grown. Professionally trained nurses and teachers are the guides and companions of these children. Their life is entirely apart from that of the rest of the colony. They have their own eating room and living rooms. They have their own work, and manage their own affairs. They have a most interesting library of books for their entertainment and study. When grown to early youth, the children take their places in the adult community, or go off to some other colony, or—as has once happened—band together and establish a colony of their own.

The general organization of these communal colonies is much the same. The source of authority is the community as a whole, which meets together at stated intervals for discussion and determination of community affairs. Executive direction is placed in the hands of an executive committee of seven or nine members. In "Dilb" there is also an inner committee of three. This executive committee, or in some cases a special "work committee," exercises the important function of planning the work of the colony, and assigning each member to his appointed task. In no colony did I find any man (or woman) who was recognized as the official head; but in every colony I seemed to find the man who by experience, intelligence, or force of character was the *de facto* leader of the group. The spirit, however, was the common spirit, and the life the common life. For better or worse, it was "each for all, and all for each."

THE "KVUTZOTH," OR COMMUNAL COLONIES

Discussion of the Jewish colonies in Palestine inevitably turns upon the communal colonies. These are everywhere the center of controversy. If one believes in these communal experiments, it is inevitable that one should be indifferent to the colonies of the more conservative variety. If, on the other hand, one believes in the individual basis of social organization, then it is inevitable that one should regard the *Kvutzoth* with suspicion and distaste. I, as a Gentile and a first visitor, was in the fortunate position of being able to view the situation without prejudices or commitments of any kind. I did my best to keep my eyes and mind wide open, and found no difficulty in feeling intense and sympathetic interest in all I saw. Especially was I stirred to admiration for a directive agency which was willing to foster colonies of various types, and open the way for heroic Jews to settle upon the land on their own terms and in their own way. There may be better or worse, even right or wrong, ways of rebuilding the ancient homeland in Zion, but there is only one spirit, and no atom of this spirit is the Zionist movement permitting to be lost. None the less, the communal colonies are the challenge of the hour. To them I found myself flung back in every discussion, and my whole attitude thus determined by my

ACHIEVEMENTS

reaction upon this single group. Hence the necessity of beginning—and ending—with the Communists!

It is from this standpoint that I must regard it as tragic that I studied the communal colonies under the worst possible conditions, and therefore saw them in the least favorable light. In the first place, I did not visit at all the best, because the oldest and most successful, of these colonies. Daganiah, founded in 1909, and Merhaviah, founded in 1910, were on my route, but I missed them both owing to the impossible conditions of storm and flood which prevailed when I came into their neighborhood.

In the second place, the four colonies of this type which I managed to see were living under such extraordinary conditions of cold and wet that nothing was normal. Inwardly, in the psychological condition of the colonists, as well as outwardly, in the physical condition of their homes and barns, everything was awry. Nevertheless, in "Dilb," where I spent an afternoon, in Ain Harod and in Beth Alpha, where I spent the night, and in the Girls' Settlement near Petah Tikvah, I made careful observations, had conferences with members, and gathered abundant facts. The whole experience was somber enough, but there may be advantage as well as disadvantage in seeing things at their worst. One at least escapes the charge of being duped.

Taking all adverse conditions into full account, and with the best will in the world, I must still record as my first impression the barrenness, grimness, even ugliness of the life which these communal workers are living. In other colonies, some of them of more recent growth than the *Kvutzoth*, I saw pretty gardens, lawns and trees and flowers, but none in the communal settlements. In the homes which I visited in the individualistic colonies I saw abundant evidences of modest beauty and adornment, but in Ain Harod and Beth Alpha there was nothing but the bare rudiments of existence. I can remember seeing in the common room of the Girls' Settlement some two or three pictures of Zionist heroes; in a private room at "Dilb" there were family portraits on the wall; in the room in which I slept at Beth Alpha there was a tiny picture on one wall, and a pathetic little sprig of flowers on the table. But with these exceptions, I saw nothing in these colonies but objects of sternest and meagerest utility.

This aspect of life was most apparent, perhaps, in the matter of eating. Food was hospitably given wherever I went; and I am in the habit of accepting what is placed before me by my host in the grateful conviction that he is sharing with me the best he has. But the serving of food, if not the food itself, may properly be judged as an evidence of living standards. In Beth Alpha, I ate twice with the members of the colony. At both meals, the members ate all their food from a single bowl and with a single spoon. In this colony, as in the other communal colonies where I ate, the rough wooden tables were uncovered, and were utterly bare of even the simplest adornment. Am I unfair in contrasting this experience with my experience in colonies of other types—in Herzlia, where I partook of a full dinner, served with extreme simplicity, but with the nicest sense of refinement and delicacy, or in Kfar Aaron, where I took tea, with tablecloths, napkins, pretty dishes, flowers and fruit, to give grace and beauty to the function. On these occasions, as at Beth Alpha, there was no wasteful expenditure—life was here also reduced to a minimum! But in the one case there was the roughness, the crudity, the ugliness of a mining camp; in the others, there was that regard for those basic amenities which mark the advance of civilization.

It is this contrast between ugliness and some attempt at least at beauty, between the utilization of sheer brute necessities and the cultivation of those gracious conventions which make life human, which remains as my last, as it was my first, impression of these colonies. Generalizations are always dangerous; there are exceptions in detail to every sweeping assertion. Yet I feel that I am not far wrong when I state that, as I moved toward the right, toward the individualistic type of colony, I felt myself moving toward the higher standards of cultured life, whereas in moving toward the left, toward the communistic type of colony, I seemed to be moving back toward the conditions of primitive existence. The matter of roads is a perfect illustration of what I mean. It was to me a shocking thing to find the houses in Ain Harod and Beth Alpha lost in an indescribable mire of mud and slime. Did nobody care enough about decency and comfort, or have adequate anticipation of bad weather in the winter season, to provide at least a row of stepping-stones between one building and another? Inquiry brought no better reply than that of the shiftless man who failed to shingle his leaky roof—in good weather they did not need roads or paths, and in bad weather they could not make them. Friends suggested that these colonies, founded some seven or eight years ago, were new, and conditions therefore still very crude. But in Herzlia, which is only three years old, I noticed roads. Here the people had had the desire and the will to provide excellent channels of communication between house and house, and between the village and the outer world. In this place as not in the other two there were the external aspects at least of human existence.

Other phases of the situation, which soften the picture, are not to be forgotten. Conditions such as I found in certain colonies in the worst season of the year are by no means the rule in all places and on all occasions. Thus in the older *Kvutzoth* which I was not able to visit—Daganiah, Merhaviah, and others—there have been attained standards of comfort and beauty which are still beyond the reach of the younger colonies. Even in Beth Alpha I saw an old piano, a pile of torn and tattered sheet music, and an ancient talking-machine. In Kirjeath Anavim ("Dilb"), fortunately located within a few miles of Jerusalem, there is established in the common treasury a so-called "cultural fund," out of which the members are each paid fifty piastres a month for the enjoyment of books, lectures, music, theaters, and "movies" in the Holy City. In the kindlier months of the year lecturers and musicians visit the remoter colonies. A recital given by Jascha Heifetz in the natural auditorium of a stone quarry, where assembled hundreds of colonists for miles around, has become a legend of the countryside. A workers' dramatic organization in Tel-Aviv [2] is accustomed to send out its players on a tour of all the agricultural settlements of Palestine. In the hot months of the year, when all the life is out-of-doors, there is much folk dancing and singing in the cool hours just before bedtime. In nearly all the settlements there are impressive libraries, narrow shelves crowded with volumes pitifully torn and dirtied from much reading. In Beth Alpha, there was a special library for the children, housed in a separate room for their exclusive use. Always, in and out, pour the books from the loan library maintained by the trade unions in Tel-Aviv.[3] There is a lovelier side to the life in these struggling colonies. I thought of it as I saw in my last few days in Palestine the flaming "lilies of the field," blossoming like the poppies in Flanders, and covering the bare and dripping earth with sudden beauty.

The one constant fact in the life of the *Kvutzoth*, for the

[2] See Chapter IV, pages 223-225.
[3] See Chapter I, page 43.

ACHIEVEMENTS

present at least, is their poverty. Other colonists, like the newest settlers at Nathanyah, have begun their life upon the land with capital resources of their own. The Communists, *per contra*, have invariably had nothing but what they could borrow from the Zionist agencies. Even this has not always been provided them as agreed, owing to unexpected failures in Zionist income. What is more, the Communists, just because of their poverty, have been unable to be pickers and choosers of the land upon which they would settle. They have been obliged, like any other beggars, to take what they could get. In many cases, these heroic *Chalutzim* have themselves deliberately chosen to take the hardest and most hopeless land in Israel, that they might do for Zion what other and less determined men, perhaps, were loathe to do. Almost invariably, therefore, these communal colonies represent the slenderest resources planted upon the most stubborn soil. I have never seen anything more heart-breaking than the rocky earth out of which the settlers at "Dilb" were wresting an existence. The story of the draining of the marshes in the Emek was a veritable saga of heroism. To see these things is to see the indispensable place which these communal colonies hold in the whole campaign for the recapture of Palestine. For these colonies are the only ones which can survive in certain areas of the country; these colonists are the only men and women who have at once the capacity and the destiny to grapple with the most primitive and cruel conditions of human survival. In a large part of Palestine, if the land is to be reclaimed and Israel redeemed, life must start again at the very lowest levels of labor and culture, and there for a considerable time it must remain. The Communists, and apparently the Communists alone, are able to meet this challenge. And it is very largely because they alone have the courage and the sacrifice to meet it, that I found them alone among such conditions as I have described. They are not to be blamed, therefore, but praised. Yet does there linger in my mind the question as to whether, after nearly a decade, such crudities as I witnessed are still inevitable; the fear that the very absorption of these people in the physical struggle may be killing out certain æsthetic and cultural interests which in the long run, and from the higher point of view, are as necessary to men as bread; and the speculation as to whether, in the communist system of social organization, there may not be an atrophying of individual responsibility which produces such crudities and neglects as I have emphasized.

But these are surface facts. The great thing, after all, is the shining spectacle of these heroic men and women coming to the worst land with empty hands, not merely to make a living but to restore a commonwealth. They are like the early New England pioneers, with the difference that the Americans had the easier lot and the simpler task, for these latter were taking over virgin soil of abundant richness, whereas these Jews are cultivating a wasted land which will yield its fruits only when watered with men's sweat and tears. Under the worst conceivable conditions these communal colonies are registering success. They are showing signs of eventual economic stability. If they made no profit at all, these colonies would be a good investment for the Zionists, for common homes and common farm buildings are cheaper than individual houses and sheds; and equipment, which would have to be immediate and complete in the case of separate individuals, can be spread over a period of years in the case of a coöperative group. The *Kvutzoth* have therefore made practicable an extension of the Zionist movement which would otherwise be impossible. But, apart from this, these colonies have made good. Daganiah, for example, is now entirely self-supporting, and is already preparing to begin the payment of interest on its debt. "Dilb" last year made a clear profit over all obligations and charges. Other colonies are making excellent progress toward economic independence. If the communal experiments are financially unsound, it is only because the whole Zioniest movement is unsound. Which has been charged, but never proved!

More impressive, because more fundamental, is the success of the communal colonies in building a radical type of society which is holding together under conditions of severest trial. Whether these colonies will survive as a permanent part of Zionism is doubted by many. Communism, I was told, is a type of organization which belongs, and is peculiarly useful, to a social movement in its early and more primitive stages of development, and thus never survives into later stages. The early Christian churches in the Roman Empire, like the original Plymouth settlement, were communistic in organization and ideal, but they did not remain so. Signs of disintegration are appearing in Palestine in the drifting away of individuals who become tired, or who desire to use their training in the *Kvutzoth* under easier or more profitable conditions. This creates a steady leakage from the communal to the more individual type of colony. Most of the settlers in Nahalal, for example, had originally been members of a *Kvutzah*. This leakage is not excessive, but has significance. On the other hand is the careful training of their children by the Communists, and the success of this training in binding the children to the practices and ideals of their parents. Furthermore, many of these colonies are not new; the older ones have weathered a generation of storm and stress. Whatever be their future, they constitute to-day a group of communities of the Utopian form which are meeting on the whole successfully those stubborn facts of human nature before which all other experiments of the kind have sooner or later foundered. I searched this question with every curious inquiry which I could make. Always I was impressed with the frank and full replies which I received. There was no evasion of issues; no avoidance of facts; no ignorance of experience. These Communists had thought their problems through, and had wrought out their convictions with an honesty and fearlessness which were thrilling. I have never in my life faced clearer minds or more humble, stalwart, steadfast spirits.

"What about slackers?" I said. The problem of the man who is willing to let the other fellow do the work? Very quietly there came back the reply. "The problem exists—we cannot escape it." Then came the further word, that this is a problem which cures itself. The steady impact of public opinion acts as a potent expulsive force. Sooner or later the slacker finds that he is in the wrong place, and voluntarily seeks a more congenial climate. Not yet has the slacker become in any colony a permanent source of weakness. The great majority of Communists are hard workers, loyal comrades, trained and disciplined members of the common group. The patience, serenity, and unquenchable zeal of these men and women are among the most impressive things I saw in Palestine.

"Is there any quarreling?" was another of my questions. Were the colonists on their good behavior in my presence? What about frayed nerves, uneven tempers, unmastered temperaments, envyings, jealousies, malice? To this the response was direct and emphatic. Personal frailties of this type did not appear. Quarreling was not a problem. Tempers were tamed by hard work. There were no jealousies, for in a communal society there is nothing to get jealous about. Idealism was proving its capacity to purge the heart of petty personalities. And always, of course, these communities are purely voluntary associations, and the backbiter, like the slacker, is free to leave.

But what about family life? Do husbands and wives suffer for lack of a home? Does the communal relation lead to broken marriages? Do children, separated from parents, lose affection for their parents, or parents for their children?

At the heart of these questions lies the fact that the women in these communal colonies live and work on a basis of absolute equality with the men. In the economic life of the settlements, as indeed in personal appearance, the women are indistinguishable from their husbands, brothers, and comrades of the other sex. I remember seeing at Ain Harod a stalwart Amazon, clad in knickerbockers and high boots, mounted upon a cart which again and again sank in mud up to the hubs, lashing a team of four heavy mules across the courtyard. At "Dilb" I watched two young women, dressed exactly like the men, doing some of the hardest labor in a great barn filled with some fifty odd cows. On the edge of Petah Tikvah is the small settlement, above referred to, in which all the inhabitants are women, who of course do all the work. In the regular colonies, on the other hand, men share on equal terms with the women the labor in the kitchens and the dining halls. Only one occupation did I find limited to one sex alone, and that was the armed watch at night. For obvious reasons this duty belongs exclusively to the men.

Under conditions of this kind, the women develop a distinctive type of appearance and character. Those whom I saw in various colonies, under a great variety of conditions, were uniformly magnificent physical specimens. They were not beautiful in the luxurious sense of the word, nor even in the smart, competitive sense. Their clothes were too rough, their limbs too powerful, for such description. No silks and satins here, no paints and powders and perfumes, no languishing glances, no soft, alluring bodies! Not an atom of sex appeal in any one of these women! But such strength, such vitality, such glowing health, such a sturdy, native pride of capacity and self-reliance!

"How do these women stand childbirth?" I asked a physician in Ain Harod.

"No trouble at all," was the reply. "It seldom bothers me, or them. It is rare for a woman to be in labor here more than an hour or two."

These facts are central in the problem of family life in the *Kvutzoth*, and of relations between the sexes. Marriage is common; divorces or separations are rare; sex difficulties are not a serious menace. At bottom, in these colonies, is an absorption in an inspiring and laborious task which leaves neither time nor strength for bickering inside or philandering outside the family relationship. The rigor of the life, if not an established code of law, tends to create a standard of morals more stern than anything the Puritans in their day ever knew. Added to this, in the communal system of society, is a mutuality of experience between families which makes broken marriages improbable if not impossible. "Marriage is frequently a failure in capitalistic society," said one of the pioneers in Ain Harod, "because of economic conditions. It is the struggle for a living, the comparisons and competitions in a community where money is the measure of all things, the pride of success and the humiliation of failure—it is these things that wreck the private home. Here we are all in the same boat. Husbands and wives are members together in the larger community. Our marriages hold not because our human nature is different, but because the conditions of our common life are favorable to the permanency of the marital relation. We have solved the economic problem, and therewith are solving the marriage problem."

The question of the children was answered in an equally encouraging way. Do children in a communal colony know their parents? I shall not soon forget the conduct of the two-year-old in the nursery at "Dilb," when his father, our guide about the place, unexpectedly made his appearance. A shout, a cry, uplifted arms, and in a trice the little one was in his father's embrace. And such a wail when the father put the youngster down, and went on his way with us! Are the parents in a communal colony fond of their children? I like to remember the young father whom we found on our arrival in the nursery at Ain Harod. The rainstorm was so terrific that work in the colony was at a standstill, and this young man was choosing to spend his free time with his first-born. We met him helping the youngster, with the most tender and solicitous devotion, to learn the art of walking. We went away after a while to inspect the settlement, and were gone over an hour. When we came back, we found this young man playing so intently with his child that he hardly gave us a glance of recognition. Here were love, loyalty, patience, utter sacrifice, all enthroned forever in the heart of this young father. Equally impressive was the young man who accompanied us from Jerusalem to Beth Alpha. He had been absent from the colony for three days, on a visit to relatives in the Holy City. We reached the colony about four o'clock in the afternoon, and he immediately disappeared. We did not see him again until seven o'clock, at dinner. "Here is an interesting sidelight on life in this colony," said Dr. Magnes, after a moment's chat with the young man in the Hebrew tongue. "He has been up to the children's house ever since his arrival, playing with his children."

I should say that nothing seemed to me quite so healthy, quite so wholesome and encouraging, as the life of the children in these communal colonies. This is not perhaps surprising, for, quite apart from all personal domestic questions, the members are lavishing an attention and devotion upon their children which constitutes the central passion of their lives. They are doing this, of course, for the children's sake. But they are also doing it for the colonies' sake. Right here in these children, they well know, is the final answer to the question as to whether their great communal experiment is going to succeed or not. Will these children be willing to endure the hardships and make the sacrifices that are the commonplace of their parents' lives? Will the second generation "stand by" and "carry on," or will they, as they come to manhood and womanhood, feel the itch for gain, the temptation to selfish ease and luxury, and drift back into the competitive world in quest of its glittering baubles of success? If these children fail, then, no matter what the parents have done, their adventure will fail as well. Hence a care for the children, a devotion to their interests, a sacrifice of all else to their needs, which is one of the loveliest and most touching things that I have ever seen. And the children are wonderful youngsters! I cannot believe that such stock, reared and trained with such clear-visioned service of high ends, can ever fail.

The question of religion in the *Kvutzoth* was naturally of interest to me as a clergyman. In the older and more conventional colonies—Petah Tikvah, for example—I saw synagogues, just as I saw them in cities like Jerusalem and Tel-Aviv. In the communal colonies, where most of the buildings are hardly more than barracks, and life is being lived on so primitive a basis of social organization, I did not expect to see a synagogue or meet a rabbi. But I was on the alert to catch some evidences of religious practice, either in the common house, or in some room set apart for worship and devotion. Nothing of the kind, however, could be seen. So far as the external physical aspect of the colonies was concerned, there was no religious life.

In answer to inquiries, I was told that the outward appearance of the settlements did not belie the inner reality. There were no synagogue services in these places, no rites and ceremonies of religion.

"You do not observe the Jewish Sabbath?" I asked.

"As a holiday," was the reply, "but not as a holy day. We stop work one day in every week, and that day is the Sabbath day of our race. But our observance is secular, not religious. We are obeying not the laws of Moses, but the laws of health and sanity."

"The real law behind the Mosaic law," I suggested, without objection from my host.

"But what about the children?" I continued. "Don't you teach them the Bible?"

"Yes," came the answer, "but not as a religious book. We teach the Bible to our children because it is the literature of our people. That is all!"

"How about marriages?" was my next question.

"Most of them are civil marriages," was the reply. "Some of our people are married in the synagogue, but they are few."

"But you don't object to religion?" I persisted.

"O, no," said my patient host. "Here, for example, in Beth Alpha," he continued, "we have one member who is devoutly religious. He and his family keep the Sabbath in the traditionally pious way, and are scrupulous in their observance of all the Sabbaths, holy days, dietary laws, etc. Such a member in our colony is not altogether a convenience. It is particularly difficult in the matter of food. But he is a good worker, a sincere man; we respect him, and do all we can to help him in his faithful observance of our religion."

Then I put a question which had been stirring in my mind during all this conversation. The gist of it was this: "You have come here to Palestine," I said, "to restore Israel. Now the unique genius of Israel was its spiritual genius, and its unique contribution to the world was its religion of Jehovah. Yet the Israel you are building in this colony does not foster, encourage, even formally recognize this religious ideal which was the glory of ancient Zion. How do you reconcile these facts? How are you restoring Zion, if you leave out the religion of your fathers?"

The answer was somewhat lengthy, but the burden of it, even in translation, was plain. "Our interpretation of religion is the interpretation laid down by the prophets. We have come here to this inhospitable land to give our lives to the restoration of Israel. We have left behind us comfortable homes, prosperous fortunes, some of us promising careers. We are living here in utter poverty, and laboring day and night to the limit of our strength. We shall never live to see the fruits of our toil. We simply trust that what we are doing will on some day, when we are gone, fulfill the dreams we dream, the visions we see. This, to our way of thinking, is religion. The life we live and the work we do is the practice of our faith."

There was something impressively familiar in this. I seemed to hear the ancient cry, "To what purpose is the multitude of your sacrifices unto me? Saith the Lord. . . . When ye come to appear before me, who hath required this at your hand? . . . Bring no more vain oblations; incense is an abomination unto me . . . it is inquity, even the solemn meeting." But does this mean that religion shall be reduced to the purely routine processes of the secular life? Is there to be no deliberate and well-ordered attempt to

ACHIEVEMENTS

cultivate those sanctities of inner thought and outer observance which are commonly associated with the religious spirit? Did not the prophets of Israel identify their social idealism with Israel's God, and did they not constantly call that God to the remembrance of his people? How can Israel be Israel any longer, if this God of her fathers be not kept in remembrance, and worshiped in recognition of his justice and mercy? These questions may be all a matter of "words, words." There is no doubt that the *Chalutzim* of Beth Alpha and other colonies of the type have within them the pure essence of religion. It would be a tragedy to impose upon them, for its own sake, the ceremonialism of the ancient synagogue. But should there not be developed out of the experiences of their own lives, the ideals of their own souls, a new synagogue which shall speak their language and cherish their faith? I cannot believe that religion, even of the freest type, can permanently survive as a merely latent, hidden thing. It cannot flow forever through a people's life as a buried river which never rises into the sunlight of human consciousness. Especially in Israel, if Israel is to preserve her peculiar character and genius, must there be developed in the new Zion, as in the old, some method of glad and free communal expression of a people's faith in the spirit that leads them on.

This brings me to the last and greatest thing that is to be said about these communal colonies. In all the Palestinian colonies, whatever their character, one feels the thrill and stir of an heroic movement for a great ideal. This movement does not quicken in the old colonies to-day as it does in the new—in Petah Tikvah and Rishon le Zion, for example, there is the calm content of deeds done and achievements wrought. But still, even in these older places, there is the uplift of this great adventure of the Jewish people for the redemption of Israel. Here are men and women who have come from the four quarters of the earth, left behind everything familiar and dear to their accustomed ways, hazarded all that life had to offer them, for the fulfillment of the dream of the Jews restored to the sacred soil of the land of Moses, David, and the Maccabees. These men and women have labored, and are laboring, like the slaves of old, only they are now free men cherishing a dream of larger freedom. They are planting vineyards in desert places, sweetening water that has long run with poison and decay, lifting songs in hills and vales long silent with the blight of death. They are reclaiming Israel—making sacred again and in a nobler way the homeland of their fathers. And the thrill of such a work is in the air these people breathe, and in the very dust they tread.

This you feel in the communal colonies, as in the others. But in the communal colonies you feel something else as well. It is the spirit of dedication not merely to the homeland, but to the world; it is the contagion of an enthusiasm not merely to reclaim the land of Palestine, but to fulfill therein those ideals of justice, righteousness and peace which through her prophets are Israel's greatest gift to humankind. The thought of the Communists far outreaches and transcends the bounds of any purely nationalistic movement. These Zionist dreamers see nothing to be gained, either for the Jews or for the world, in populating and planting Palestine as one more nation added to the already too many nations now existing upon the earth. What they see and welcome in Palestine is the chance to build a new kind of nation—to begin the age-old social experiment all over again—to avoid the mistakes that have cursed and ultimately destroyed all civilizations hitherto, and, by laying deep and sure at the start the durable conditions of brotherhood and peace, establish at last an ideal society of men.

This, to these Communist Jews, has from the beginning of her history been the unique mission of Israel. If the Jews are not here to lead mankind in ways of justice and larger freedom, exactly as taught by the ancient prophets, then they have no special calling; they have endured and suffered through the ages in vain, and now in this late day of liberation may as well merge their destiny with other men. But they *have* a special calling! God has called them to build the new Jerusalem, that shall be a light to all the nations. And this the Communists would do! More than any of the other colonists do these Communists embody that idea of spiritual fulfillment which lies at the heart of Zionism in its noblest, truest form. In these *Kvutzoth* one feels already the escape from that impulse of nationalistic reversion which is the besetting peril of the Zionist Movement. If the soul of Israel is saved, and her promise in Palestine redeemed, it will be more because of the *Kvutzoth* than of any other single influence.

It is this conscious sense of an ideal social mission that gives the communal colonies in Palestine a uniquely glorious character. Whether they succeed or fail, they are bestowing upon Zionism a luster of dream and vision of the ideal day to come, that already makes this Movement to be unparalleled among the pioneering movements of history.

"These other colonies are splendid," said a distinguished Palestinian leader to me, "but I can't get a bit excited about them. They are doing what has been done a thousand times before. It's the old individualistic system, working by the same old selfish methods to the same old selfish ends of material gain and power. But these communal colonies—here is something new! It is the heart of man refusing to be defeated in its eternal quest for brotherhood. The prophets are speaking once again in the lives of these pioneers. I had rather see Zion try and fail in the *Kvutzoth*. than succeed in the old fat and prosperous ways that we know so well in other countries underneath the sun. If man has any future, it is in these bitter, cruel struggles of undaunted men for a better way of life."

We had been talking in the common room at Beth Alpha for hours. The rain, lashed against the walls and windows by a driving gale, smothered our voices. The air, untempered by a ray of heat, congealed our breath to foggy vapor and chilled us to the bone. Dr. Magnes and I were dressed exactly as when we had arrived—our feet encased in heavy arctics, our bodies wrapped in our greatcoats, our hands covered with damp and soggy gloves. I looked at the room dimly lit by a central lamp suspended from the roof, the board floor smeared with the mud of many tracking feet, the long, rough wooden tables running the length of the room, the shabby piano in the corner, the low walls bare of picture or decoration. I looked at the colonists—sitting alone, or talking quietly in groups, two playing silently at chess in the dark farther end of the room. The night watchman came in, his boots heavy with mud to the knees, his coat dripping with rain, his rifle slung across his back. There was no animation, no gayety anywhere—scarcely a sound except the wind and rain. We were too cold to move, too wet to be of good cheer. Was it not time for bed?

I pondered the men with whom I had been talking. One was the man who had led us in to Beth Alpha that day. He was the son of a prosperous, middle-class family, a university graduate, a Doctor of Laws. Across the table was a second man, who had answered my questions. His dark, earnest, careworn face seemed to match his scholarly standing as a Doctor of Philosophy. We arose, took lanterns, and went out into the drenching night.

Industry

The second stage of social organization and development, next above agriculture, is industry. This is naturally in its infancy in Palestine. One wonders that in such a land, in so comparatively short a period of time, it has appeared at all. Yet the capital invested in industrial enterprises in Palestine since the War amounts to not less than six million dollars, of which at least ninety per cent is Jewish. In recent years alone, more than a hundred and fifty new undertakings have been launched. All of these are small, not a few failed in the years of industrial depression, but the great majority are successful and of momentous significance for the future.

Thus at Haifa, I saw just outside the city a large cement factory, which was white with the dust of a twenty-four hours' schedule of work each day. In this same city are a well-equipped and prosperous vegetable-oil factory and a modern, power-driven flour mill. In Tel-Aviv I visited and thoroughly inspected a busy hosiery factory.[4] This plant employed over a hundred men and women, and was projecting an addition to the factory which would double its capacity. An export trade to Egypt and Syria, as well as the domestic trade, was well developed. Other established industries in Palestine, all built and manned by Jewish labor, include soap, honey, salt, brick and tiles, and silk. Just ahead loom the vast developments promised by the exploitation of the hidden but rich mineral products of the Dead Sea.

The progress of industry in Palestine, along modern, competitive lines, is of course greatly handicapped by the lack of cheap and abundant power. This need is now being met

"Isn't that factory funny," cried an English woman in Jerusalem, when I told her of my visit. A characteristic remark!

by the great power works under construction at the falls of the Jordan and its branches by the famous Russo-Jewish engineer, Pinchas Rutenberg. I was unable to inspect this huge piece of engineering work, owing to the flood conditions prevailing when I passed by. But I could see at a distance its vast extent and its enormous potentialities. Already light and power are being supplied to Jaffa, Tel-Aviv, Haifa and Tiberias. Soon to all portions of the land, perhaps to Arab villages as well as to Jewish colonies, will extend the cables and wires that transform a world. To industry and its needs, of course, the Rutenberg Works mean the opening of a new era. These Works, by the way, were the only enterprise in Palestine that seemed to win the approval, even stir the enthusiasm, of the English officials. Here was something practical, business-like, up-to-date. They could understand it.

Among the cities of Palestine, Haifa promises to be the chief industrial center of the country. This is the reason, perhaps, apart from the natural features involved, why Haifa has been selected for the enormous harbor development which will soon be under way. Ten million dollars has been set aside for this vast undertaking. What the fishers, drawing their nets on the beach at Acre, will do when this work is completed, is a question which the toilers perhaps have not considered. But such fishing will be difficult, to say the least, when a port, second to none in the eastern Mediterranean, the natural outlet of the foreign trade not only of Palestine but of all the Near East, is opened to the shipping of the world.

Alone, in a class all by itself, is the city of Tel-Aviv. In every other place in Palestine, even in the youngest of the agricultural colonies, there is the feeling of antiquity. The land holds ancient memories of Israel, the horizon is dotted with the sacred names of kings and prophets. But everything is new in Tel-Aviv. Twenty years ago, in 1909, its site was nothing but a desert-like stretch of sand dunes on the Mediterranean shore. To-day it is a thriving city, with homes, schools, shops, synagogues, public buildings, all bearing the stamp of Western life and of our modern age. It gives one a curious feeling to walk the streets of this city, and try to realize that this is Palestine. Were it not for a passing camel train, or an occasional Arab in his native costume, one would never imagine that this bustling town was located within many thousand miles of the holy places of Zion.

Originally intended as a garden suburb for Jewish merchants, clerks and laborers working in the harbor city of Jaffa, Tel-Aviv in the days of rapid expansion after the War suddenly took on a civic life of its own. Growing in all directions along European rather than Oriental lines, it developed thriving commercial and business quarters, manufacturing enterprises, a trade union center which radiates its influence throughout the land, social and cultural institutions, schools, hospitals, and public health centers. The garden or residential features of the town are by no means lost. Plans for homes and playgrounds along the lovely shore of the Mediterranean give promise of a great population living happily together under ideal conditions of health, comfort and natural beauty. As Haifa is destined to be the great industrial and trade center of the future Zion, so Tel-Aviv is obviously destined to be the civic and social center of this Zion. The life of the new Israel, rooted deep in the reclaimed soil of the hinterland, will here blossom into those arts and cultures which are the fruits of labor and the justification, as they are the adornment, of civilized existence.

The picture of Palestine's economic future, which will come through whatever agonies of struggle and sacrifice, is not difficult to draw. All through the land will grow the colonies, like flowering oases of the desert or fruitful fields sprung from the empty prairies of America or Argentina. From these colonies, in ever swelling streams, will flow to the ports of Haifa and Jaffa, and across the borders of Syria and Egypt, the products of the labor of the *Chalutzim* —oranges, grapes, wine, olives, almonds, honey, dairy products, poultry, grains and vegetables. Modern railroads and automobile highways, threading the land along the old camel trails and mountain paths, will speed the flowing of these streams to coast line and frontier, and in exchange bring back the imports which for so long must supply the wants of Israel. In Haifa and at the Dead Sea will develop industries driven by enormous power plants fed from the falls of the Jordan. Tel-Aviv on the Mediterranean, like Tiberias on the Sea of Galilee, will become a civic center of the land. A fruitful hinterland, thriving ports and commercial centers, trade routes, factories, and homes— these constitute the basis of civilization. They are the rock foundation of the new Zion.

Schools

But civilization is more than economics, as "the life is more than meat and the body than raiment." On the foundation of agriculture and industry must be reared the edifice of culture. This marks the third and climactic stage of social development, upon the success of which depends the ultimate justification of all civilized existence. That the Zionists, in this early and difficult period of their Movement, have already reached this stage of development, and, amid the poverty and hazard of their days, are not forgetting the higher arts of life, is demonstration, if one is needed, of the character of the Jew and of his vision for mankind.

The cultural life of any people begins with its children

ACHIEVEMENTS

and their education. In Palestine, as I have already hinted, there is no public school system of the American, or even of the English, variety. By this I mean a system of schools maintained by the state for all children under a compulsory order of attendance. In the Holy Land any such system is precluded by the division of the inhabitants into Arabs and Jews, each group of which insists upon instruction in its own tongue. The Mandatory attempts to meet the situation, as I have pointed out, by money grants for educational purposes on a basis of actual population. The net result [5] is a system of Arab schools and Jewish schools, the former maintained by the public funds as "Government Schools," the latter supported in larger part by the Zionist organization as "Zionist Schools." Each group is enlarged by certain private schools and academies. In addition there are numerous Christian schools, maintained by missionary funds from abroad.

My acquaintance with Jewish schools began in Jerusalem. Thanks to the guidance of the enlightened Dr. I. K. Berkson, American Jew, graduate of Teachers' College, New York, member of the faculty of the Jewish Institute of Religion (on leave), head of the Zionist Schools in Palestine, this acquaintanceship constituted at the start a lesson in social evolution. We began with a Talmud school, privately supported, of the tightest traditional order, and then climbed step by step until we reached schools of the extreme modernist type. In Palestinian life all ages of the past, as well as all peoples of the earth, are represented.

Bright and early, on a chilly Sunday morning, we started our educational pilgrimage by a visit to a famous Talmud school founded in Jerusalem in 1841 by one of the great orthodox synagogues of the city. We learned upon inquiry that the institution had no endowment and charged no

[5] See Chapter III, page 155.

regular fees, but from the beginning had been supported by the voluntary offerings of the pious in many lands. Its curriculum is the study of the Bible (Old Testament) and the Talmud; its equipment, a building with rooms provided with tables, benches, and tattered copies of the sacred text. Instruction begins with very small boys in the Pentateuch and Prayer-Book, and extends in the next few classes to the Prophets. At eight years of age, the boys begin reading the Talmud, and continue the study and discussion of this mighty tome until they leave the school. In answer to some questions as to whether anything else was taught, we heard some vague references to arithmetic in the lower grades and astronomy in the upper grades. But we saw no signs of these or other studies. The boys, with their curious garb, their curling earlocks, their Hebrew texts, were learning the Law of their people. That was enough!

Shall I ever forget the classes in this school, as I passed from one room to another? In the lower classes, the boys clustered like swarming bees about a central table, at the head of which sat the teacher, a venerable bearded man, with peering eyes and kindly smile. Usually the boys were reading in unison—their fresh young voices shouting the text in a lusty singsong chant, their little bodies swinging back and forth from the hips in rhythmic beat with the words. As we entered, every voice would cease, every body stop its swaying as though suddenly frozen, every eye become riveted upon us as though we were some strange creatures from another planet, as indeed we were. Then, after a moment's salutation and explanation with the teacher, the signal would be given, and the chorus of voices would again be shouting, and the bodies swaying like the swing of oarsmen in a racing shell. The clamor became deafening, the excitement terrific. How much did these boys know of what they were thus reading with such rigid, mechanical precision? It was not until we came to some of the higher classes that this fearful singsong passed away. We now encountered discussion—as, for example, in a group of nine-year-old boys who were vigorously debating the Talmudic law of compensation for damages in person or to property. In still higher classes, we found the students ranged separately along the walls, each reading and swaying alone by himself, with the teacher pacing slowly up and down the length of the room, ready to answer questions or give explanation upon request. In the last room of all, studying silently by themselves, were the students who were giving their lives to the study of the Law, and thus never leaving the school at all. Some of these were of college age; others of mature years, married and the fathers of children, proudly supported by hard-working wives or parents; one was a venerable man with long white beard, not less than eighty years of age, who had been in the school longer than any teacher could remember. I watched this man, the oldest student I had ever seen, for some few moments. Never once did he lift his eyes from the book; only once was there any slightest motion—when he turned the page. Chanting and swaying had both disappeared before an inner absorption which was absolute. Here was the living symbol of one of the strangest phenomena in history—a people held together for ages without land or government, hearth or home, friendship or pity, through the mystic power of a book. It would have been easy to laugh at that old man. I felt only reverence for him. Yet I knew that his day was past, and his mission accomplished. For the feet of Israel are now set in new and happier paths.

We stepped into the street again, and it seemed as though at one stride we had moved from the Middle Ages into the modern world. The closing of the door was like the dropping of a curtain on a thousand years gone by. Yet we were not to "arrive" all at once. For our next school, while a Zionist institution supported by Zionist funds, was a sort of halfway station between the orthodoxy behind and the modernism before.

This school also was a Talmud School, but we quickly found that more emphasis was laid upon the Bible than upon the Talmud itself. As in our first school, all the students were boys; and instruction in the lower classes took the same form of singsong repetition of the sacred text. It was amazing how this material was drilled into these little heads. Without warning, the principal caught up a book and read a sentence here and there. Immediately these sentences were identified, chapter and verse, by a dozen eager shouters. As we went along from class to class, we were interested to discover instruction in other subjects which were made to grow naturally and easily out of the Bible study. Thus, blackboards began to appear, with figures and words and geometrical designs in the familiar chalking of our American schools. Here were modern maps for teaching in geography and history. Could the boys find New York? Why, here was a boy who came from New York, and there was a great laugh at the expense of the visitor. These boys were not merely looking into the Book; they were looking out from it as well. Was it significant that in this school I saw only one boy with the traditional earlocks upon his cheeks?

This school was representative of a distinct type of school supported by the Zionists—the transition type it may best, perhaps, be called. But most of the Zionist schools are of the more general modern type, and these I saw, this same morning, in the form of a kindergarten at the one end and a girls' grammar school at the other.

There is little to be said about these schools, so beautifully do they conform to all that is most progressive and enlightened in our modern methods of education. The kindergarten was a delight to eye and ear and mind. The rooms were modest, rather poor, but light, airy, clean, equipped with the familiar paraphernalia, surrounded by ample playgrounds and crowded with happy, healthy children. It was pitiful to hear that funds were lamentably scant for educational work of this kind.

As for the girls' grammar school, I could see no difference from our American schools, save that instruction was in Hebrew, and that there was definite study of the Old Testament literature. The standard of instruction I was able to test in an English class, where to my delight I found the girls reading a fairy story by Hans Christian Andersen. I noted with especial interest the fine system of health inspection, the lunches cooked by the pupils themselves in the school kitchen, the large vegetable gardens grown by the pupils, and the up-to-date athletic playground. Schools of this kind are dotting the land, yet they are hard to support, so scant is the English dole, and so inadequate the Zionist funds for all the pressing needs of the Movement.

No account of educational work in Jerusalem would be complete which omitted mention of the Open-Air Playground maintained by the Guggenheimer Foundation. Located in a large space of sloping ground at the base of an old Crusaders' wall, and looking out eastward over Kedron to the Mount of Olives, this playground is frequented daily throughout the year by an average of some three hundred children. This would be no remarkable thing, perhaps, in America, but it is a remarkable thing in Palestine, primarily because the children are indiscriminately Arabs and Jews together. Here is a deliberate attempt to lay the ax at the root of that alienation between these two races which threatens the future of Palestine more terribly than any other single fact. And it is a successful attempt!

Trouble was not infrequent in the beginning. But long since it has disappeared, not only among the children, but gradually also among their parents as well. I searched the little faces, the day I visited the Playground, for any consciousness of difference, any evidence of prejudice or fear. I could find none. Indeed, I had difficulty in deciding which were Jewish children and which were Arab. All were playing happily together, and seemed to be members of one family. Children know how to be friends, even if adults do not.

The modern schools seen in Jerusalem are typical of the Zionist schools planted all over the land in Jewish centers. The schools in Tel-Aviv are remarkable from every standpoint—buildings, organization, teaching. They include kindergartens, elementary schools, secondary schools, technical schools, a gymnasium or high school, a normal school, and a school of commerce. Even in the agricultural colonies, in the remotest sections of the country, there are schools of the highest standard. In Beth Alpha I saw the superintendent of instruction—a university man, relieved of all manual labor that he might give his whole time and strength to training the children. It is a remarkable achievement, this spread of education through an ancient and now newly settled land, comparable to nothing but the founding of the early schools of colonial New England.

I visited some special and higher educational institutions during my stay in Palestine, which are of equal importance with the general school system of the country. In Haifa, for example, I found the splendid Technicum, a high-class co-educational technological institute, with preparatory school, housed in fine buildings erected by the German Jews before the War, and now taken over by the Zionists. The Technicum maintains two departments—civil engineering and architecture—and is prepared to organize other departments as soon as money can be found. It receives Jews and Arabs alike, conducts evening classes for workers, and maintains a lending library of technical books open to all citizens of the town, irrespective of race. In Tel-Aviv, I inspected the Herzlia Gymnasium, a private collegiate institute for boys and girls. Here were seven hundred and fifty pupils following a twelve-year course (through second year in college) under instruction of a high order.

At the head of such institutions as these, the crown of the whole educational system of Zion, in some ways "the best gem upon (the) zone" of Jewish Palestine, is the Hebrew University. This institution was founded in 1918, as a superb gesture of faith. As Dr. Weizman laid the cornerstone of its first building, the British army had just entered Jerusalem; the beaten Turks were retreating to the north, leaving death and destruction in their path; the country lay silent and desperate, and the people starving. What the far-visioned leader of Zionism did on that day was scarcely noticed and soon forgotten. But when the wounds of the land began to heal, and its homes and haunts to be rebuilt, especially as the new tide of Jewish settlers began to pour in from every quarter, it was remembered. Land was purchased on Mt. Scopus, ground was broken and the first buildings erected, and in the month of Nisan (April), 1925, the Hebrew University was formally opened and dedicated by Lord Balfour. To-day the university has teachers, students, research workers, and a few world-famous scholars, such as the great Joseph Klausner. It has a number of permanent and beautiful buildings, notably the new Library. In a decade this institution has developed a Chemical Institute, an Institute of Physics and Mathematics, an Institute of Jewish Studies, a Medical Library, with a medical center, hospital, and school of tropical medicine in the offing. Lecture hall, dormitories, homes for professors, are still to come.

The Chancellor of the University, Dr. Judah L. Magnes, formerly of New York, is one of the ablest scholars and most brilliant teachers in the Jewish rabbinate. It was good to share his enthusiasm as he led me through the scattered rooms, rented here and there in the city, in which the newborn institution had started and was still continuing much of its life. It was touching to see his devotion to his colleagues, distinguished scholars of Hebrew literature and lore, of world science and religion, whom he had gathered about him to lift the torch of learning in this ancient land. It was like a pilgrimage to climb the slopes of Mt. Scopus, and see the buildings which now crown this noble crest, the nucleus of the great university which is to be.

Surely, no institution ever had a nobler site. Scopus, the camp of all the conquerors of Jerusalem from Titus to Allenby, is the loftiest elevation above the Holy City. From it may be seen, to the east, the River Jordan and the Dead Sea; to the west the mountains of Judæa; and all before, the spreading beauty of the City of David. Upon this hill stand the research laboratories, the Einstein Building for scientific instruction, the amphitheater, and the great Library. Two hundred thousand precious volumes, rich with the treasures of Eastern lore, are to be housed in this new structure. Notable among these books is a collection of Arabic literature which in character and worth is unexcelled. For, with the vision of a prophet matching the wisdom of a scholar, Dr. Magnes has determined to make his university a center for the restoration of Arabic as well as of Hebrew culture. The Arabs of Palestine, as we have seen, are a neglected, a forgotten part of Islam. Hence the chance to serve Arab as well as Jew, and in the rekindling of the love of knowledge to find that road of reconciliation which the feet of both must some day tread! In these early years of the University, Dr. Magnes has wisely laid emphasis upon research study by chosen scholars rather than upon routine teaching of hastily gathered and ill-prepared students. And in no field of research has he opened a nobler path than this renaissance of general Oriental culture.

We climbed to the roof of the library building, to survey the landscape. It was a noble prospect which lay before our gaze. It seemed to me to be the outward image of the noble spiritual prospect which the Chancellor had been spreading before my inward gaze that day. Dr. Magnes said little about how he raised his funds. I saw in what utter simplicity he and his faculty members are living. I noted the narrow inadequate quarters in which much of their work is being done. That this university should have been started at all is one of the glories of Zion. That it has grown so fast and so far is one of the miracles of Zion. That it should languish, even amid present horrors, would be one of Zion's tragedies.

Health Work

From the beginning of settlement in Palestine, nothing was deemed to be more important than systematic health work of the most extensive and thoroughgoing character. If the Jews were to survive at all, the land must be cleansed and the native inhabitants taught how to live. The cities, before the coming of the English administrators, were open cesspools of waste and filth. The open country was poisoned with foul springs and vaporous marshes. Typhoid, malaria, tuberculosis competed in an orgy of death for the lives of the population. Trachoma and other diseases of the eye were taking their pitiful toll of blindness. Before the pest-laden atmosphere of this land, the first pioneers of Israel fell like charging soldiers before machine guns. As the Pilgrim fathers in Plymouth were stricken by the cold of their first winter, so the pioneers in Petah Tikvah were stricken by the pestilential heat of their first summer. In the one place as in the other, more than half of the original group of settlers perished of exposure and disease. The survivors in Palestine fled their homes as before the attack of an enemy. The land must be drained, the waters purified, the settlements equipped with physicians and nurses, if the work was to go forward to success.

To this vast work of sanitation and public health, the Zionist Movement has given itself with tireless energy, trained skill, and boundless generosity. All through the land to-day are hospitals and diet kitchens. In the slums of the cities and in the remote settlements of the open country are the medical stations of Hadassah, with physicians and trained nurses at the disposal of the people. It was an amazing experience to step through a doorway in a narrow Jerusalem street, crowded with camels, asses, berobed men, veiled women—all the cluttered circumstance of Eastern life—and find oneself in hospital wards, operating rooms, X-ray laboratories, as modern, if not as elaborate, as those familiar to me in New York. It stirred me to pass the low archway and tread the narrow passages of a stone tenement built in the days of the Crusaders, and in a little room open to the wintry weather, crowded with a wretched family of children and animals, find a trained nurse teaching a sick and discouraged mother how to make the most and best of her wretched home. It lifted my heart to visit the nurses' training school in the Holy City, and the great health center newly built and lavishly equipped by Nathan and Lina Straus. But nothing quite so opened my eyes as the hospital which I found in the distant colony of Ain Harod!

I had been riding through the wet and cold of the bleakest countryside I had ever seen; I had been sharing the barest and most comfortless living conditions I had ever known.* Heroic men and women housed in barracks, set in a sea of mud, in the waste and empty spaces of the Emek valley! I was splashing and floundering about on a tour of inspection of the settlement, and came suddenly to a building that seemed different from the rest. In the first place, it was fenced off and set back from the road, as though in a little park. It was pleasantly surrounded by shrubs and plants which I knew in the sunny weather of this tropic clime must be gorgeous and fragrant with blossoms. A welcome path led from the gate on through clustering bushes to a doorway which opened on a roomy hall. To the left was a reception room; to the right an office, equipped with business-like desk and chairs, a telephone, diplomas and charts upon the walls, and in the center an alert young man, clad in surgeon's coat and apron, who beamed upon me with smiles and open hands. I was in a hospital, and this was the head physician.

I have seldom had so curious a feeling as that which dogged me as I examined this hospital. Here I was six thousand miles distant from New York. In recent weeks I had passed through countries and dwelt in cities which were bestrewn with the crumbling monuments of dead civilizations. In all these lands I had seen native populations whose primitive conditions of meager and dirty living had come down unchanged from ages not yet uncovered to the historian's eye. This very day I had seen reeking mud huts of the Arab such as had dotted this land for a thou-

* See Chapter I, pages 20-22.

sand years; I had passed shepherds and sheep which might have been specters from Abraham's day; my path, as lonely as the trails of all the dead, had been crossed by wild animals and beset by the waste and ravage of forces untamed by man. At last I had come to this lone settlement of Zion where life was so poor, conditions so forlorn. And here, as though a magician had waved his wand, I was moving through a hospital which, apart from the contracted spaces and crude architecture of the simple wooden building, might have been a wing of some institution on Fifth Avenue.

Everything was on a small scale, of course. There were no quiet laboratories, no X-ray rooms, no operating arenas. But here, in this remote corner of a lost and wasted land, was all that science needed for its essential work. To right and left of the hallway, in the rear, were the men's and women's wards—clean, wholesome, bright with snowy linen, warm with the smiles of contented faces. These wards had sixty beds, I was told, eighty in emergency, with a new wing now under construction for many more. I expressed surprise that so many beds were needed for a settlement no larger than Ain Harod. Whereupon I learned that this hospital was not a local institution, but a medical center, maintained by the great workers' organization in Palestine, for all the valley. When a prospective mother approached her time, for example, she was conveyed here from her village, near or far, and in this hospital brought her child into the world. I saw one such mother returning home after such a visitation. Her little baby in her arms, her stalwart husband by her side, she was taking the train up Jordan way.

I was interested in these maternity cases. "How many do you have," I asked the head physician. "We average about two hundred and fifty a year," he said. Then, with a proud and eager smile, he continued, "Last month (January), we had thirty-one—a baby a day. That was a record."

I marveled at what I was seeing. I marveled again, in a more modest way, when later on we met the trained veterinary riding his horse through the mud and rain to visit the cattle. Was there ever such a combination of primitive living with the best of scientific method and equipment? It was as though the Pilgrims had crossed the Atlantic with physicians as well as clergymen, had built hospitals along with their churches in Plymouth and Duxbury, and had seen their offspring reared by trained nurses and expert child specialists. What can Zion not do under such conditions? Never in history has a pioneering movement been so equipped with the knowledge and technique necessary for the realization of ideal social life upon the earth. These *Chalutzim* have all the spirit of devotion and sacrifice that ever men and women have had anywhere. In addition they have what their predecessors in other ages, in strange, forbidding lands, have never had—the resources of the most highly developed and carefully organized body of knowledge that the world has ever known. Just because of this fact these Jewish settlers, whatever the initial difficulties and the recurring dangers and disappointments in their adventure, are already far advanced toward the fulfillment of more than man has dared to dream before.

Cultural Life

But there are higher ranges still in modern Israel. Not only the bodies, but the minds and souls of the people must be served! Hence, in Tel-Aviv, which promises to become the cultural center of the Jewish homeland, are the beginnings to-day of the arts and crafts which are to flourish so abundantly in days to come.

I had my introduction to the cultural life of the Jews in

Palestine on my second evening in Tel-Aviv, when we attended a public performance of the Ohel Dramatic Studio, an amateur organization of players drawn from the ranks of the working men and women of the community. This particular performance was in honor of a lamented comrade, Joel Engel, a musical composer of distinction who had died unexpectedly two years before in the full flower of his genius. Four one-act plays, all of them original dramatizations of stories of Jewish life, were chosen for this evening's program because of the incidental music which had been written for them by Engels. A portrait of the composer, adorned with a wreath, hung at the right of the stage. A brief memorial address was given by the director of the players, a talented Jew from Russia. An invisible orchestra and chorus furnished thrilling music at well-timed intervals during the performances, which were given in the extreme form of the *grotesquerie* associated with the futurist school of dramatic art, and with a verve, devotion and artistry by the actors which were impressive. I learned that these actors were all volunteers, who gave freely of their time and strength to the cultivation of a native drama in Israel. Players, musicians, stage hands, scene painters, carpenters, electricians, all were wage earners in Tel-Aviv. Not satisfied with productions in this city and in Jerusalem, the members of Ohel were accustomed, at severe personal sacrifice, to go out into the working centers and agricultural colonies in various parts of the country, and present their plays to the hungry toilers who crowded any available shack, or looked on in the open air. I was told that, at this very time, the players had just finished the production of an original dramatization of the Isaac and Rebecca story, and were now preparing a production of Stefan Zweig's great Biblical and poetic play, "Jeremiah." A large audience was gathered on this night of the Engel memorial, most of them young men and women, all conspicuously of the working class. There was no interruption of the plays by applause, though the players were familiar and popular figures, but there was rapt, almost reverential attention throughout.

The next evening in Tel-Aviv, I was promised a concert by the local orchestra, the Palestine Ensemble. A Beethoven symphony was on the program, and I was all excitement. To my deep regret, circumstances interfered with attendance upon this occasion, and I thus missed the chance of hearing an orchestra which for three years, under expert direction, has presented the best classical music to packed audiences of Jewish men and women.

And there is not only an orchestra but an opera in Tel-Aviv. Its performances were suspended, and its company scattered at the time of my visit to the city, but the director, absent in America in the interests of the opera, was due soon to return and resume performances of the standard works in the repertoire. It stirred me to hear of the festival performance of Verdi's "Aïda" which had made notable the latest season of the company.

As a community center for plays and music, a cultural shrine of the masses, is Beth Ha-Am, the People's House. At first, in the early days of Tel-Aviv, this house was nothing but an open, sandy plot of land, enclosed by a tall fence and furnished with a makeshift stage. On this stage, crude as it was, Jascha Heifetz played his violin, and Dr. Weizman spoke, to thousands of men and women standing or squatting on the ground. Later a more permanent stage was built, a cement flooring laid, and chairs arranged. An adequate building is now projected for this great center. Here all public performances of plays and operas are presented. And here, when professional recitals, concerts and lectures have been heard by selected audiences in hired halls, it is the custom to present them once at least for the general public. Prices of admission to such performances at the Beth Ha-Am are kept at a minimum by city ordinance.

Oneg Shabat (Sabbath Rejoicing) is a remarkable institution founded and maintained by the great poet, Bialik, leader in the contemporary renaissance of Hebrew literature in Palestine, "for the recapture of the traditional Sabbath pleasures by the study and discussion of all questions pertaining to Judaism, past and present." Twice every Saturday, morning and afternoon, Bialik and his colleagues lecture, lead discussions, or open debates on pressing problems of the day. To accommodate the crowds who throng to these assemblies, a great edifice, to be known as Ohel-Shew, is now in course of construction.

Activities of this kind, springing up spontaneously in a prosperous community like Tel-Aviv, reveal the genius of the Jew for things of the mind and spirit. They are an answer also to my complaint of the æsthetic poverty of life in the communal settlements. This amazing race cannot be satisfied with material achievement. Long excluded from the cultural life of the civilizations which beat like an unfriendly sea upon their ghetto walls, driven by the cruel circumstances of their unnatural existence into narrow, tortured grooves of self-expression, the soul of the Jew has had no more chance to develop normally and beautifully than the fettered feet of the women of old-time China. But now he is liberated. The Jew is back on the land, his own land, starting all over again, from the beginning, the evolution of his racial life. And already his cultural genius is made manifest. Even while the roots of his endeavor are reaching down desperately to grip the new soil and draw from it a meager sustenance, the plant itself is beginning to blossom and bear fruit. Out from this weary struggle with the land, in the midst of daily peril from the savage aggression of hostile native tribes, under the rule of an unfriendly government and the regard of an indifferent world, there spring the art and song, the poetry and drama, which mark the higher reaches of man's soul. The hardy New Englander, battling with his ax against the forest and with his musket against the redskin, built no theaters, wrote no poetry, composed no music. *His* Old Testament flowered in no beauty of this description. But the Jew, from out his battle against the enmity alike of nature and of man, makes

"New arts to bloom of loftier mould."

By some divine alchemy of the spirit he achieves in the first half-century of the life of his new Zion not only the labors but the arts of civilization. I saw many wonderful things in Palestine. None more wonderful than the blossoming culture of the land!

The Hebrew Renaissance

But I have yet to mention the most romantic and in some ways the most remarkable event in the history of the cultural development of this new land. I refer to the revival of the Hebrew language as the spoken language of a people.

For centuries this ancient tongue has been as dead as Greek and Latin. It was used by rabbis and scholars in the synagogues, as the languages of Greece and Rome are used to-day in the ancient churches and modern universities of Christendom. But to the Jewish people, wide-scattered in many lands, this traditional language was only a language of prayer. In the business of daily life, the Jews used the vernaculars of the regions of their sojourning, or in the ghetto the debased medieval German known as Yiddish.

That the Jews would ever learn again to speak the language of Isaiah and Jeremiah, which began to be displaced by Greek or Aramaic even before the Roman destruction of Jerusalem, seemed as improbable a few years ago as that Europeans would learn again to speak the language of Cicero or Plato. I remember how, when I entered the theological school, I was discouraged from studying Hebrew on the ground that this language was deader even than the dead languages of the classic world. Yet in the space of two generations one lonely and heroic scholar, the immortal Eliazer Ben Yehudah, resolved that this miracle should be achieved. He started the task in his own household. I have heard the son of this reformer, the distinguished Palestinian journalist, Ittamar Ben-Avi, tell of the despair of his young mother when her husband solemnly announced one day that, from that moment forth, he would never speak to any living soul, not even to his wife and children, anything but the Hebrew tongue. He kept his word. Silence reigned within the home until painfully, word by word, the mother had learned something of the ancient language. The children must learn this language as well—and *only* this language! For years, Ben-Avi told me, he and his sister were kept rigorously apart from all other children, lest the purity of their Hebrew speech be defiled. Not until the language had become fixed within them beyond the possibility of corruption, were the children released into the school and on to the playground. It was amusing, and also pathetic, to hear this ardent son of his father tell of his amazement and confusion when he met other children, and found that they could not understand his speech, nor he theirs. At how great a price are all reforms bought!

From this one center of contagion, the influence spread. To-day in all of Jewish Palestine no other language is used but the ancient language of the prophets. In homes and lecture halls and public meetings, in newspapers and books, in letters and public documents, the Old Testament

ACHIEVEMENTS

tongue is the universal medium of intellectual exchange. With this language, long dead but now miraculously alive again, merchants sell their wares, women sing their songs, children play their games. There is a highly developed Hebrew profanity and Hebrew slang. Even animals to-day have Hebrew ears. Thus, a stubborn horse, which I was riding on a trip in Palestine, could not be moved until eloquently addressed in the language of the Old Testament. To perpetuate and glorify the work which single-handed he had begun, Eliazer Ben Yehudah dedicated his life to the production of a huge encyclopedic dictionary of the modern Hebrew tongue. To keep the language pure and up-to-date, a committee of scholars sits in Jerusalem, and issues once a month a list of approved new words, to name objects and describe phenomena unknown to the orators and writers of Old Testament days. The marvel of this achievement is well-nigh incredible. In the life time of one man an entire people has gained the familiar use of a language dead and buried for more years than the span covered by the Christian era. To match it, there is nothing known to the historical experience of mankind. To imagine it, one must think of the people of our world all suddenly learning to speak the Latin of Cæsar or the Greek of Homer.

I had not known of this revival of Hebrew until I arrived in Palestine. I had heard, of course, that the ancient tongue was spoken, but had not realized that its use was universal among all classes of the Jewish population. My first reaction upon the amazing phenomenon was one of dismay. Are there not enough languages in the world, that still another must be added? Is there not already abundant confusion in Palestine itself, without the Jews contributing their peculiar tongue to the existing Babel of tongues? Is any fact in human relationships more manifest than that differences of speech lie at the bottom of differences of temper and feeling as between nations, races, and religions? The great need of the world to-day, if men are ever to know one another and dwell together in peace, is a common language in which they may all be heard and understood. The whole tendency of our age, in this matter of speech, is in the direction of simplification—a common alphabet, a universal tongue. Yet the Jews complicate matters by reviving an old language, happily dead; and by deliberately choosing, in a land rife with international and inter-racial rivalries, to speak a tongue which nobody can understand but themselves! Is this not an unhappy evidence of that race pride which it should be the first business of Zion to subdue? What does it make of Jewish Palestine but the very thing which we have deplored and feared—one more nation among too many nations, with a narrow and bitter nationalism of its own to vex mankind?

Such objection to the revival of the Hebrew language is obvious, and also superficial. It altogether ignores one central factor in the Palestinian problem, familiar to the Jew, but unfamiliar to the Gentile. The new Zion, as we have seen, is to be the homeland of Israel. It is to be built, sustained and cherished by the whole world of Jewry. Already pioneers to the ancient land have come from Russia, Poland, Roumania, Czecho-Slovakia, Hungary, Germany, France, England, America, Bokhara, Turkestan, Dughestan, South Arabia (Yemen), and Morocco. They bring with them their children, their household goods, their capital (if they have any), their religion, their native ways—and their native language! How are these *Chalutzim* to communicate with one another? How can the Jew from Samara talk with the Jew from Frankfort, or the family from Yemen do business with the family from New York? It is true, to be sure, that most of the pioneers come in groups, and settle as groups in agricultural colonies or city neighborhoods of their own. But they cannot remain apart in such colonies or neighborhoods. Nothing could be more fatal to the life of Zion than a separation of its people into a congeries of little, isolated groups, divided along lines of local and national origin. The homeland must be a single community. It has no reason for existence, at such expense of sacrifice and labor, if it does not unite the Jews, after their long centuries of tragic dispersion over all the face of the earth, into an organism which flows with a single life-stream propelled from the beating heart of Israel. The Jews of Palestine must from the beginning be one family. Which means that, from the beginning, they must have one language which all can speak and all can understand!

What shall that language be? What can it be but the language which was spoken by the fathers when Israel was once a people, which preserves to this day the sacred literature of the race, and which in its memories and traditions has held the race to the only unity it has known in the days of its dispersion? Any other language would be alien and artificial. It would from the start cut off the Jews from that common heritage and character which it was the very purpose of Zionism to restore and preserve. If they adopted Arabic, or English, or even Yiddish in any form, as their common tongue, they would sooner or later degenerate into that mongrel type of life from which they are now so laboriously striving to escape. The restoration of Zion means the restoration, as vital forces of contemporary life, of the ideals which once made Zion great and distinctive among the nations of the earth. The restoration of these ideals involves the understanding and love and *use* of the language which they kindled into flame upon the lips of the ancient prophets. As a matter of fact, the Hebrew tongue is not, and never has been, dead. Latin is dead because Rome is dead. Greek is dead because Sophocles and

Plato and Demosthenes have no spiritual descendents. But Hebrew lives because Jewry lives. It has slept, as Zion has slept for ages, awaiting the hour of awakening. That hour has now come. With the restoration of Israel comes the restoration of Israel's speech. As surely as the city of God shall be reared again upon Mt. Zion, so surely shall the words of its prophets be spoken again within its homes and upon its streets.

The revival of the Hebrew language met a social need which could be met in no other way. It was an integral part of the tremendous task of reuniting a people, long divided and far scattered, in the ancient homeland of their race. It was as natural as it was inevitable. It thus had none of the deliberate artificiality, was tainted by none of the egoistic race pride and national antagonisms, of the Gaelic revival, for example, in Ireland. This revival had no basis in the vital needs of a people. The Irish had been persecuted, as only the Jews had been persecuted before them, but they were living together in their own country, on their native soil, and were speaking a common language. This language, to be sure, was the language of their conquerors and oppressors. But it was now also their own by long usage, and in its usage had assumed a flavor and produced a literature as native to Ireland as "the old sod" itself. The Gaelic movement, an attempt to teach the Irish to abandon English and return to the ancient tongue of centuries before, was just a part of the revolt against English tyranny, and passed when that revolt achieved its aim. It had nothing essentially to do with the renewal of Irish life, and therefore found no rootage in the Irish heart. Gaelic did not suddenly become a people's language in Ireland, as Hebrew did in Palestine. The plaything of certain sincere artists and scholars, it produced for a while in Dublin an exotic literature, but never produced, as Hebrew is now producing in Jerusalem and Tel-Aviv, a literature which springs as naturally from the life of the people as oranges and grapes from the soil which they plow. In nothing is the revival of the ancient Hebrew tongue in Palestine so remarkable as in this production of a contemporary, native song and story for the new homeland of the race. At the center of this movement stands Bialik, poet, novelist, publisher, prophet. I met this man, and heard the "rapt, seraphic fire" of his speech. His poems, I was told, had the beauty and power, as they had the form, of the Isaiahan prophecies. His stories for children revealed the simplicity and native folk-genius of Hans Andersen. As a translator, he was indefatigable; one of his most popular works in this form was "Alice in Wonderland." And his songs, like the songs of Burns and Moore, were the ballads of a people's heart.

Where Bialik leads to-day, young men and women are eagerly following. Hebrew journals and magazines are multiplying beyond the capacity of the new country to support them. Wandering poets, after the style of Vachel Lindsay in America, pass from colony to colony, from home to home, and chant their verses for food and the night's lodging. Ohel has no difficulty in finding and producing native plays. And back into the lore of their ancient people go these eager questing minds, to find legends and folk tales, ritual songs and ghetto superstitions, which they may add, as living treasures of memory, to the riches of the race. If the new Zion has a new culture, it is because it has again, as a new experience, the old language of the fathers. The rebirth of Hebrew was the rebirth of Israel's soul. In this achievement, more than in all else beside, is Zion justified.

As I write these words, my mind goes back over the pageant of Palestine. I see at "Dilb" those thousands of little trees planted on the hill slopes above the colony, that savage bull staked and chained in a remote corner of the settlement, that happy group of men and women binding grapevine twigs into bundles for sale as fuel. I see that deep well just dug on the open and empty plain of Nathanyah, and the eager pioneer descending gayly into the cool depths of the excavation to bring up a handful of the wet sand, to prove that they had found water. I see those thousands of oranges, piled up like heaps of gold, in the sorting room at Petah Tikvah, with the silent, busy workers, Arabs and Jews together, quickly dividing large from small and good from bad. I see that lively girl in the Girls' Settlement, standing tall and slender as a cypress tree, with soiled trousers, heavy, mud-stained boots, upturned sleeves, laughing and chatting with her hundreds of hens inside the poultry yard. I see the dust and hear the clamor of the cement works outside of Haifa. I stand on Carmel, and look down upon the waters of the port where lie quietly at anchor two ships, forerunners of the fleets which will ride within this roadstead in days not far ahead. I walk the streets of Tel-Aviv, and watch the passing of camel trains and modern automobiles through crowded streets, directed by traffic policemen. I watch the teachers in the schools as they teach the elements of modern knowledge to the eager minds of Jewish youths and maidens. I run through the elaborate card catalogue in the library of the University. I speak to the sick in hospitals, and listen to scientific experts expound the intricate details of research experimentation. I go to the play, and listen to the music of instruments and voices. I talk with Henrietta Szold, Arthur Ruppin, Judah Magnes, and learn the statescraft of Zion. I sit with Joseph Klausner among his books,[7] and examine his new manuscript on

---

[7] One of the earliest excesses of the August (1929) outbreaks of the Arabs was the sacking of Professor Klausner's home and the destruction in large measure of his library.

St. Paul. I hear Bialik's flaming speech, and listen as he recites his latest verse.

Fifty years ago all this was but a dream. Over the barren hills of Palestine wandered Arab shepherds and Bedouin horsemen. Little groups of goatskin tents, black with sun and rain, showed where the Bedouin were squatting for a few weeks' pasturage. A hundred mud huts, clustered beneath the shelter of a hill, revealed the village of some Arab sheik. Wooden plows scratched stray sections of the soil for a scanty harvest. Along narrow trails moved camels and asses bearing the rude products of the countryside to market. In fetid cities traders quarreled, and bought and sold. A thousand holy places marked the landscape, while Moslem and Christian priests kept jealous watch. And Jews, wretched but pious, observed the holy Sabbath, and waited to mingle their bones with the dust of Abraham and Isaac. A dead land, parched with sun, poisoned with rain, blasted with all the lusts that curse men's souls! Where did the Jews find courage to reclaim this waste? What but the tortures of their tribe, and the besetting dream of Zion, could bring them hence? And they have come! In what must seem to them like a single tick upon the dial of their racial history, they have reared secure and firm, leaping sheer from foundation to pinnacle, the structure of civilization.

"The seed shall be prosperous; the vine shall give her fruit, and the ground shall give her increase, and the heavens shall give their dew . . .
And it shall come to pass, that as ye were a curse among the heathen, O house of Judah, and house of Israel, so will I save you, and ye shall be a blessing. Fear not, but let your hands be strong."
Zechariah 8:12-13.

CHAPTER V

THE PROMISE

Success

THE achievements of Zionism are the answer to all doubts as to its success. In a scant half-century of time, a hundred and fifty thousand Jews have migrated to Palestine; more than a hundred colonies (two a year!) have been planted on the land; industries have been established and an export trade developed; kindergartens, schools and technical institutes have been founded, and scholars and students gathered in a university; hospitals have been opened, and a network of health stations flung over the land; and seeds of culture, sown in the soil of the ancient tribal speech, are already springing to the life and beauty of a racial renaissance. In less than the space of two generations, Zion has become a deep-founded, full-rounded society.

This is success. But is it permanent success?

It must be permanent! There is an imperative in this undertaking which is inescapable. The Jews are a frustrated people. Defeated, driven, degraded, they have lived for ages as prisoners in a dungeon. They have been confined behind the walls of outlawry, fed with the bread and water of affliction, subdued to the will of jailors and persecutors. Through all these centuries they have been able never to express but only to possess their souls, waiting for some deliverance that would restore to them their thought and life as a free, self-mastered people. What has kept them alive, as we have seen, is the conviction of this deliverance. Burning within their tortured breasts was the inextinguishable faith that some day they would be free and thus able to fulfill their destiny. Dreams and visions, fixed for fruition upon Palestine, were literally their "meat day and night" in these generations of suffering. Should these now fail, it would be the end. For this would be a defeat of the Jews at their own hands. Not by the sword of the conqueror nor by the rod of the oppressor would they be overthrown, but by their own inadequacies and futilities. Their failing faith, their meager courage, their spirit not strong enough to match the temper of their desire! As a climactic irony of fate, frustration would have come to the Jews at last not from without but from within, and such frustration would be final. The Zionist Movement, to my mind, marks a turning point in the history of Israel. Jewry will now rise, never to fall again; or else it will now fall, never to rise again. It is because the inner crisis is now so great, that I feel there must be a success in Palestine which will endure.

And there *will* be such a success—if Jewry does not falter or fail in its support of the *Chalutzim!* During the War, we learned the importance of the nation, as contrasted with the army. If victory were won, we were told, it would be won not so much by the soldiers on the battle front as by the workers on the home front, who provided the food, the clothing, the guns, the ammunition, which kept these troops an effective fighting force. There was no question about the fitness of the men in the trenches—their discipline, efficiency, and valor. They could be trusted to fight to the end—as they did, on both sides! But what about the men and women, far from the battlefield, whose labor, money, sacrifice, devotion, must sustain the cause? Would these

THE PROMISE

fight to the end? The nation that collapsed first at home, was the nation that would lose the war. And so it proved!

The situation in Palestine, in its cruder aspects, is similarly a war. A battle is being fought by heroic Jews, not with the weapons of death but with the implements of life, to overcome the terrific resistance of nature and of men to the hopes of Zion. These Jews, the *Chalutzim*, are being supported by the resources of Israel, as they must continue to be supported until the country is enabled to produce by the toil of its own citizens its own resources. In the long campaign ahead, the *Chalutzim* are not going to fail. They are watering the sterile soil of their ancient fatherland with the sweat of their labor and on occasion with the blood of their sacrifice. They have no intention, however bitter and prolonged the struggle, of giving up. Witness, for example, Bne Benjamin, who have taken upon themselves the solemn pledge to stay in Palestine and carry on what their forebears have so nobly begun! Hitherto Zion has recruited its strength exclusively from without; with the organization of this society of youth, it begins the recruiting of its strength from within. The new generation as·well as the old, in other words, are highly resolved to finish the work they are in—to see their heroic undertaking through to victory, if not for themselves, then for their children and those others who come after. But will the people at home, in their security and ease, finish their work? Will they see this undertaking through? Will the world of Jewry outside of Palestine sustain the fight in Palestine?

Upon this question hangs the whole destiny of Zion. The investment in the enterprise of the Jewish national home is a long-term investment. It has run for fifty years without return in terms of economic self-support. It is true, as the skeptical English official told me, that Jewish colonies in Palestine are sustained exactly like Christian missions—

by offerings from abroad. It is also true that this situation of support from abroad must continue for another fifty years. No man can yet see the day when Zion will be standing upon its feet, upheld alone by its own independent strength and effort. But if the *Chalutzim* are undismayed by an outlook of a hundred years,[1] why not the supporters of these *Chalutzim*, who themselves are never to feel the privations and sufferings of these years? Who that knows the Jew, and what he has already triumphantly endured through centuries of hope deferred, can doubt his determination and capacity to endure this last trial of his faith? One thing is certain—that, if the world of Jewry stands by the national homeland unfalteringly, without complaint or niggardliness, a long investment will become a safe investment. This is the fundamental point of difference between the Christians and the Jews in Palestine. The Christians are beggars, and therefore must be supported forever. The Jews are workers, and ask only for time to attain to self-support. These Jews are sowing good seed. If not left to wither and die for lack of nourishment, the seed will yield its harvest.

What Kind of Success?

So sure is the success of Zionism, on the conditions named, that I feel no informed and sympathetic observer can regard it longer as in doubt. The real question to-day is not a question of success or failure in material terms, but of success which may become failure in the higher spiritual terms which are the life of this adventure. It is conceivable, in other words, that Israel's success in Palestine may be her own undoing. For the Jews have returned to Zion not to gain wealth and establish power. On the contrary they have gone there to achieve an ideal, to fulfill a dream. They have been moved, as they are moved to-day, by the

[1] See Chapter III, page 104.

compulsion of an inner spirit of sacrifice for a vision of justice, righteousness and peace upon the earth. This is the prophet's vision—and it is as true to-day as it was in the days of Isaiah and Jeremiah, that worldly success is the enemy of such vision. For success creates the very conditions under which ideals die, decay and disappear. It is the poison which eats away the spiritual vitality not only of individuals but of nations. There is this deeper question, therefore, in the lot of Zion. What kind of success is Zion going to achieve? What is this success, or any success, likely to do to the idealism which is the life of Zion? How is the new Israel to save herself from the inward failure which is so frequently identical with outward triumph?

It is just here that the various problems which beset Zionism, the difficulties which seem so inescapable, so insuperable, and hence so desperate, suddenly take on the aspect no longer of liabilities but of assets. The Jewish homeland is not, and never will be, free to compete for the ordinary rewards and prizes of national life. This homeland is held permanently fast within certain limitations which, from the worldly point of view, doom the enterprise to failure, but, from that higher point of view which is traditionally the concern of Israel, mark merely the bounds within which it can prosper without hazard to its soul. Zion will succeed, but never greatly or splendidly, and therefore never corruptly and proudly. Inhibited from the quest of power, it will be saved from the use and abuse of power. Denied the luxury of all excess, it will likewise be denied the degeneracy to which excess of any kind is a door which sooner or later opens, and opens wide. Its disabilities will be its salvation.

The most insidious snare of success is riches. Few men can stand prosperity, and fewer nations.

> "Ill fares the land, to hastening ills a prey,
> Where wealth accumulates, and men decay."

It would seem as though this snare were not yet laid in Palestine; and yet already, in this comparatively early day of settlement, there are depressing signs that the pioneers are not immune from the love of money and its ills. Thus, in the older colonies, there is distinctly evident what I have called a settling-down tendency. In these colonies, of course, the early struggles are over, and a certain degree of security has been attained. With this has come a passing of the zest for adventure; and with this, in turn, the desire to enjoy a life which has been so hardly won. The citizens of Petah Tikvah and Kfar Aaron are men and women who have become comfortable, and therefore are becoming conservative. They are beginning now to think, more or less unconsciously, in terms not of giving but of getting. They are gaining possessions—land, houses, gardens, automobiles, bank accounts—and, as always in such circumstances, these possessions are gaining possession of their possessors. In these older and larger colonies, in other words, there has already started the dangerous process bemoaned by Goldsmith in his familiar lines just quoted above.

But this process is not confined to members of the older generation, who have done their task, made their sacrifice, and perhaps now, in the evening of their day, are entitled to some reward. I seemed to find the same process at work among the new recruits of Zion in Bne Binjamin. These hundreds of young men, resolved to give their lives to the Jewish homeland instead of seeking their careers in other and easier lands, are moved by a lofty heroism. They are also directed by an intense practicality. Their colonies are all organized on strict capitalistic principles. They invest their money, and other people's money, with the distinct idea of making profits. Zion is being served, of

THE PROMISE

course, but so is the capital invested, at six and eight per cent. The idea of giving their all to Zion and asking no return, at least within the period of their own lifetime—the idea so conspicuously and beautifully present in the communal colonies—seems utterly foreign to the minds of these pioneers. It was disturbing to hear these young Jews speaking with contemptuous levity of their communal comrades, whom I had so recently seen living under conditions of such dreadful privation in the remote areas of Zion's territory. They had no sympathy with these Communists—no appreciation of their invaluable contribution to the cause. They talked about them precisely as the English did—not with suspicion, to be sure, but always with impatience and scorn. The members of Bne Binjamin—fine, upstanding, heroic fellows, with clear minds aimed straight at a specific goal—were yet primarily business men, who were conducting their enterprise on business principles, and therefore inevitably in the business spirit. It may be that their principles and this spirit are sorely needed in Palestine. It is high time, perhaps, that something was done with the idea of making it pay from the start. But there is peril here, apparent to anybody familiar with "the deceitfulness of riches."

Or there would be peril, if riches were conceivable in Palestine. But they are not! The eternal safeguard to disaster in this direction is that Palestine is a poor land, and Zion therefore must always be a poor home. Not a poverty-stricken home! Not a perpetual haunt of beggars and paupers! On the contrary, this land, poor as it is, can be made beautiful and fruitful, as it has already been so made in many places, and its people can eventually sustain themselves on a level of decent and modest comfort. But the land will never produce riches, and the people will never be able to accumulate wealth. The economy of Palestine, in other words, can neither create nor sustain the profit motive. Nobody will ever come to this country, as millions have come to America, for example, to make money. The dominant motive alike of immigration and of residence must be the cause to be served, the homeland to be built. Which means that Zion will forever be protected from those perils of prosperity which are almost inseparable from any degree of material success!

In Palestine, if in no other region in the world, practical necessities may be said to coincide with ideological principles. This is the real answer to the question of the permanency of the communal colonies.[2] This type of colony as we have seen, is at present indispensable to the Zionist Movement because of its perfect adaptation to the stern conditions of primitive struggle which prevail over so large a part of the country. The communal colonies are the ones which can meet these conditions with a minimum of expense and exhaustion—the only ones, under certain conditions, which can survive at all. The passing of these rigorous economic conditions might well be assumed to mark the passing of this type of social life, as it has similarly passed in other times and places. But in a certain sense, these conditions will never pass. Life in this land will always be hard and labor severe. Men will have to work on a narrow margin of subsistence. There will develop, no doubt, landowners, landlords, lawyers, money lenders—a more or less leisure class of persons. But such class will be small. Few men will be idle in this country, since it cannot afford to have men idle. There will exist, from necessity, conditions of mutual responsibility, and from such conditions must follow equal conditions of mutual opportunity. The universal sharing of work must lead to the universal sharing of re-

[2] See Chapter IV, page 195.

ward. There must develop, in other words, in the interests of the safety and happiness of all, just such a type of cooperative, economic endeavor as we now find, in its more primitive aspects, in the *Kvutzoth*. As labor prospers and life becomes easier, as the whole community of Zion moves gradually from the level of economic dependence to that of economic self-support, it is highly probable that the communal type of social organization, as seen to-day in the *Kvutzoth*, will be modified in the direction of larger personal initiative, wider and deeper individual experience. But I am persuaded that, whatever the ultimate fate of the communal colonies, these foreshadow at this hour the future life of Israel. From the sheer hard necessities of the case, Zion will make itself a community of brothers. In other lands such a community, bravely started, has been rent apart by the competitive struggles of men for riches easily acquired. Individuals have persistently broken away from the group, separated their personal destinies from the destinies of their fellows, and launched out on private quests of private fortunes. Like the struggle when gold is found, it is "each man for himself, and the devil take the hindmost." But there is no gold, not even oil, in Palestine. Wealth is not at hand to reward the eager, selfish seeker after fortune. The single man cannot separate himself safely from his group. Each man must live and work with every other, if any of the number is to prosper, or even survive. Under conditions of this kind, the only sound social principle is the one already implied—"each for all, and all for each." In Palestine, therefore, the group, the community, as the unit of social organization, will endure. What men in other lands have failed to do, because wealth has rotted the state and corrupted the fiber of men's hearts, the Jew in Palestine will at last succeed in doing, because

"For him light labors spread her wholesome store,
Just gave what life required, but gave no more:
His best companions, innocence and health;
And his best riches, ignorance of wealth."

The worldly concept of success includes the profitable mastery not only of nature but of men. It projects the idea of power as well as of wealth. The story of the entrance of Western peoples into undeveloped regions of the earth, and of their contacts with the native populations of these regions, is a familiar one. It runs all the way from the tragedy of the extermination of proud and rebellious races, such as the Incas, the Aztecs, and the roving redskins of North America, to the equal tragedy of the deliberate exploitation of more docile races, such as the inhabitants of India and China. Its details differ, but it is always the same in its essential elements of an alien conqueror taking over the possessions, the culture, the very life of a weaker people to his own advantage and for his own purpose. What we invariably find is force working its will and way upon those unable, for lack of strength or knowledge, to resist the hand of the invader. Success is achieved when the native population is either eliminated, or profitably subdued.

It is difficult to associate success of this familiar imperialistic type with the Zionist adventure in Palestine. It is obvious that the native Arabs, while no less stubborn and savage than the American Indians, cannot be removed from the scene. They are there to stay, for better or worse. It is obvious also that the Jews, newcomers to the land, have little power, and no intention whatsoever, of exploiting the Arabs. The *Fellaheen,* so far from being enslaved and used for the profit of the Jews, are being economically emancipated by the Jews, and thus released to the enjoyment of a freer and more abundant life than they have known before, or perhaps could ever know under any other conditions. It is this fact which so disturbs the feudal leaders of the race, and tempts these latter to stir up revolt against invaders who would liberate the native masses from an economic, social and spiritual subjection so profitable to the dominant classes of the land. To the *Fellaheen* the Jews are emancipators. In its results as in its initial purpose, this Jewish settlement of Palestine offers no parallel to any other settlement of a highly developed people in a remote region among a weak and primitive population. Its atmosphere and color do not suggest in any slightest detail the colonial enterprises of imperialism. The Jews have not come to an alien land from motives of selfish profit. They have not sought out a rich country and a helpless people for purposes of conquest and exploitation. They are not explorers and adventurers—not even capitalistic investors. They are a stricken and unhappy race returning to a land which is their own, to build again the homes and altars from which they were driven by the sword. They would not use this sword, from which they have suffered so terribly, upon others. They would not drive the Arabs from the country, as they themselves were driven by the Romans. They would not exploit these Arabs, for they seek no wealth— only comfort, security, and a sense of glad possession. Of course they must live, but not on the inhabitants, nor even at their expense. The Jews of Zion propose to live by their own labor, and the fruits of this labor share freely with their neighbors.

Yet the temptation to power and the use of power is present. The relationship of Zion to the natives of Palestine is not altogether unique. For these natives, just to the extent that they are emancipated, are in the way. They own or occupy the land which the Jews must have if they are to establish themselves upon the ancient soil of their race. The return of the exiles to the national home is not unlike the return of a grandson, or great-great-grandson, to an old homestead which has been the abode for several generations of another family. This family is obviously in the way of occupancy by the old possessors.

But the Arabs present a second and still more serious obstacle to the establishment of "the Jewish national home." These Arabs, as we have seen, have nationalistic ambitions of their own. Their dreams of an Arab state match point by point the Jewish dreams of a Zionist state. They would organize and rule Palestine for the Moslems exactly as the Jews would organize and rule Palestine for Israel. Obviously the two states cannot exist together at Jerusalem, any more than two settlers, Arab and Jew, can own and work the same strip of soil in the Emek. The political aspirations of the Arabs are in the way of the Jewish government of Zion, as the Arab ownership and occupancy of the land are in the way of its Jewish settlement.

In these conflicts of interest, there are two things that can be done. The Jews can recognize the rights claimed by the Arabs as having a validity at least as great as those which they claim for themselves, and seek through friendly intercourse the ways of reconciliation and peace. They can point out to the Arabs that, whether it was wise or not in the beginning, both races are now rooted in the land, and must henceforth live side by side. The expulsion of either race from Palestine is as unthinkable as its extermination. For better or worse, they are together, and must now remain together. Hence it is for the mutual advantage of the two peoples to accept a common country, and make of it as surely and speedily as possible a common home. Nothing is to be gained from conflict, everything from co-operation. Already, in a land wide enough for both, the Jews and Arabs are finding it possible to work together on

THE PROMISE 251

the soil, and in this partnership of labor find prosperity and happiness. If the two races can thus work together as farmers and artisans, why can they not live together as citizens? If there can be one economic life, which is profitable to both, why not one political life which is safe for both? There is no essential conflict between the hopes of Zion, and the basic rights and privileges of the native population of Palestine. There need be no civil war between competing sovereignties for power. As the Jews have brought the Arabs prosperity, so they now also would bring them liberty. Zion but seeks the way not of denying the Arabs anything, but of sharing with them all those material standards, industrial methods, and political and social liberties, without which the Jewish homeland cannot itself survive. Common agricultural undertakings, common industrial enterprises, common coöperative societies and trade unions, common hospitals, common libraries, common schools, a common government, a common home—this is the one end for which together Jews and Arabs should increasingly and unselfishly labor.

This is one way out of the dilemma of conflict—the way strenuously favored by the more idealistic among Zionists. To the more practical minded it seems, at least in any immediate or unrestricted application, the hazardous, the dangerous way. The Arabs of Palestine are illiterate, superstitious, and savage. It will take decades, perhaps generations, to reach them by the slow infiltration of Jewish life. Meanwhile, the Arabs are afraid. They shrink from these strange invaders with their superior methods and higher culture. They see their lands stolen, their children robbed, their country lost, their religion outraged. They are sensitive to agitation. Faster among them than any reassuring sentiments of good will from Jewish settlers, travel the fierce exhortations of their native leaders to a national, or a holy war. In the mountains lurk the savage hillsmen; on the frontiers hover hordes of barbaric Bedouin. Safer than conciliation at such a moment is the British sword sheathed in the Mandate of the League of Nations, to subdue undisciplined Arabs and thus prevent them from interfering with Zion during its early years of critical development.

Some few of the Jews, of the chauvinistic type, would make of this a thorough piece of business, and annihilate Arab power in Palestine forever. Most of the Zionists have too much respect for the rights of the Arabs, work with them too happily in mutual coöperation, to desire for them any permanent injury or frustration. But even these moderate Zionists show a disquieting tendency to take for granted Jewish ascendancy and control throughout the land and over all its people. They would make no appeal to the sword, save in defense of life and property. They do not think at all in terms of violence, or repression. Yet they were silent when England and the Allies tore to tatters the nationalistic aspirations of the Moslem world. They have refused the request of the Palestinian Arabs, presented in not immoderate terms, for coöperation in securing some form of popular government, and thus have conspired, as an obstructive minority backed by alien power, to deny to the majority their public rights. And they visualize a future, for the coming of which they are determined patiently to work and wait, when the Jews will be the majority in the land, and forthwith take over the political sovereignty which through all these years they have so stoutly denied to their Arab neighbors. These Zionists cannot seem to see a future Zion except in terms of Jewish supremacy. Darkly implicit in the whole Movement is the conviction that, if Zion is to endure, Palestine must in its own right be a Jewish state. But a Jewish state means, obviously, a non-Arab state. A non-Arab state means, in turn, repression of the Arab, or at least his subordination to Jewish authority and force. It even means, to some Zionists, the withdrawal of Arabs from Palestine to other near-by Moslem lands. A diaspora of the Arabs, to follow the diaspora of the Jews! Wherein does such consummation of Israel in Palestine differ from similar consummations of France in Syria, England in India, America in the Philippines? And what is native revolt against it but one more uprising of a colonial people against the alien rule which denies to them their own?

However temperate the spirit of the Jews in Palestine, however wise their counsels of prudence, however idealistic their expectations of the future, the logic of the policy which they are tempted to follow is repression of a native population, interference with its rights, frustration of its ambitions, with all the inevitable consequences of sporadic rebellion and ultimate civil war. In such policy of force, the whole destiny of Zionism is at stake. It is the one policy, of course, best calculated to precipitate those very chances of destruction and slaughter which it was instituted to appease and if possible remove. As grapes do not grow from thorns nor figs from thistles, so security does not spring from violence, nor peace from power. But, worse than this, it is the one policy most surely destined to wreck from within whatever it may save from without. For it is not the business of Israel to overcome or overbear, to repress or conquer, to prosper or even to survive, by means of force. A Zion which resists and subdues another people is not the Zion which has captured the imagination of mankind. A Zion which can exist only under the shelter of armored airplanes and behind a barricade of British bayonets is not the Zion of which the prophets dreamed. "Not by might, nor by power, but by my spirit, saith the Lord.". This is the ideal of Israel. To have vindicated this ideal at so costly a sacrifice through so many centuries of persecution, is the glory of Israel. If this ideal is not to be perpetuated, by whatever further sacrifice, then is the glory of Israel departed. Zion is too high a dream, too fine a spirit, too beautiful a dream, to survive in Palestine only as the rule of empires survives in their dependencies. It were better that she perish utterly than by such survival bring mockery to a sublime tradition; or, if she survive by such betrayal of her destiny, be known as Ichabod forever.

The occasion of this temptation to power was of course the conquest of Palestine by British arms, and the placing of the Jewish national home under the protecting shield of Britain. We are now ready to see how this intrusion of the Great War into the Holy Land, with its consequent identification of Zion's future with the might and favor of the British Empire, was in its essence a calamity. The union with Britain under the Mandate had immense material advantages. It brought swift acceleration to the Movement—resources for its development, confidence in its future—which could not have been acquired under other circumstances in fifty years. It also, perhaps, gave the protection necessary to Zion in the chaos of the War and post-War periods. But at what a price were these advantages purchased! In every deeper and truer aspect of the situation, the entrance of England upon the scene was a tragedy —a triple tragedy. First, it aroused and mobilized the Arabs to an aggressive nationalistic and religious passion for independence, and thus enlisted them for generations in a "holy war." Secondly, it involved the Jews of Zion in this war between East and West; arrayed them definitely, as responsible agents in Palestine, on the side of repressive world power, and thus against the aspirations of the native population among whom they must live and fulfill their destiny. Lastly, it subtly, insidiously changed the psychology of the Jewish mind, and thus the temper of the Zionist cause. In Allenby and his victory was established for the first time in Zion the war tradition. In the Balfour Declaration and the British Mandate were recognized for the first time the precedent and the prestige of arms. In Trumpeldor and his fellow-patriots, slain in the first battle between Jews and Arabs, was created the romantic legend of fighting and dying for one's country. Hitherto in Palestine the Jews had lived alone and unprotected, trusting to patience and pity for the triumph of their cause. In their extremity they had no weapon but suffering, and no shield but faith. Suddenly, with the coming of the English, there intruded, like Satan into Paradise, the consciousness of power. The first reliance of the Jews was now the Empire. Not to the righteousness of their cause merely, nor to the justice of their principles, nor yet to their own ways of gentleness and peace, need they now look for protection, but to the overshadowing might of British arms. This was a change of status; inevitably this change of status brought a change of spirit. In the raging contentions of the Eastern world, the Jews were certain still to be the victims, but not so certain the innocent victims.

It would be easy to despair over this situation. The resort of Jews to alliance with world power for the sake of success, or even security, is not a lovely spectacle. It awakens memories not of Isaiah trusting resolutely in the God of judgment, but of Ahaz going down "to Egypt for help," and trusting "in chariots because they are many, and in horsemen because they are very strong." For there is in Israel a tradition of foolish kings as well as of wise prophets! But there is reassurance in the fact that this can be no permanent nor even protracted period in the history of Zion. The genius of the Jew must sooner or later assert itself against the policy of force. The ideals of the national home are too plain and too precious to be long compromised with the standards of empire. Bitter experience must itself teach Israel anew the impracticability in Palestine of reliance upon anything other than her own inherent strength and rectitude of purpose. For conditions in the Holy Land do not allow to the Jews any ultimate success through predominance of political or military power.

The Arabs are in Palestine, as they are in the Near East generally, to stay. The Jews have in themselves no permanent power to overmaster or even to control this formidable Moslem world. They can only seek or accept the power of alien nations who have purposes other than their own. Already the Mandate as granted to England by the League of Nations is proving a weak reed upon which to lean. On the one hand England has no intention, whatever her pledges, of serving the interests of Zion at the expense of her own interests of empire, and thus no intention of advancing the cause of Zion at the expense of the Arabs. On the other hand, England's presence in Palestine on behalf of Zion, and under her promise to place "the country under such political, administrative and economic conditions as will secure the establishment of the Jewish national home," is a perpetual affront to the Arabs, and an occasion of alarm and hostility against the Jews. What would have happened at the close of the War had England not come into Palestine may be a question. What did happen is a certainty. The people among whom the Jews must live, and without whose friendship and coöperation they cannot hope permanently to survive, were alienated in fear and hate. So long as Zion shelters herself behind the British sword, this alienation between the twin populations of the country will continue. So long as this alienation continues, the future of Zion is uncertain. If Zion is to endure—a light to Jewry, and a challenge to mankind—this alienation must be dissolved, as it can alone be dissolved by the cleansing detergents of confidence and good will. By sheer force of circumstance, if nothing more, the Jews will more and more dissociate themselves from British interest and power. They will avoid alien alliances, and thus the more surely identify themselves with the land of their adoption and the people of its habitation. They will trust to the Arab, and make his cause their own. Unceasingly by prudent example, patient influence, and much sacrifice, they will make two races one, and thus reveal to each that its strength and happiness and hope are in the other. Conditions in Palestine all conspire to this solution of the dilemma. The impact of circumstance reënforces the spirit of Israel, to save her from the perils of power as from the corruptions of wealth. If not by herself, then in spite of herself, will Zion be redeemed.

In this same compulsion is found the answer to that deeper problem already presented [3] as the final problem of Israel's life in the ancient homeland of her tribe. Is the new Zion to be one more nation added to the other nations now existing upon the earth? Are we to have in Palestine only another confusion of flags, frontiers, languages, coinages, the trappings and attributes of sovereignty, to make existing nationalistic confusion worse confounded? Is Jewry to follow in the path of empire, and become another people feverish with pride and quick to aggression? What does the Jew find in such a prospect to please him, and what can the world find in it of enlightenment and progress?

In consideration of these questions, already shown to be so pertinent to the whole destiny of Zion, it may be said that there are two types, or concepts, of human society.

On the one hand, there is the political concept, which is

[3] See Chapter III, pages 162-168.

embodied in what may be called the state, or nation. The state is fundamentally a government. Its life is political sovereignty, as its structure is political organization. The end of the state is power; and the means to this end, authority imposed by force and violence. The instruments of the state are its armies and navies, its officers and princes, diplomats and soldiers. The state flourishes in the imposition of its will upon other and weaker sovereignties; it languishes in the subjection of its will to other and stronger sovereignties. The state finds its natural operation and its perfect fulfillment in war. There is good reason why the state is with such difficulty persuaded to abandon the use of arms.

On the other hand, there is the cultural concept of society, which is embodied in what may be called distinctively the community, in contradistinction to what has just been called the state, or nation. The community is fundamentally a people rather than a government. Its life is a spirit or ideal, and its institutions only such temporary or permanent organizations as may be needful for the expression of this life. The end of the community is the general welfare of its citizens, and the means to this end education, agitation, public discipline, and humane leadership. The instruments of the community are schools and colleges, churches and synagogues, libraries and art museums, orchestras and opera houses, parks and playgrounds, hospitals, trade unions, coöperative societies, committees of public welfare, organizations of scientific research and literary endeavor. Its important men are authors, artists, engineers, physicians, teachers, scientists, philosophers, publicists, reformers, experts of social welfare, statesmen of the commonweal. The community flourishes in the health, happiness, prosperity, ordered and peaceful life of all its people; it languishes when disease, poverty, strife and violence disturb the homes and distract the minds of men. The one great enemy of the community is war, and the conditions of its stability and survival peace.

In most societies the struggle between these two types—the community and the state, as thus conceived—goes on perpetually, like the struggle between life and death within the physical organism. The immortal dramatization of such struggle is the story of the kings and prophets of ancient Israel. Eventually, if civilization is to endure, the state as such must disappear, and its institutions mingle and be transmuted into other and higher institutions created for the proper functioning of what we have somewhat arbitrarily, perhaps, called the community. Meanwhile, there are, as there have always been, societies which, from the sheer necessities of the case, must flourish as cultural entities, and thus live, if they are to live at all, as anticipations and prophecies of the future society of men. These societies have no power, and under the given circumstances of their existence, can gain no power. They may desire it, and even strive for it, and in their striving divert the energies and wreck the destinies of their people. But the power which they seek is permanently denied them. From lack of territory, or numbers, or natural resources, or inner temperament and spirit, they are shut out from the rivalry of states, and must live, if they choose to live at all, as communities—centers of enlightenment and spiritual culture.

Zion is such a society, for Zion can never be a state, or nation. If she is to live at all, it must be as a community. There are Zionists, to be sure, who dream of their new country taking its modest place among the powers of the earth, and thus discourse on government and politics, flags, and armies and navies. In the same way there are Englishmen, like the admirable Josiah Wedgewood, who argue for the incorporation of Palestine into the British Commonwealth of Nations, and thus visualize the future Zion as a "seventh dominion," after the pattern of Canada, or the Irish Free State. But what is the reason for such destiny; and, if there be one, where are the conditions of its fulfillment? What elements of political and military power, necessary to the life of any state, exist in the Palestine of Israel? Where are the people, the wealth, the resources, the ambition, the will? The picture of a Jewish state is absurd, as the picture of a Jewish dominion seems curiously beside the point. Both pictures are unreal. From the sheer necessities of the case, Zion belongs in the category not of political but of cultural societies. Her future is directed by the unalterable conditions of her environment to the world not of governmental organization and power, but of intellectual and spiritual enlightenment. In coöperation with the Arabs, the Jews of Zion must work out methods of local control, and establish institutions for the proper ordering of domestic affairs. Like any other people, they must assume and discharge the functional activities of community existence. But beyond this the energies of Zion must of necessity be poured into the social and cultural life of her people—into their farms and factories, their schools and university, their art and song and faith. For they have no other channel in which to flow. There looms no other destiny toward which to move. Permanently debarred by the inexorable rigors of circumstance from wealth and power and glory, Zion, if she would live at all, must become ever more and more that "spiritual center . . . of study and learning, of language and literature, of bodily work and spiritual purification," of which her greatest modern prophet, Achad Ha-Am, has so surely dreamed.[4]

It is because the Communist settlers in the *Kvutzoth* see

[4] See Chapter II, page 81.

THE PROMISE

this fact so clearly, and work for it with an eye so single to the ultimate goal of economic and cultural brotherhood, that they remain, for all their weakness, so significant a part of Zion. More than all others in Jewish Palestine, these men and women live close to the basic realities of their undertaking. They know the limitations within which the Zionist experiment must proceed, and the probable bounds set to its ultimate development. The conditions of this experiment permit no hope, as indeed they should stimulate no desire, for the building of a state which shall compete with other states in pomp and circumstance. What they not only permit, but dictate, is the creation of a society, a glad and free community of souls, in which men shall not "labor in vain, nor bring forth for calamity," but be "the seed of the blessed, and their offspring with them." The Communists, inspired by no dreams but the prophets' dreams of brotherhood and peace, are setting themselves deliberately to the task of constructing that cultural type of society which can alone endure in Palestine. If they have faith and cheer to-day, amid their poverty, it is because they have conviction that in their colonies is the Zion of the future.

The ideals of Zion are thus confirmed by her realities. Necessity binds her to her farthest vision, as gravitation binds the stars to their remotest flight. We need not fear. This new nation will not be another political state added to the states which now rend and tear our common heritage of earth. These Jews in Palestine will never be one more proud, aggressive, jealous, martial people, contributing new vexation and terror to the world. This way there lies for them "no thoroughfare." From such corruptions and perversions of the spirit they are delivered, if not by the ideals of their inner life, then by the inescapable conditions of their outer existence. Their task, whether they would have it so or not, is permanently a discipline to far adventures of the soul—to culture, enlightenment, social justice, peace, and brotherhood. Zion, therefore, will be a people and not a state, a culture and not a government, a commonwealth and not a power. Driven to Palestine by the compulsion of sacred memories and tried traditions, the Zionists have found a narrow, barren land, and an unfriendly people. In this land, and among these people they have built a home, which can give them nothing for which the nations strive and cry—neither wealth, nor power, nor independent sovereignty. But, for this very reason, it can give them everything of which the prophets dreamed and for which their stricken tribe has yearned in darkness and despair. For what Palestine denies the flesh is but the price of what Palestine may give the spirit. Zion is a vision, and Palestine is a land where visions thrive. Therefore, for Zion, is Palestine once more "the Promised Land."

In every enterprise of men's hands and hearts, there lurk two perils. The first is the peril of failure. This has been overcome in Zion. The second is the peril of easy and great success. This, in Zion, of all enterprises I have known, has never existed.

The spirit of Zionism, like the valor of the Zionists, has never been doubted. Only its success! Now that success is achieved, or being achieved by labor that grows not tired nor afraid, the nature of this success is doubted. Yesterday the skeptic cried, It can't be done! To-day he complains, It isn't worth doing!

If the Jews are doing in Palestine under difficulties only what others have done, or they themselves may do, in other places, under more favorable conditions, then men may well have doubt as to whether the enterprise is necessary, or

THE PROMISE

worthwhile. But there is a spirit in Zion which is unique. This spirit has been generated and preserved through the centuries by the weakness of an heroic people in the face of outrages and persecutions they had not the strength to end but only to endure. This spirit is now in its fulfillment preserved anew by the weakness of this same people in the face of difficulties and dangers they have not the strength to overcome but only to use. If these difficulties and dangers persist, this unique spirit will endure, even as it has endured through death and agony until this day. If they are lifted, or pass away, then this spirit may die for lack of sustenance upon which to feed. But Palestine is itself the perpetual guarantee that such conditions, while they may be tempered, cannot be changed. The land serves the genius of the people it has bred. The task sustains the ideals of the workers it has called. The mission of the Jew remains still what it has always been—to find strength in weakness, and victory in suffering.

What Such Success Means

The establishment of Zion, as thus defined, means great things for the world.

First of all, it means the preservation of the Jews. This is important to the Jews themselves, but more important to the world. There is tragedy in the loss of any people. Governments may come and go, be merged in one another and happily disappear, but people should endure. For each people brings to humanity, as each child brings to a family, a unique character, a special genius, which enriches the human spirit and its achievement upon the earth. Especially is this true of the Jews, who, like the ancient Greeks, developed a type of culture and enlightenment unrivaled in the history of mankind. Unlike the Greeks, the Jews were saved from degeneracy and ultimate disappearance as a people. They survive to-day not in the relics and ruins of the civilization which they produced, but as a vital force in the life of contemporary society. This force must be preserved for the intellectual power it embodies, the spiritual values it conserves, the vast influence of prophetic insight and vision it can contribute to mankind. Yet it was never in such peril of extinction as it is to-day. For the Jews are still a scattered people. If they are to survive as something more than a memory and tradition, they must have some rallying center to which to cling, and from which to draw the peculiar nurture of their tribe. For ages this rallying center was the ghetto, in the darkness of which burned the unquenchable flame of the Messianic hope. But to-day the ghetto walls are down—the flame is in danger of being lost in the bright light of outer day. What now shall hold the Jews to one another, and to Israel?

The answer to this question is Zion. It is the new rallying center which shall "bind all Jews together," to quote again the words of Achad Ha-Am, by holding them fast to the recovered ideals of their race. In Zion the far-flung sons of Jacob have a common work to do, and a common hope to cherish. To this new homeland, the Jews of Russia, Poland, Roumania, Czecho-Slovakia, Austria, Germany, England, America, Bokhara, Turkestan, Morocco, turn with a common affection and desire and thus feel kinship with one another. And it is kinship on the highest level of racial experience! For amid these ancient hills, upon this sacred soil of Palestine, they see Israel reborn and thus redeemed. Here the Jew is become himself again. He stands upon his own ground, and feels within the quickening of his own spirit. This spirit he obeys. For he need no longer now be obsequious, or imitative, or submissive. The hour is past when he need bow his head and "wash his hands" before his betters, and thus by his debasement buy the favor wherewith to live. In Zion he has achieved his independence, recovered his self-respect, and thus may be true to his essential genius. "If you wish to see the genuine type of Jew," writes Achad Ha-Am, "where it be a rabbi, or a scholar, or a writer, a farmer or an artist, or a business man—then go to Palestine and you will see it."

It is this vision, this achievement, not only in Palestine but throughout the world, which is remaking the Jew into the likeness of his own spirit, and thus saving him, in the hour of his emancipation, from disintegration and decay, and thus from ultimate dispersal and disappearance as a people. To many an ardent Zionist, the vindication of the great adventure lies not so much in what it is doing for the pioneers in Palestine as in what it is doing for the great host of Jewry outside the borders of the national homeland. Two perils beset the Jews in this modern age. The one is the peril of atrophy in the traditions and ceremonialisms of an ancient faith. The other is the peril of corruption from the gross materialism of a machine-made civilization. In the one case, the Jews would wither away into a sect, and perish. In the other case, they would become absorbed into the substance of a worldly society, and disappear. That in either case they would vanish as a racial entity is as unlikely as that the Negroes will be so lost in any time that can now be foreseen by the mind of man. But that in both cases they would vanish as a spiritual force which can redeem mankind, is certain. To save the Jews from such a fate, and humanity from such a loss, nothing can serve but the emergence within the life of Israel of that which Israel was born to serve—a task, a mission, an ideal. The religion of Israel must be made real again. The visions of the prophets must become not words but deeds. And it is this, precisely this, which Zion brings! In the hope of the homeland Jewry lives again, and therewith brings light and leading not merely to itself but to the world.

A second thing implicit in the establishment of Zion was pointed out by George Eliot as long ago as 1876, in the flaming speech of Mordecai, the Jew, in "Daniel Deronda," who saw in Palestine "a new Judæa, poised between East and West, a covenant of reconciliation."

This reconciliation between East and West has been long delayed. For centuries the struggle between the two halves of the human family has waxed and waned, but never ceased. In our day this struggle threatens more terribly than ever, for the mystic and mysterious East is now stirring to its utmost depth and its remotest range. In China, India, Persia, Syria, Arabia, the nearer and the farther East, the unnumbered multitudes of men are shaking themselves as from a mighty slumber, and preparing to face the West on its own terms and to its own ends. The gulf between these hemispheres of culture and civilization is one of the most terrifying phenomena in the world of our time. Deep down in its dark and unprobed depths lurk the hidden forces of war and revolution that may yet annihilate the race. What influence can bridge this gulf? How can these two divisions of mankind be brought together in a harmony of inquiry and understanding? Where can they learn to coöperate, and thus to avoid the rivalry and struggle in which both are doomed to perish.

George Eliot's Mordecai saw an answer to these questions in Zion—and so do Zionists to-day! Already in their schools and university, their playgrounds, settlements and hospitals, they are building the institutions and generating the forces which may develop this much desired "covenant of reconciliation."

"East is East, and West is West, and never the twain may meet," says Rudyard Kipling. But they *do* meet in Palestine. The peoples of the Orient and Occident have always met in Palestine. This land for ages has been the frontier between these severed worlds. As such, to be sure, it has been crossed and recrossed, fought over and died for, by an unceasing stream of contending armies—Egyptian and Babylonian, Greek and Persian, Roman and Parthian, Christian and Saracen, English and Turk. The wide valley of the Emek is sown with the bones of countless armies from both horizons. But a frontier not merely divides but joins. It is a place where peoples meet to clasp hands as well as to fight. For centuries Palestine has been known as the "bridge" between East and West. But over a bridge pass not only soldiers, but also travelers, traders, teachers. Where better than in Palestine, thus "poised between East and West," can the work of acquaintanceship and cooperation between these two worlds begin? And who better than the Jew is equipped to do this work?

For the Jew is himself an Oriental. His racial origin lies far east of Jordan, in the dim valleys of the Tigris and Euphrates. His mind flowers naturally into the poetry and parable of Eastern lore. His wisdom is the wisdom of the Orient, and his spiritual vision a product of the basic religious genius of this world. In body and blood, in temperament, in psychology, in inward range and depth of mystery, the Jew is a child of the East. But he lived his life for centuries on the frontier of the West. Then he crossed this frontier. Even before the destruction of his nation, the tribe had drifted by thousands and tens of thousands into the Græco-Roman world. Greek thought and speech, and Roman citizenship, had become a part of Israel's experience. Finally with the fall of Jerusalem, came that far scattering through Europe, and ultimately to America, which has made the Jew a denizen of the West. Unchanged in nature, in his love of wisdom and his passion for religion, he has long been familiar with the languages, the modes of thought, the habits of life, the practical interests and activities of the peoples among whom he has dwelt, and now, in these days of wider enfranchisement, has become the master of their political insight, scientific knowledge, and technical equipment. Still the inward, he is become the outward man as well. Feeling the East and its dreams, he knows also the West and its ways. In him, as in no other man upon the earth, the Occident and Orient have met and mingled. The soul of the Jew represents a confluence of these two worlds. And now he comes again to the frontier in Palestine. What better work can he do, what work can he better do, than serve as an interpreter, a friend, a mediator between these worlds which are so truly both his own! In nothing is the Jew in Palestine so fully vindicating himself as in this work, already well begun, of bringing East and West together. Prejudices must long be bitter, and misunderstandings dark. Political intrusions from the one side will match religious fanaticisms on the other, and of both the Jew will be the victim. But he has but to endure, as he has endured from the beginning. In his dual genius is "the covenant of reconciliation." In Zion is the laboratory where will be found the formula of peace.

But Zion is a laboratory for other experiments as well. It is a universal laboratory for the study of social ills—and therein is the third and greatest aspect of its significance to the world.

The basic problem of men's lives upon this earth is that of learning to live together in peace and happiness. To ask why men should ever have allowed themselves to become divided into mutually hostile groups is a superficial way of probing into the fundamental and vastly intricate question of human rivalries and antagonisms which begins with outward facts of economic and political determinism, and ends with inward mysteries of psychological and spiritual reaction. Meanwhile, whatever the explanations, the hostile groups are here, and man's continued life upon this planet depends upon the discovery of methods of adjustment and reconciliation.

Now in Palestine would seem to be found all the occasions of diversity, all the issues of antagonism, which vex humanity. This little land appears as a kind of microcosm of all the hostilities which rend and tear the human organism. Is it racial differences?—here you have them in the intense race prejudice between the Arab and the Jew. Is it political differences?—here you find them in the clash between Arab nationalism, Jewish nationalism, and British imperialism. Is it religious differences?—here they are in the fierce fanaticisms of Christians and Moslems and the orthodox piety of Jews. Is it economic differences—here they flourish in the basic contention for the land upon which men must feed. Is it social and cultural differences?—here they abound in the *Fellaheen* shepherd, the Arab landlord, and the Jewish *Chalutzim*.

It is because Palestine has always been the unhappy meeting place of differences of this kind, that the history of the land has been so tragic. And is so tragic still! But these same differences present opportunity, as well as prepare calamity. It is where diseases rage in pestilence that remedies are found. Palestine, in other words, may be made not merely a battleground but a laboratory. It needs but the presence of a determined mind, a courageous heart, an idealistic spirit, to make this country an experiment station for the healing of the ills of man. And it is just this which the Jew brings to Palestine in Zionism. Here in this adventure is the dream of a society of justice, righteousness and peace. Here on the scene of this adventure are all the diversive and divisive elements out of which this dream must fashion the substance of its reality. If the Jew succeeds in what he has so heroically undertaken, he will have discovered the solution of all social problems. It is in this sense that Zionism is far more than the hope of Israel. It is the hope, also, of the world.

Conclusion

Zion has thus a universal significance. This significance resides at bottom in Zion's vindication of man's insistence upon a spiritual interpretation of life—his belief in the triumph of right over wrong, of good over evil, of the spirit over the flesh. "The meek shall inherit the earth."

On my return from Palestine, I passed through Rome, and made a pilgrimage to the Arch of Titus. Proudly spanning the Appian Way on the high crest of the slope at the entrance of the Forum, this Arch was reared by the Emperor to celebrate through all future years his destruction of the Jews. Never had there been a greater military victory. Jerusalem, besieged and taken, was leveled to the dust, and all its people who were not butchered were strewn to the four winds of heaven. Here upon the Arch to-day are the sculptured pictures of the deed—the Jewish captives yoked to the Emperor's car, the table of shew bread and the seven-branched candlestick borne in triumph in his procession. When Titus died, so soon after his task was done, it must have been with complacent calm at the glory of his achievement.

The Arch still stands—and so does Jerusalem! And the Jews still live, though Titus is dead and his grave forgotten. And, wonder of wonders, these Jews are back in Jerusalem. The story of Rome and all its emperors ended more than fifteen hundred years ago, but the story of the Jews is beginning all anew. What irony is in these moldering stones and battered sculptures! An emperor's arch, which has now become the memorial of his slaves and victims! I smiled, as I gazed, at the littleness of kings and the feebleness of swords. And I thought of a story which had been told me by a certain Jew in Palestine.

This man had met Mussolini, and had been able to do him certain personal services. The Italian dictator was grateful, and at the moment of parting said that he would be glad to do anything in his power to show his appreciation.

"What can I do?" he said.

"There is one thing you can do," said this gallant son of Israel. "You can take down the Arch of Titus, stone by stone, and give it to the Jews, to be erected again upon Mt. Zion."

Mussolini did not grant this bold request. It is perhaps better so. Let the Arch stand in the Eternal City, to proclaim eternally, in its most appropriate setting, the truth which Napoleon discovered in the midst of his greatest triumphs, and phrased in immortal words:

"There are only two powers in the world, the spirit and the sword. In the long run, the sword will always be conquered by the spirit."

For Product Safety Concerns and Information please contact our EU
representative GPSR@taylorandfrancis.com
Taylor & Francis Verlag GmbH, Kaufingerstraße 24, 80331 München, Germany